Why this shift? (...This wide and deep hunger for s██████ years of atomization and collage.) Contemporary media promotes proliferation and content on independent demand, advertising selection among a range of narratives: the creation of personal narratives. Through choice of the form of a play, writers insist there are ways to compare and entwine our split histories, fusing them into collective experience. Deconstruction helped us recognize a fractured world, and broke open borders between disciplines to facilitate art's witness to our brutalized social and physical environment. In post-deconstructive, post-disciplinary circumstances, we crave a way past recognition and into response. There's great future in writing that acknowledges the atomic but pushes to... the molecular (and from there, to a world). If the nineties belonged to the girl with the most cake, tomorrow goes to the baker.

Apocalypse. . .

These plays are acutely aware of mutability: how it is violent and how it is funny. They hold that emotion is a natural/national landscape; that the

boom
bust

cycles of our utopian adventurings force us to honesty and the admission that we prepare ruin (causing it, releasing it, and calling it into our lives).
They also hold to hope: that fire brings things forth as well as bears them away.
New writing revitalizes the jeremiad;
draws the impossible demands of apocalyptic thinking into practical discourse.
The old (what we own and know) is passing away…
this is useful;
this is always true.

Why this shift? (…To immanent meaning, to vision of life pressured by a sense for the need to change, to radical transformation dosed with cynicism's clarity – what Norman Klein calls "paranoid utopianism.")

The enormous change for which we've been preparing, the wheeling that brought us through WW I – its technologies, reorganizations, economies – and through the genocides, rapes and geo-rapes that followed… this change is twisting to antipodal revolution. The dynamics we've pled for and bled for – this world of ambient, wildly liberated resources, this world of rapid distributions and concentrations, this (potentially creative) chaos of selves – has clicked the bulleted chamber into line with time's barrel. We've gotten what we've asked for. We've got to ask again, the perpetual quest of the better question. We cannot have utter hope without an appreciation of our comprehensive failure (synapse of conception is despair; all that is wonderfully possible is knit by carbons of all that has perished; we generate in the shadow of genocide). Our hope is great because our loss is great. An authentic way of finding and facing glory is by mourning it, missing it, insisting on it… vs. speaking with assumed moral certainty from the presumed center of it. In a variety of voices and styles, these plays come up to impossible questions with wonder and abandon, with alert and graceful waiting and witness.

This time of mutation

(presto

cha nge-o)

– made crucial through the
screaming volatility and
elusiveness of social purpose
and shared discourse

(boo)

– puts writing, especially
theatrical writing, in fine
position to agitate for
wakefulness, convergent
aspiration, and new-
made symbols

(hello)

Since nothing is certain

and we are alive in a biology of loss,

everything (e v e r y t h i n g)

may be given over to ritual projects

of regeneration and their sacramental

destructions – the manifesto

of all live theater.

Erik Ehn

man·i·fes·to (man-*uh*-**fes**-to) A public declaration of principles, policies, or intentions, especially of a political nature.

MANIFESTO series

edited by
Erik Ehn

Volume I

Glen Berger

Yussef El Guindi

Bret Fetzer & Juliet Waller Pruzan

Sung Rno

Heidi Schreck

Amy Wheeler

CONTENTS

ACKNOWLEDGEMENTS

The editors wish to thank the following for their assistance in compiling this volume.

4 CULTURE
KING COUNTY LODGING TAX

Frank Chiachiere
The Shunpike
Jennifer, Brontë & Rowan Neel
The patrons and performers of Ukalooza
(along with Steve Wells and Ian Bell of Re-bar)

FOREWARD

What is Rain City Projects? Seattle's sixteen-year-old playwright service organization. Our mission is to support, promote and develop professional regional playwrights. The archive of Rain City Projects scripts is an astonishing documentation of theater activity in the Pacific Northwest over the past sixteen years. During that time RCP has gone through many incarnations: we've published playscripts by Pacific Northwest playwrights (199 to date); provided travel grants; produced play readings; published theater journals; and quite naturally, hosted riotous Ukulele-themed events. But we want to do more.

The Pacific Northwest is a great arts mecca! In fact, Seattle alone has more equity theatre and performances than almost any other city in the country (NYC and Chicago being the notable exceptions). There is a staggering panoply of artistic diversity here. And yet for the most part that diversity goes unread, unpublished and unproduced outside of the Pacific Northwest. It's time that changed. These are damn good plays and we think the world ought to know about them.

What is the Manifesto Series? The book you hold in your hands is not your grandfather's play collection. It's a compilation of great Northwest plays, edited with extreme prejudice by a nationally recognized playwright who has a vision of what theater can be—should be—will be (dammit!). This is not best-of collection—it's a call-to-arms: experimentation, new writing, and emerging artists are essential.

The purpose of the Manifesto series is to get plays by Northwest playwrights in the consciousness of the theatre makers and lovers around the country and to provoke debate about the direction of new theater in the United States.

The plays in this collection represent where Erik Ehn thinks theatre should be going in this country. We agree.

Enjoy.

Darian Lindle
Board Member, Rain City Projects
www.raincityprojects.org

GLEN BERGER launched his playwriting career in earnest as a member of Annex Theatre in Seattle. He spent a decade in New York and now lives in the Hudson Valley with his wife and two children. He is a fifth-year member of New Dramatists. His plays include: *Underneath the Lintel* (Over 450 performances Off-Broadway, 2001 Ovation Award (Los Angeles) and 2003 Sterling Award (Edmonton) for Best Play, and one of Time Out New York's Ten Best Plays of 2001, productions in over 55 cities in 8 countries), *The Wooden Breeks* (nominated for Best Writing by the L.A. Weekly, 2001), *O Lovely Glowworm* (2005 Portland Drammy Award Winner for Best Script; 2002 "BugNBub" Primary Stages Award), the musical *A Night in the Old Marketplace*, (Loewe Award,), *Great Men of Science, Nos. 21 & 22* (1998 Ovation Award and 1998 L.A. Weekly Award for Best Play), *I Will Go... I Will Go* (published in Applause Book's 2001 Best Short Plays Anthology), and *On Words and Onwards* (Manhattan Theatre Club/Sloan Foundation Fellowship). Glen has received commissions from the Children's Theatre of Minneapolis and the Lookingglass Theatre, was selected for the 2003 Old Vic/New Voices program, participated in the 2001 A.S.K. Playwrights Retreat, and was playwright-in-residence at New York Stage & Film. He has written several episodes for the PBS children's series *Arthur*, (for which he was nominated for two Emmys), its spin-off *Postcards From Buster* (one Emmy nomination), *Time Warp Trio* (NBC), *Peep* (The Learning Channel), and is the head writer for *Fetch* (PBS).

Glen Berger

Great Men of Science, Nos. 21 & 22

Act 1: Life, the Canard

Act 2: A Frog He Would A-Wooing Go

FORWARD: There are Three Facts, confirmed and undeniable, that I try to keep in the front of my brain instead of tucking them away in some musty corner in the back where I can conveniently forget them—

1) The observable universe contains well over 500,000,000,000 galaxies, with each galaxy containing over 1,000,000,000,000 stars, of which, our vast, blazing and life-bestowing sun…is one.

2) The Earth is 4,600,000,000 years old, in which time—from the Pre-Cambrian Era to the Present—a dizzying, terrifying number of inhabitants—amoebas and trilobites, dust mites and Neanderthals—have all struggled to live from one hour to the next. (Indeed, more living creatures are in my stomach (and yours) at this moment than the total number of human beings that have ever existed.)

3) I will die. I will be dead in sixty years, though it's entirely conceivable that I'll be dead before the week is out.

These facts prompt what I call The Great Question—"**To What End?**" What am I doing here, What are we doing here, and what is Anything doing here?
And if the Great Question will never be satisfactorily answered, then where and how do we find Meaning? Or why do we even attempt to look for it? Or as the Housekeeper puts it in Act II, "Why does anyone do anything?"

The Great Question prompts The Great Answer, which does in fact answer the Great Question, but only temporarily, before prompting the Great Question again, which prompts the Great Answer again, and on and on the Answer and Question tumble, like two boys wrestling down a hill.

The Great Answer, of course, is **Love**. And just as the Great Question can never be satisfactorily answered, the Great Answer can never be satisfactorily defined, despite the tireless work of poets and scientists. What in the hell is Love?

And, again, why are we here? What is Life?

There used to be a Museum of Automata in York, England (I believe it was purchased and moved wholesale to Japan). On one of the pages of the catalogue of this defunct museum is a one-page description of Vaucanson's life, with a photo of an enormous contraption with a duck on top and the caption "photo purporting to be of Vaucanson's duck." In the midst of the most miserable writer's block of my life, I was staring at this photo one day wondering a) what do they mean "purporting"? If it isn't Vaucanson's duck, then what the heck is it? and b) why a duck?

I might have forgotten about this moment if I hadn't been listening to very serious stirring music from a modern string quartet at the time. I had read a paragraph about Spallanzani's famous experiment with frogs just the day previous, and the juxtaposition of music, the image of the duck, and the reminder of Spallanzani's experiment, gave birth to *Great Men of Science, Nos. 21 & 22*. I had known that the Royal Academy of Sciences in the 18th century sponsored annual contests, so I devised a contest for 1738 to prove or refute a statement by mathematician Abraham DeMoivre—"The Apparent Randomness of Events in Nature Will, if Subjected to Calculation, Reveal an Underlying Order Expressing Exquisite Wisdom and Design."

Is DeMoivre right or not? I don't know, but I do know that the endless revolutions of the Great Question and Great Answer provide the engine that sends humanity hurtling forward in bewilderment and awe.

I hope you enjoy the play.

ACT I: Life, the Canard

The Story of Jacques de Vaucanson's Great Labour

CHARACTERS:
Jacques de Vaucanson
Gabrielle du Chatelet
Abbe
Le Cat
Lazarro Spallanzani
Citizens #1-#4, Member of Academy, etc.

2

Note for Act I Set: Slide projection suggested. Consider as well utilizing projection screen as a screen for 18th century-style silhouette-tableaus.

Note for Act I Music: Music is strongly recommended for the production. Modern, yet evoking the 18th-century, intricate, repetitive, and stirring.

TIME: 1738

> *Lights up slowly to reveal GABRIELLE DU CHATELET, dressed as the Goddess of Reason. She sings—*

CHATELET: *(singing)* Awake my Paris...
  Stir from thy slumberings!
  The worlds you now strive in
  Shall be snuffed and forgotten,
  come the Dawn....
  Bid farewell and return to
  This one Dream we share...
  Paris.... Awake....

  Embrace the streets
  Embrace the anvils
  And sewers
  And markets
  And furnaces

  light up on VAUCANSON asleep in thinking pose

  And you...Jacques de Vaucanson...
  Great hope of our time...
  Whose mind burns with the
  Incandescency
  Of Genius...
  Now Dispel the mists from your eyes
  So you may dispel the great mist from ours
  So we may be brought
  Ever nearer...ever nearer....
  To the Age of Light....
  Leave your dreams behind....
  Behold!... the world....is thine........

  We see drawings of Moon and Sun. A ticking watch increases anticipation:

VAUCANSON: With its face always facing us, The Moon in this Minuet,
  moving counterclockwise, six tenths of a mile with every tick of the clock,
  bids Paris adieu for the day, and now we bow to the Sun, and Morning
  comes as Morning must!

  *The city awakes with cock crow and stirring music. Vaucanson conjectures to
  himself in his studio, perhaps utilizing quill and paper—*

VAUCANSON: *(conjecturing, not narrating)* A hammer, in a 34 degree arc, strikes
  a nail, one two three four times and Pause....

  *We see a man hammering a notice of heavy paper, one two three four times,
  pause. Then silence while—*

  ...And in the pause, in a puddle...the birth of a gnat. For now, at least, it
  lives. A fifth time hammer to nail and one more for good measure—

  The hammerer hammers once and one more for good measure

HAMMERER: The Annual Contest, sponsored by the Royal Academy of

Sciences, has today been made public! Devised for the year of our Lord Seventeen Hundred Thirty Eight!

CITIZEN #1: *(reading notice)* "With the highest Degree of Persuasiveness, Prove or Refute the following statement, uttered by the eminent mathematician Abraham de Moivre—"

> *Projected on a screen, or on a large banner unfurled, De Moivre's statement is written, and visible throughout the play. We hear the voice of DeMoivre, and, perhaps, see a rendering of DeMoivre, with moving mouth*

VOICE OF DE MOIVRE: "The Apparent *Randomness* of Events in Nature—

CITIZENS: The Apparent Randomness

VOICE OF DE MOIVRE: Will, if subjected to Calculation, Reveal an *underlying Order* Expressing Exquisite Wisdom and Design."

CITIZEN #1: *(reading)* "Prove or Refute."

> *For the following section, Citizens #1-#5 move with precision in a sort of minuet in the "street." ABBE is to the side, unseen by citizens. Vaucanson remains in studio.*

CITIZEN #2: What minds have turned to this question!

CITIZEN #3: To prove or refute is to prove or refute the existence of God—

VAUCANSON: Dear Lord grant me the courage and wherewithal to unveil Your secrets...Surely You do not mean them to be secrets forever....And surely now our gnat touches down on a hat. The right elbow bends, the hand is carried upward, and by pressure of thumb, the hat, with the gnat....is lifted.

> *The right elbow of Abbe bends, he takes off hat and bows*

CITIZEN #4: *(to Citizen #2)* Have you heard from D'Alembert?

CITIZEN #2: *(excitedly)* Oh yes—in affirmation of DeMoivre, he will show that Newton's Third Law of Motion applies to both freely-moving *and* stationary bodies.

CITIZEN #1: And what, pray tell, of Fontanelle—

CITIZEN #3: —the secretary of the Royal Academy is refuting the possibility that random events are anything but random. He said, and I quote, "It is beyond the reach of scientific investigation."

VAUCANSON: A gnat in the nose, and a sneeze!

> *Abbe sneezes*

CITIZEN #1: And what of Jacques de Vaucanson?

VAUCANSON: A sneeze.

> *Abbe sneezes*

CITIZEN #1: And what of Jacques de Vaucanson?

> *long pause*

VAUCANSON: A sneeze.

> *And an enormous sneeze from Abbe*

CITIZEN #4: Jacques de Vaucanson!

CITIZEN #2: A most promising young scientist—

CITIZEN #4: Startling—

CITIZEN #3: Insolent—

CITIZEN #1: Jacques de Vaucanson!

CITIZEN #2: Yet I have heard he has over-reached himself this time—

CITIZEN #3: It is a mathematical problem, and he is known for mechanical things—

CITIZEN #1: His rooms have been given over to every manner of machinery—

CITIZEN #3: He returns his meals uneaten—

CITIZEN #1: Only the Jesuit, the Abbe deFontaine, knows just what he labours on—

CITIZEN #4: Yes, the Abbe, whose fondness for Vaucanson is rivaled only by his fondness for a drink—

The Abbe, a dissipated older Jesuit, enters, carrying a parcel under his arm and putting a flask surreptitiously to his lips

CITIZEN #2: And I say! Isn't that the Abbe now—

VAUCANSON: A gnat near the mouth now flies to the eye—

ABBE: I have been—

Abbe swats gnat by eye with hand

VAUCANSON: A miss.

ABBE: —requested by Monsieur Vaucanson not to reveal the nature of his work. You will see soon enough.

CITIZEN #3: And that parcel you conceal from us—is it not for your young upstart?

ABBE: You will see soon enough.

CITIZEN #1: But you must give us something!

ABBE: I gave him my word—

CITIZEN #2: But he's the only one missing from our list—

Citizen #4 reads from his checklist, and checks "refute" or "affirm" in turn

CITIZEN #4: Clairaut will examine the variables in magnesia and quicklime.

ALL: Refute!

CITIZEN #4: Maupertuis will address the case of the polygon curve.

ALL: Refute!

CITIZEN #4: Couboursier will account for the irregularities in the observed motion of the planets.

ALL: Affirm!

CITIZEN #4: Burke will forecast the month in 1751 when Halley's comet shall return—

5

ALL: Affirm!

CITIZEN #4: Lavoisier will show that Halley's comet shall never return—

ALL: A refutation!

VAUCANSON: If I can but do it...

CITIZEN #3: So you won't let on?

CITIZEN #2: Come come, what is Jacques concocting?

VAUCANSON: If I can but do it—

CITIZEN #4: All of Paris wants to know—

VAUCANSON: Eyes will weep in gratitude—

CITIZEN #1: Divulge this at least: Will Vaucanson affirm or refute DeMoivre's statement?

CITIZEN #2: Will he affirm or refute DeMoivre's statement?

> *The music builds. We hear the rumble of carts on cobbles, the tension builds, and as church bells ring out across the city—*

ABBE: Affirm! He will affirm! And with a ringing declaration that will bring tears to the faithful and turn all the treatises of the Fontanelles and Buffons into so much bumf!

VAUCANSON: From the noblest man to the humblest gnat. Life!

CITIZEN #3: *(to Abbe)* Your neck, Monsieur.

> *Abbe swats neck, smashing gnat.*

VAUCANSON: and Death—

ABBE: *(exiting)* Good day!

> *Music intensifies, isolated light on Vaucanson*

VAUCANSON: *(passionate to tears and heroism)* —Nothing is random...Nothing is random, and I will prove it...Employing Newton's laws of attraction by which the tides behave and the planets are known to rotate; Using calculations plotting the movement of the stars themselves across the heavens; Utilizing a system of springs and weights, gearwheels, cogs and escapements of my own construction fashioned in ratios of proven mathematical laws and proportion.... I will create.... a Duck.... that flaps its wings, eats, and excretes...just like a duck!

> *The music ends, the stage clears. We then hear a number of insistent knocks on the door of the garret of Vaucanson. We become aware of the quack of ducks. Vaucanson is deeply engrossed in hard thought and pained study and intense labor.*

ABBE: *(unseen through door)* Monsieur Vaucanson, it is I —

VAUCANSON: *(quite in the middle of work)* It's open.

ABBE: It's not open.

> *Pause. Then knock knock knock*

VAUCANSON: It is open.

ABBE: Jacques it's locked.

VAUCANSON: It isn't. You have to push.

ABBE: I am. I am pushing.

VAUCANSON: No, push.... push.

ABBE: I'm pushing.

VAUCANSON: Hold the handle and push.

ABBE: For God's sake, it is locked.

VAUCANSON: It is not locked. I was occasioned to unlock it an hour ago.

> *Pause. More knocking. Pause.*

ABBE: Jacques. The door is locked.

VAUCANSON: I'm telling you it's open, stop knocking and push.

ABBE: Jacques, we do not have much time—

VAUCANSON: *(half to self)* I know....I know......in less than nine months I'm to present to the Academy a deterministic, dynamic model that yet will elucidate irregular, unpredictable behavior...how....how to accomplish all that needs doing when I haven't a sou to my name and I've lost my peruke...

> *pause*

ABBE: What? Your what? Jacques, I can't hear you.... Look, I have something here to show you if you would only—

> *tries door again*

...I think it will be a great aid in the solicitation of funds.... Please, I beg of you open the—

> *Vaucanson pulls on door, unfastens bolt, opens door*

VAUCANSON: It was locked after all. My apologies. Everywhere I turn, unexpected Impediments.

ABBE: You look terrible.

VAUCANSON: The work...The work involved..

ABBE: There's food outside the door—

VAUCANSON: Leave it outside.

ABBE: *(retrieving it)* You must try to eat a little.

VAUCANSON: I cannot.

ABBE: When was the last time you ate?

VAUCANSON: I don't remember. I can't even look at it.

ABBE: It is nourishment.

VAUCANSON: Put it out of sight.

ABBE: If you want it, it's over here.

VAUCANSON: Fine.

ABBE: Do you see? Over here.

VAUCANSON: Fine!

7

ABBE: Jacques, How are you proceeding ....

VAUCANSON: *(erupts)* **What contrivance can I use to make this artificial duck take up the corn and suck it up quite to its stomach I don't know! I don't know! I don't know!** calming.....the obstacles seem...insurmountable...

ABBE: But can you do it?

VAUCANSON: There is this. If I do not manage it, another will, in time. For all knowledge will be Man's, in time. I know I am at least 50 years ahead of my time. Perhaps 60. But perhaps this idea of mine is 80 years ahead of its time.

ABBE: And what then?

VAUCANSON: I'll have no choice but endeavor to stride yet another 20 years in nine months and only hope it wasn't 30 years I needed to traverse.

ABBE: What? Look, Jacques, sleep, there's such a thing as that....

VAUCANSON: I know, but when I finish. If I finish.

ABBE: And then it will be the sleep of the just.

VAUCANSON: Oh more than that my friend, more than that. With such exuberance will the angels dance in Heaven that the crowns will fall off of their heads!

ABBE: And yet you do not believe in heaven.

VAUCANSON: Not as such. Sit and I will explain to you the whole of my beliefs.

ABBE: Jacques de Vaucanson doubles over, clutches his abdomen, profanes the Lord and takes off his trousers.

> *Vaucanson doubles over in great pain*

VAUCANSON: Jesus.....God....!

> *Vaucanson hastens to unbutton trousers, and hops about from foot to foot to stifle the intense pain and refrain from urinating*

ABBE: What is it? Do you need the chamberpot?

VAUCANSON: Where's the chamberpot......

ABBE: Is it your bladder again.

VAUCANSON: The stones, oh the stones...

> *Vaucanson finds chamberpot and runs behind the silhouette screen*

ABBE: I thought you were improving...

VAUCANSON: No, if anything the spasms are more frequent.

ABBE: Haven't you seen a doctor?

VAUCANSON: No time. Or money....

ABBE: The suffering you endure...and yet still you continue...

VAUCANSON: *(with trousers at ankles, appearing from behind screen)* We must....We must persevere....it is all we can do...

He runs back behind screen. In silhouette, we see and hear Vaucanson urinating.

VAUCANSON: *(whilst urinating)* But what is this you were saying at the door—something about something to help us solicit funds?

ABBE: Oh yes, I was thinking we needed some sort of device to—

VAUCANSON: *(due to volume of urinating)* What? I can't hear you—

ABBE: *(raising voice to compete with urinating)* I was saying how I thought it would be —

VAUCANSON: I'm telling you, I can't hear you—

ABBE: *(raising voice still louder)* Well just that it occurred to me—

VAUCANSON: Damn it, can't you see I'm occupied!? A moment is all I ask!

Vaucanson yelps in pain, finishes urinating, and emerges trouserless.

ABBE: How are you?

VAUCANSON: Miserable.

ABBE: But are you taking anything for it?

VAUCANSON: *(pulling out a small flask)* Just this.

ABBE: What is it?

VAUCANSON: Turpentine.

ABBE: Does it work?

VAUCANSON: In theory, it should break down the stones, the stones being either calcium oxide or calcium phosphate or magnesium ammonium phosphate but I don't know. From time to time, I pass gravel. Perhaps that is a good sign.

ABBE: Perhaps.

VAUCANSON: Well there's nothing to be done.

ABBE: Surgery?

VAUCANSON: Never again. But friend, what is this about a device for raising money?

ABBE: I'm concerned about your gravel.

VAUCANSON: Never mind my gravel, if we can raise enough money to enable the realization of this duck I will be happy to pass the Alps in my urine. The Alps.

ABBE: Well. I thought to myself, how can we make our plea for funds more compelling, and this old Jesuit looked no further than another old Jesuit who invented.....this.

He opens the box he was carrying to reveal a Magic Lantern

VAUCANSON: A Magic Lantern?

ABBE: What do you think?

Abbe has set up Magic Lantern and random slides are "projected"

VAUCANSON: I think in elucidating some of the finer points in our fund-

9

raising presentations, yes the device of Jesuit mathematician, biologist and physicist Athanasius Kircher, who died in 1680, will be quite effective.

ABBE: *(showing random slides)* And if not, the images can still be most pleasing to look upon. "If what we say is confusing to you, at least take solace in viewing this picture of...

> *he changes the slide*

...a trout."

VAUCANSON: No! They must they must understand that we are furthering the case that God's world is not a whimsical and capricious one.

ABBE: And that of course is why, in the end, I am assisting you—

VAUCANSON: I do not deserve it. You have found suppliers and have been my invaluable liaison, you have raised much-needed funds, you have gone above and beyond—

ABBE: No, I'll hear no more of it. I once did you a terrible wrong.

> *A historical presentation utilizing magic lantern. We hear a hymn sung by a choir, and see slides depicting gears, orreries, angels, etc.:*

ABBE: Jacques de Vaucanson, you once had designs of being a Jesuit. You were 9 years old, a novice, and you constructed a mechanical angel. It opened its mouth in song and flapped its wings. "Just like an angel," you said. "Just like an angel indeed," said I. "How should you know how an angel flaps its wings? How naive, how presumptuous, nay blasphemous, to reduce a heavenly creature to cogs! cogs and gearwork!" "Look here you bitter ruinous old man," said you, "I wanted to see an angel come to life. You are beholding a year's labour." "And now," said I, "you will behold a moment's effort." And I smashed the angel to pieces in front of you. And you, 9 years old, replied, "Father....Man and Woman once lived in a Paradise. But this first paradise was *dependent* on their ignorance. With the first taste of knowledge, they were cast out. But it is you who are naive and presumptuous, nay blasphemous, if you believe God constructed this miracle of a world so that we may appreciate it as a blind man appreciates a painting. Just as Newton has revealed the laws governing the planets, that the planets move with a clockwork precision, those same laws must by necessity govern the natural world, and when we at last fully understand these laws, we will understand what God wants of us, what his intentions are and what our purpose is, and when we understand that, we will no longer be His helpless bawling child groping in the darkness, but His *helpmate* and His true friend and that will be the Second Paradise, the Lasting Paradise, the paradise dependent not on ignorance, not on ignorance, but on understanding, and we cannot turn back, no, not out of fear, not now." And with that you threw down your cassock, slammed the door, and left the Jesuits, striding through the city streets to your destiny.

VAUCANSON: Naked, for I wore nothing underneath my cassock.

ABBE: Yes.

VAUCANSON: Impassioned.

ABBE: Yes.

VAUCANSON: And I have carried that vision to this day, and now this!
—something much better, something real and observable...something
true....for yes like an angel, a duck too is God's creation, yes?

Silence

Why are you silent?

ABBE: I have just hit my funny bone. I am in great pain.

VAUCANSON: *(out of patience with his friend)* Have you arranged a presentation.

ABBE: For next Tuesday, but I'll need a list from you tomorrow of the images
we'll want to project, as well as a list of more necessary materials you
require for your construction as another shipment goes out Friday.

VAUCANSON: Yes.

ABBE: And perhaps knowing there will be some money for your cogs and
springs will permit you to sleep a bit easier?

VAUCANSON: Yes but... No....

ABBE: No?

VAUCANSON: No, for there is a further difficulty that threatens to undo all
our good intentions....

ABBE: A further difficulty...

pause

VAUCANSON: My ratios...I have lost all of my ratios.

ABBE: Your Ratios?

VAUCANSON: Yes....

ABBE: Are they important?

VAUCANSON: The duck cannot be made without them.

ABBE: And you cannot reconstitute the ratios?

VAUCANSON: Perhaps, but it would take me weeks of lost time, for they are
built on discoveries that have taken me years to uncover through sweat
and toil and miserable nights.

ABBE: And you don't know where you have misplaced them.

VAUCANSON: No....no, I know....

ABBE: You do know?

VAUCANSON: Yes.

ABBE: Then the difficulty—

VAUCANSON: The difficulty.... the difficulty.... oh god, the difficulty.... is
that.... I am in love with Gabrielle-Emilie, the Marquise du Chatelet.

Lights up on tableau of Chatelet

VAUCANSON: She has green eyes and had Euclid and Virgil memorized before she was 12…Entrancing, enraging, and the first to translate Isaac Newton's *Principia Mathematica* into French…Who is like her? I….I never want to leave you.

> *Vaucanson is now lying in bed. It is evening. Distant strains from a ball are heard. Perhaps a slide with title "Three Weeks Previous." The interaction between the two of them should feel as natural as possible.*

CHATELET: But Jacques, your work—that must come first.

VAUCANSON: My work, yes. This contest of which you've just informed me intrigues. But how can I prove that events in nature are not random?

CHATELET: Not with pen and paper—

VAUCANSON: No, you're right, not a treatise..I need to create…a living testament!

CHATELET: Your submission to the Annual Contest will be nothing short of genius…

VAUCANSON: If I can but manage it.

CHATELET: You will.

VAUCANSON: I don't know…Or no, yes, yes I will. I am with you and somehow nothing seems out of reach…Must we still keep the two of us a secret?

CHATELET: We must.

VAUCANSON: Your husband the Marquis.

CHATELET: My husband.

VAUCANSON: Come back to bed.

CHATELET: I am expected downstairs.

VAUCANSON: From here you can hear the ball—

CHATELET: But I'm the one who threw it—

VAUCANSON: You have set the dance in motion—now, as God does, let it run, in perfect harmony, without you.

CHATELET: *(kissing him)* No..no… I really must return, and you must go.....

VAUCANSON: I can't bear it!

CHATELET: Go forth and astonish the world.

VAUCANSON: I'll do my astonishing from this bed.

CHATELET: That's not what the Academy has in mind.

VAUCANSON: Who would even think to disprove DeMoivre?

CHATELET: Well, Fontanelle for one.

VAUCANSON: Let him try.

CHATELET: Francois Arouet for another....

VAUCANSON: Ah. Francois Arouet.

CHATELET: Yes. Francois Arouet.

12

VAUCANSON: Francois Arouet?

CHATELET: Yes, Francois Arouet.

pause

VAUCANSON: By Francois Arouet you mean of course Voltaire.

CHATELET: Yes.

VAUCANSON: *(feigning nonchalance)* So you have heard from him? Voltaire?

CHATELET: Yes.

VAUCANSON: So he is back from Prussia?

CHATELET: Yes.

VAUCANSON: And you have spoken with him.

CHATELET: I have spoken with him.

VAUCANSON: But did you not say yourself...*(now erupting)* that you were through with him?!

CHATELET: Only I can keep his imagination in check. The mischievous man must be kept out of mischief, his wings clipped. Whereas you....your wings require nothing less than the sky's infinite expanse.

VAUCANSON: But all the same, do you not find his company anything but trying?

CHATELET: You mean excepting those days of poetry and picnics? Or the evenings in the laboratory? Our coach last year overturned on a freezing winter's night and help had to be sent for...How did we pass the time? Curled up together in a pile of Russian rugs, identifying the outlines of the lesser constellations....

We see slides depicting constellations of Delphinus, Cepheus, etc.

That for one was a beautiful night...

VAUCANSON: It sounds indeed beautiful. *(Brooding—)* Even if you took me as a lover only to spite him...

CHATELET: No Jacques, don't believe it—

VAUCANSON: Even if I am merely a pawn in a lover's quarrel, it has backfired, for I am smitten, utterly, and there isn't a set of calipers in the universe that could measure the length and breadth of it, and I will devote myself to convincing you—

CHATELET: Make this contest then the definitive argument—work and prove Voltaire and his skepticism are misguided....

VAUCANSON: I will Gabrielle, I will, yes, let me show you....

CHATELET: Done then.

VAUCANSON: And perhaps, in the meantime, you should not see the man.

CHATELET: Voltaire? No, I will still see him.

VAUCANSON: So you will still see him?

CHATELET: Yes.

13

VAUCANSON: I see. So you will still see him then.

CHATELET: Yes.

VAUCANSON: As a friend.

CHATELET: Yes, as a friend.

VAUCANSON: Good. For he is an old friend.

CHATELET: Yes.

VAUCANSON: So as a friend. *(pause)* And as a lover?

CHATELET: You mustn't fret over such things.

VAUCANSON: I mustn't fret because of course you will not see him as a lover, or I mustn't fret because it will just upset me tremendously?

CHATELET: The latter.

VAUCANSON: The latter.

CHATELET: I have seen him. I am still seeing him, and in fact, he is on his way here as we speak.

VAUCANSON: As we speak?

CHATELET: Yes.

VAUCANSON: *(exasperated)* "As we"—How could you invite him here!? Where are my trousers! He is approaching as we speak?! Mon Dieu! What do you see in that man!

CHATELET: You have a rare and noble spirit Jacques de Vaucanson..... But he is wittier.

VAUCANSON: For holding nothing sacred he is to be admired?

CHATELET: Perhaps you are right.

VAUCANSON: Perhaps not.

CHATELET: He declared DeMoivre's statement the desperate hope of a febrile old man.

VAUCANSON: He said this? When all of nature argues against it?

CHATELET: He often speaks of you.

VAUCANSON: Does he.

CHATELET: He has great admiration for you.

VAUCANSON: Does he.

14

    A servant enters.

SERVANT: Monsieur Voltaire has arrived.

VAUCANSON: God my god....

CHATELET: You will return to the dancing?

VAUCANSON: No.

CHATELET: Where will you go?

VAUCANSON: I need some air.

CHATELET: He would like to meet you.

VAUCANSON: Yes, and you and all your guests can have fun at my expense. Gabrielle... I can prove him wrong, and if I do succeed, I must know, I must know...will I have your favour? Will you pledge yourself to me alone?

Pause

CHATELET: It's likely.

VAUCANSON: That is enough.

CHATELET: *(handing him peruke)* Take this.

VAUCANSON: I am missing a shoe.

CHATELET: By the window, and please do not be upset.

VAUCANSON: I'm fine I'm fine. But I have to go. Fine then...I'll be off.

CHATELET: Your peruke is crooked.

VAUCANSON: My peruke?

CHATELET: Jacques de Vaucanson, scientist, lover, erupts with an expletive—

VUACANSON: Fuck my peruke!

CHATELET: Right hand clutches, throws down, peruke, and off he storms, slamming door, leaving peruke.

Vaucanson throws down peruke, turns, Storms out of room, slams door. Lights up again on Abbe.

ABBE: So you threw down your peruke...

VAUCANSON: Yes, and I felt great about it. At the time.

ABBE: But what does all that have to do with your ratios?

VAUCANSON: The ratios are in my peruke.

ABBE: Ah, I see. You keep your ratios in your peruke.

VAUCANSON: Yes.

ABBE: And when was this?

VUACANSON: I don't know...three weeks ago.

ABBE: Well good god man, get them back!

VAUCANSON: *(tortured)* I can't.......I can't.......because....no doubt...Voltaire is there as we speak....they are in each other's arms as we speak.....

Pause. Vaucanson broods.

But friend, perhaps you could retrieve my peruke.   15

ABBE: *(matter-of-factly, in one sentence—)* I would do anything for you, but you know in this instance that I cannot. I am that man's sworn enemy after I criticized his work on Newton and he denounced me in his pamphlet *Le Preservatif*, and I responded with the stinging condemnation *La Voltairomanie*; and we who once were friends! But of course, he still thinks I should be indebted to him but it is because he is under the mistaken assumption that it was he alone who sprung me from prison after the spurious charge that I corrupted young boys.

VAUCANSON: Damn Damn this peruke. As if I hadn't other things to think about....

ABBE: Do you think it's still in the bedroom?

VAUCANSON: (resigned) Perhaps a servant has carried it away.....or thrown it away...

ABBE: (alarmed) Yes, oh christ, or thrown it away. Look, We must take a coach there together immediately—

VAUCANSON: (spurred to action) You'll make inquiries with the servants, and perhaps I can enter the bedroom, if it is unoccupied, via the window...and seek out the curséd hairpiece!

ABBE: We'll find the fastest coach.

VAUCANSON: Until then, every moment is a moment lost.

> The Abbe and Vaucanson exit. Lights up on Minuet Interlude. Stirring violin, harpsichord. Chatelet, dancers. Vaucanson and other characters take their places in minuet.

CHATELET: Before we can consider the Minuet, we must consider the complexity and harmony inherent in a single step! We must go Neither fast nor slow—The former is Folly, the latter is Indolence. And Above all, no affectation; the steps must progress naturally, and yet in each step, there is effort, there is premeditation. The knees boldly stretched—The legs slightly turned outward—Head upright, waist steady—

With the left arm forward, we advance the right foot...

We have begun...

> A knock on Vaucanson's door. Door opened tentatively. LE CAT enters. Finds no one. Makes himself comfortable. Peruses papers scattered about. LeCat glances at his pocket watch. As diagrams of setting sun, and of rising moon, are projected, Le Cat muses—

LE CAT: Though standing still, and still as still as it has always stood, the Sun, notwithstanding, steals from view as we pirouette west to east never ceasing never ceasing, and Evening descends as Evening will....

> Vaucanson enters worse for wear.

VAUCANSON: My pardons, I attempted travel this morning only to reach midway and watch the wheel of our carriage fall off and roll away and now the wheel and day are lost... irretrievably....

LE CAT: Monsieur Vaucanson.

VAUCANSON: Do I know you?

LE CAT: You do not. But it is an honor to meet you, I have heard much of your abilities.

VAUCANSON: How did you get in?

LE CAT: The door was open.

VAUCANSON: No no I locked it.

16

LE CAT: It was unlocked.

VAUCANSON: It must have been locked.

LE CAT: But it was not.

VAUCANSON: It was locked, surely.

LE CAT: No.

VAUCANSON: But I take pains to secure the door whene'er I leave.

LE CAT: It was not secured.

VAUCANSON: Are you sure?

LE CAT: I am quite sure.

VAUCANSON: The window perhaps?

LE CAT: I did not come in through the window. Nor did spontaneously generate from that plate of meat.

VAUCANSON: I did not wish to suggest that you had. My pardons if you thought I thought you had generated spontaneously from that plate of meat. I suppose the secrecy I cloaked my project in was a privilege I'd have to relinquish sooner or later. You've been here long?

LE CAT: Long enough to examine your sketches... An artificial duck that stretches its neck to take corn from your hand!

VAUCANSON: *(growing excited again)* Yes, from the hand! then swallows it greedily, and doubles the swiftness in the motion of its neck and gullet to drive the food into its stomach where it will be digested by dissolution, not trituration as some would have it. The matter digested is conducted by pipes quite to the Anus, where there is a Sphincter that lets it out.

LE CAT: So you have set out to refute DeMoivre's statement.

VAUCANSON: No, I have set out to prove DeMoivre's statement.

LE CAT: But you are constructing an artificial duck.

VAUCANSON: Yes sir, were you not listening?

LE CAT: If you don't mind my saying so, you will never accomplish it.

VAUCANSON: So far, Courage and Patience have overcome everything. And now if you'll excuse me, I have much work to do, Monsieur... I'm sorry, what was your name?

LE CAT: Le Cat.

VAUCANSON: Le Cat? If you are Le Cat then you are the most celebrated surgeon in Paris.

LE CAT: I am Le Cat. Now please, undress, and I shall peruse your penis.

VAUCANSON: You'll what? Ah, You have heard of my adversity.

LE CAT: I have.

VAUCANSON: Madame Du Chatelet recommends you highly, but I cannot afford a doctor.

LE CAT: Do not worry about the cost, for it was Madame who sent me here. I

17

was with her this morning.

VAUCANSON: This morning?

LE CAT: Please, your trousers.

VAUCANSON: You were with the Madame this morning?

LE CAT: Yes, Monsieur Arouet was distressed at her condition and had me summoned.

VUACANSON: Monsieur Arouet?

LE CAT: Yes.

VUACANSON: Francois Arouet?

LE CAT: Yes.

VAUCANSON: By Francois Arouet you mean of course Voltaire?

LE CAT: Yes.

VAUCANSON: He was there was he...Voltaire...

> *Vaucanson, trouserless, picks up a very large book and reads a page to hide his thoughts while Le Cat speaks*

LE CAT: Oh yes, they are much in love, I don't usually believe in such tripe but you can feel it in the air, their love...

VAUCANSON: Fine.

LE CAT: —and early this morning he was alarmed to find Madame suffering from great swoons and any amount of vomit.

VAUCANSON: My God is she all right?

LE CAT: In a manner of speaking. She is pregnant.

VUACANSON: *(to self, with delight)* Great swoons... and any amount of vomit... are two reactions contemplated then suppressed by this scientist upon hearing the news of a pump beating in tiny 2/4 counterpoint to the greater pump above it and all this occurred in the time it took for a large book to slip from the hands and fall at a velocity proportional not to its weight but to the time elapsed in its falling.

LE CAT: *(rewinding to previous line:)* In a manner of speaking. She is pregnant.

> *The book falls from the hands of Vaucanson with a thud*

VAUCANSON: I see.

18

LE CAT: Yes, and true to her nature, she said never mind her, she would foot the bill if I went straight away to the studios of the suffering Jacques de Vaucanson.

VUACANSON: *(failing to disguise excitement)* But this is.....this is staggering....

LE CAT: Is it.

VAUCANSON: ...How truly... miraculous... for her..

LE CAT: Yes, well Shall we get on? If you may, please bend from the waist to 85 degrees.

VAUCANSON: (*bending*) A child... Well!...(*ready to compute—*)... And how pregnant is she?

LE CAT: There is another eight months before the infant receives the first of many rude shocks....

VAUCANSON: Eight months... yes, that would do it... amazing... amazing... a tiny life....

LE CAT: Well you seem certainly more moved by the event than Voltaire...

VUACANSON: (*sobered by possibility of paternal rival*) Oh yes, Voltaire. (*testing*) How did he take the news?

LE CAT: I can't say favorably. After all, in less than a month, Madame's husband is expected home from the military campaigns in Corsica—

VUACANSON: (*still more sobered*) Oh yes, her husband....

LE CAT: (*examining rectal area*) There's quite a scar I see... You've had surgery before?

VAUCANSON: Three years ago.

LE CAT: It's a perilous operation. One's chances of survival are quite small.

VAUCANSON: That fact was made known to me only afterward. How close...how close I came to obliteration.... And all for a stone.

LE CAT: A trivial death is the most appropriate sort of death for it does not obscure, nay in fact it underscores, the irrefutable insignificance of individual life. Don't you agree?

VAUCANSON: No I do not, and the stone they removed was the size of a tennis ball.

LE CAT: I don't doubt it.

VAUCANSON: And I still pass gravel in my urine. No, never the knife again.

LE CAT: Well, if you change your mind, I have developed techniques that avoid many of the complications caused by this sort of surgery in the past.

VAUCANSON: What sort of complications?

LE CAT: Well, sterility for one.

  pause

VAUCANSON: Sterility?

LE CAT: You were made aware that a procedure like the one you endured almost always results in sterility.

VAUCANSON: (*devastated*) Sterility. No. No I was not made aware.

LE CAT: Do you have children?

VAUCANSON: Do I have children?

  A slide is projected—a lateral view of the male reproductive system with penis

LE CAT: It's a lateral cut of the perineum to reach the urethra, where the stone is impacted, and the slightest slip of the knife will sever the vas deferens which connects to it.

VAUCANSON: *(profound dejection)* And the vas deferens carries the juice of the testicles.

LE CAT: Yes. I'm sorry to have to tell you but it's a near certainty. I thought you knew...

VUACANSON: *(half to self)* ...and we can be reasonably assured then that Voltaire has not the same curse upon him....

LE CAT: I should say he has amply proved otherwise...

VAUCANSON: ...no little chicks... and my life will end with me... and all that will live on... *(taking solace)*… is my work....

LE CAT: And all because from the same tube men emit both waste and life...which perhaps is why waste and life are so difficult to distinguish from one another....

VAUCANSON: You say so, but I do not think so....

LE CAT: You do not think so, but think of Needham, who through the tube of his microscope witnessed in a teardrop the swarming of little eels so small that a cluster of a million could not be discerned by the human eye. A cluster of a million! And no doubt this universe is but another teardrop, containing all of mankind and all his great grand history besides. Blot it up with a handkerchief and who, pray tell, will take notice?

VUACANSON: You may well ask!

LE CAT: I needn't ask, for I know the answer. No one. And no thing.

VUACANSON: No sir, no sir, no event goes unfelt, and even the flap of wings on a gnat now dead may no doubt be amplified through space and time into a thunderclap, for all things are ineluctably connected—

LE CAT: I assure you sir, the stars stand aloof, and so do I.

VUACANSON: You can try, but I tell you not a particle in the universe can make such a claim, much less a surgeon—

LE CAT: —One who sees all this soup of living and dying for what it is—a dish of laughable insignificance.

VAUCANSON: There is nothing laughable and nothing insignificant. Do you not see that in the infinite chain of beings, our earth, our body, are among the necessary links? In every droplet of sea water you'll find Needham's little eels. Look and you'll see the movement of one little eel affecting and affected by other little eels, and other little eels still other little eels, until the entire droplet is affected, and each droplet affecting other countless droplets until it is the very sea that is affected, yes the sea, that engenders clouds, and the clouds that furnish the rain that nourishes the earth that binds the moon that makes the tides that affects the ships, and sailors on ships, and the wives of those sailors on ships and the handkerchiefs of those wives waved at departing sailors on ships, and the teardrops in those handkerchiefs and the eels in those tear drops, the eels sir, the eels sir...To say nothing of the sailors' wives' grandfathers' uncles!

20

LE CAT: To say nothing is right. You have said nothing as to the purpose of it all. To what end?

VUACANSON: That we will discover in time, and in the meantime we have this... *(searching for word)* this dance.... And there is no begging out of it—you say you stand aloof, but a man who says he has left a ballroom has done nothing of the sort. He has merely stepped outside and under the stars and into an even greater, all-encompassing, incomparable Minuet.

LE CAT: A Minuet. If this Universe is a dance, sir, it is nothing more than the spasmodic dance of a boy who has just burned his tongue.

VUACANSON: *(the gracious host)* Yes, well, thank you doctor. Now if you don't mind, I have much work—

LE CAT: I have some suggested courses of treatment—

VAUCANSON: Thank you all the same, but I'm not interested, you can tell Madame Chatelet I said as much—

LE CAT: Madame Chatelet, yes, I nearly forgot—she sent this on to give to you.

Le Cat hands Vaucanson his peruke

VAUCANSON: My peruke! Say what you will Le Cat, but I will prove all your doubts wrong with this.....

LE CAT: With your peruke?

But Vaucanson realizes the ratios are not to be found

VAUCANSON: Le Cat, did you not perhaps from this wig see slip a slip of paper as you traveled from Chatelet's?

LE CAT: No.

pause

VAUCANSON: No matter.... No matter. But if you would be so good as to survey your carriage.

LE CAT: Of course. May I ask what the slip contained?

VAUCANSON: Merely... effort.

LE CAT: It occurs to me that as I was riding here I espied a spider within your peruke and I shook the peruke violently outside the window, dislodging the spider—

VAUCANSON: —and perhaps the paper—

LE CAT: It is possible.

VAUCANSON: Where was this?

LE CAT: Some miles between Paris and Cirey on the King's Highway.

VAUCANSON: Can you be more specific?

LE CAT: No.

VAUCANSON: Right, fine, thank you. I will show you now the door—

LE CAT: Thank you all the same but I can find it myself. I wouldn't recommend across this floor any unclad feet....

notices toes of Vaucanson poking through large holes in his stockings

My dear sir, your feet—

VAUCANSON: Yes.

LE CAT: They're webbed.

VAUCANSON: An incomplete separation of the digits. My father's feet were the same.

LE CAT: Were they.... And his father's before him?

VAUCANSON: I don't know.

LE CAT: Because it is a trait known to pass from one generation to the next.

VAUCANSON: Is it?

LE CAT: But of course, Sterile Sam, the trait will end with you...

VAUCANSON: *(through gritted teeth)* Yes. It will end with me. And now the door—

LE CAT: Webbed feet. So that is why you've set out to construct of all things, a clockwork duck.

VAUCANSON: No, actually...that hadn't occurred to me....

LE CAT: Come sir, surely—

VAUCANSON: No, it is coincidence.

LE CAT: Pure accident! And here you are constructing a duck to prove there is no such thing! How then did you fix upon the idea specifically of a duck?

VAUCANSON: *(suspicious)* Do you really want to know?

LE CAT: I do.

> *We hear crickets, frogs, distant ducks, and see perhaps a projection "3 weeks previous"*

VUACANSON: *(carrying shoes)* How the sky was awash with stars that night of the ball at Du Chatelet's chateau....It was about three weeks ago, I was in a disagreeable mood, I needed air, but just as I was taking my leave for the evening I was foolishly convinced in participating in that vexatious game wherein all the shoes of all the guests are piled in one enormous pile, and when all was said and done, I wound up with shoes that resembled mine in every respect except they were too small by half. As I roamed the grounds wet with dew—

> *We hear the sound of a man vomiting into a body of water*

22

I heard coming from the banks of the pond—

> *More vomiting, and Lazarro Spallanzani is revealed. Pitiful groans heard from the man as well. Italian accent, clearly exhausting for him to communicate with Vaucanson, and a struggle for Vaucanson as well. By end of scene however, they are finishing each other's sentences.*

VAUCANSON: The punch at Madame du Chatelet's gatherings tends to be quite strong.

SPALLANZANI: I cannot-a speak-a French.

VUACANSON: You are Italian.

SPALLANZANI: Yes, so... how you say... shove off.

VAUCANSON: My pardons. Never mind.

SPALLANZANI: But what is it that you said. I must try. I must try.

VAUCANSON: Merely that you've had too much to drink....

SPALLANZANI: No, no, I never drink! It is...the after-effects....

VAUCANSON: Yes?

SPALLANZANI: of... what is the word..........oh to hell with it.

VAUCANSON: No, no, What? You must try. The after-effects of what.

SPALLANZANI: The after-effects of... experiments I performed on-a myself.

VAUCANSON: Experiments? For the contest sponsored by the Royal Academy?

SPALLANZANI: No. The contest, it has-a been made public?

VAUCANSON: It hasn't, but perhaps you had gotten wind—

SPALLANZANI: No no, I do not have-a wind. But you found out this contest? From whom?

VAUCANSON: I have only just now been informed by Madame Du Chatelet.

SPALLANZANI: Ah, they say-a she is a most-a remarkable woman.

VAUCANSON: She is...most remarkable.... *(aside)* And what with Voltaire having just returned, I for now must extinguish all thought of her, or I will surely torment myself to oblivion...

SPALLANZANI: *(half to self)* Why I am here? I would not be missed if I left.

VAUCANSON: Were you not invited?

SPALLANZANI: No. Yes. I mean France. This...Earth.

VAUCANSON: *(encouragingly)* I hear there will be fireworks later.

SPALLANZANI: The fireworks will never come.... How do you say in French.... How-a vain-a is all-a human thought!

VAUCANSON: Your French is sound, but not your conclusion.

SPALLANZANI: How-a petty is all our ideas!

VAUCANSON: You are overwrought.

SPALLANZANI: Petty! And How-a poor our glories and-a all our labors!

VAUCANSON: No. Shush!

> *pause*

SPALLANZANI: How-a wretched we are!

VAUCANSON: Quiet.

> *pause*

SPALLANZANI: Wretched.

VAUCANSON: No. Cease and I will tell you the topic of this year's contest.

23

SPALLANZANI: I am very sick.

While Spallanzani retches with volume and violence, Vaucanson recites:

VUACANSON: The contest is thus.
Prove or refute the following statement:
The Apparent Randomness of Events in Nature
Will, if subjected to Calculation,
Reveal an underlying Order....
Expressing Exquisite Wisdom and Design

SPALLANZANI: I did not get any of that. Once more please.

VAUCANSON: The Apparent.......Oh what's the point...

SPALLANZANI: No no, you must tell me... you must try....

VUACANSON: *(miming/gesturing as best he can, but ridiculously)* The Apparent Randomness of Events in Nature—

SPALLANZANI: The apparent randomness...

VAUCANSON: *(miming)* Yes—Will, If Subjected to Calculation,

SPALLANZANI: yes...

VAUCANSON: *(miming)* Reveal an Underlying Order

SPALLANZANI: An Underlying Order—

VUACANSON: *(miming)* Expressing Exquisite Wisdom and Design. Prove or refute.

SPALLANZANI: Ah yes, and tell me, will you prove or refute?

VAUCANSON: Prove.

SPALLANZANI: How.

VAUCANSON: *(clutching Spallanzani)* I don't know, but I must...must think of something, Everything depends on it!

SPALLANZANI: Tonight my mood is black, yes, but I don't see how it can be done without much deceit.

VAUCANSON: No, I cannot believe that.

SPALLANZANI: It is all foul and pointless endeavorings. Instead of vomiting into this duck pond, I should drown myself in it. But the problem...is that I can swim, and I would swim through the muck and the lilypad back-a to the edge despite myself, yes? It makes-a no sense, why I should cling to this...dunghill.

VAUCANSON: You are feeling low after a failed experiment, that is all. I have often felt the same way..

SPALLANZANI: I don't-a care! But…perhaps.

VUACANSON: What experiment were you working on before being forced to abandon it?

SPALLANZANI: *(Becoming animated)* It concerned-a.....Life!

VAUCANSON: Excellent!

24

SPALLANZANI: How inert matter somehow becomes flesh...

VAUCANSON: For instance?

SPALLANZANI: Seména.

VUACANSON: What?

SPALLANZANI: *(with heavy accent)* Seména.

VUACANSON: *(not getting it)* One more time.

SPALLANZANI: Seména!

VUACANSON: One more time.

SPALLANZANI: Seména!

    pause

VUACANSON: *(straining)* One more time.

SPALLANZANI: Oh to hell with it.

VUACANSON: *(timidly trying again)* Semena?

SPALLANZANI: I said forget it!

VUACANSON: Fine.

SPALLANZANI: *(under breath)* To hell with everyone.

VUACANSON: I'm sorry?

SPALLANZANI: I said to hell with you!

VUACANSON: Well to hell with you!

SPALLANZANI: Just-a leave me alone, eh? I want to be just-a with the lilypads and the frogs...

VUACANSON: Fine. You have your liberty. The croaking's too loud for me anyway.

SPALLANZANI: They are seeking mates..

VUACANSON: *(walking away, to self—)* And they'll find nothing but heartache and despair—

SPALLANZANI: The female frog, she lays her 20,000 eggs, and the male sprays his seména on top of them, and in one week, tadpoles.

VUACANSON: *(stops, now realizing)* ...semen.......Semen!

SPALLANZANI: Yes! Yes! Semena! Inert matter! And in one week, tadpoles! How? How is this possible?

VAUCANSON: Yes —How indeed. What is it in the semen that creates life?

SPALLANZANI: No one knows, but I can tell you that it is the same for both man and frog.

VAUCANSON: Ah but look here, man is not a frog.

SPALLANZANI: Is man not a frog?

VAUCANSON: I say to you Man is not a Frog.

SPALLANZANI: The difference, it is trivial.

    duck quack and frog croak at minimum volume

VAUCANSON: I don't know his name, but Impulses from the gastrointestinal tract of my fellow scientist have been sent to his brain. The brain then sends back impulses that precipitate spasmodic muscular contractions. The pressure generated forces up the contents of his stomach, namely: bile, three prunes and a dollop of porridge.

SPALLANZANI: I do not-a know his name, but in the pelvis of this fellow, the muscular sac, holding a half a pint of urine, is irritated by a calcium concretion floating in the urine, and suddenly begins persistent-a rigid contractions.

Beat. Then Vaucanson is attacked by an intense bladder spasm, and almost simultaneously, Spallanzani begins retching with violence and misery. Quite Prolonged. Vaucanson attempts to stifle pain and prevent from urinating, while desperately attempting to undo his trousers but a button becomes stuck. He rolls on ground, he stands up again, fighting with button. Frog croak and duck quack quite voluble.

VUACANSON: (*with violence*) I can't undo the button! Come button! Cursed button!

Spallanzani, retching now waning, has collapsed on ground, and crawls toward Vaucanson. Vaucanson has sudden realization that his bladder is emptying into his trousers.

VUACANSON: Oh God.......

Vaucanson sinks to ground

SPALLANZANI: Your pants, they are damp.

VUACANSON: You see a man in trousers humiliated.

SPALLANZANI: Do not be embarrassed.

VAUCANSON: This wretched wretched bladder....I'd sooner not eat or drink anything again—

SPALLANZANI: No, no.... We eat and we grow into men.

VAUCANSON: (*stimulated*) Ah, again—inert matter into living matter....

SPALLANZANI: Yes, food! That is it. In our stomach...a...a...

VUACANSON: Yes, yes..a...a..

SPALLANZANI: A....how you say—

VUACANSON: a...a...Transubstantiation!

SPALLANZANI: A what?

VUACANSON: Food into flesh—

SPALLANZANI: That is good—

VAUCANSON: These were the experiments you conducted?

SPALLANZANI: My rival Reaumur, damn him, he persuaded a duck to swallow a sponge that the duck then regurgitated.

VAUCANSON: Go on.

SPALLANZANI: But are the juices in the human-a stomach like those in other beasts? That is the question. So I myself swallowed not just a sponge, but many-a bags of chemicals.

VAUCANSON: You shewed admirable conviction—

SPALLANZANI: But I could not vomit them up again! Reaumur's duck, he could, that god-damn duck, he could and I could not. And now I think the packets have broken open for I vomit all the time, and with blood.

VAUCANSON: I have seen a human carnival performer who swallowed stones for a living and then regurgitate them at will. You might have hired someone like him to swallow your packets.

pause

SPALLANZANI: I did not think of that.

VAUCANSON: Nevertheless, yours was a worthy experiment.

SPALLANZANI: And yet I am sure I would find the gastric juices similar between man and duck.

VAUCANSON: But look here, man is not a duck.

SPALLANZANI: Is man not a duck?

VAUCANSON: I say to you Man is not a Duck.

SPALLANZANI: The difference, it is trivial.

VAUCANSON: No. Our nobility, our reason, puts us in a different class altogether from the duck...

SPALLANZANI: And yet.....look...look at one of those creatures...

Spallanzani points at duck by pond, we hear gentle quacking

SPALLANZANI: See! It walks, it flutters its wings, it feels irritations—

VAUCANSON: Yes, you're right, it runs away, it comes back again—

SPALLANZANI: —it-a makes a complaining sound, yes? it feels pain—

VAUCANSON: —it shows affection—

SPALLANZANI: —it has desires, it gets-a pleasure from this or that....

Music more stirring, up on frogs and ducks

VAUCANSON: Yes you're right, it certainly shows all the emotions that you show!....

Music more stirring still

27

SPALLANZANI: —and it eats and eliminates just as you do.

VUACANSON: Better than I do!

SPALLANZANI: And here they say that it has-a no soul—that it's just a machine —

VAUCANSON: *(realization beginning to coalesce)* A machine? Oh no my friend, it is—

SPALLANZANI: No, that spark of life, it will never be explained.

VAUCANSON: We do not know it yet, but do not call that unknowable. Good god sir, are we not scientists? There were mysteries all around us that we... we have exploded! The formulas for that duck may be more complex than those of a clock—

SPALLANZANI: Hah! A hundred million billion times more complex—

VUACANSON: —fine! yes! but a hundred million billion is still a finite number, of course it is! And therefore, with time, attainable. I assure you sir, we are living equations—

SPALLANZANI: —machines then—

VUACANSON: —but how exquisite the Design....

Music now shimmering, inspiring—

SPALLANZANI: *(clutching Vaucanson's shoulders, with tears)* My god... it is true... it is true!.... Signore, we are living in a utopia...

VAUCANSON: *(clutching Spallanzani, with tears)* I know... I know, my friend....

SPALLANZANI: —under this canopy of stars...

VUACANSON: —aneath the music and whirrings of the spheres, it is truly—

SPALLANZANI: —the best of all—

VUACANSON: —possible worlds—

SPALLANZANI: —where even those ducks—

VUACANSON: —yes, those excreting ducks by a stagnant pond are—

SPALLANZANI: —a glorious necessity—

VUACANSON: —and contain within their atoms

SPALLANZANI: —the blueprint—

VUACANSON: —of the universe!... *(growing excited at a thought forming in head—)* ...indeed... indeed—

SPALLANZANI: *(pointing to the ground, ecstatic)* —Holy God, Signore—You have-a my shoes!

music still more stirring, and fireworks begin to be set off. A great booming, and slides of flares

VAUCANSON: *(ecstatic, clutching Spallanzani even tighter, and completing thought—)* Nothing is random!.. Nothing is random, and I will prove it!.. Employing Newton's laws of attraction by which the tides behave and the planets are known to rotate; Using calculations plotting the movement of the stars themselves across the heavens; Utilizing a system of springs and weights, gearwheels, cogs and escapements of my own construction fashioned in ratios of proven mathematical laws and proportion.... I will create... a Duck... that flaps its wings, eats, and excretes... just like a duck!

Musical coda. The slides change to another picture. Spallazani has exited.

VAUCANSON: Any questions?

It becomes clear that Vaucanson is now in the midst of a fund-raising presentation. The Abbe is assisting with the Magic Lantern slides.

CITIZEN #1: Why a duck?

VAUCANSON: I believe I have just explained to you why a duck.

CITIZEN #2: It is a clockwork.

VAUCANSON: Yes.

CITIZEN #2: Will it tell the time?

VAUCANSON: Of course not! But! Study the movement of the humerus in the wing and you will observe the same mathematical ratios that send Mars around the Sun, watch the duck stretch out its neck and you are witnessing the formulae that predict the curl of smoke from a pipe, steam from a kettle, the shape of a cumulus cloud or a plume of dust from a cart, in short, you will observe chaos itself made sensical by mathematical principles!

CITIZEN #3: Good God, you are creating the universe—

CITIZEN #2: What you propose sir is impossible!

VAUCANSON: Impossible?

CITIZEN #2: Of course you do not want to hear such an opinion.

VAUCANSON: No, no... tell me the things that are not possible, for those are the things that I will do... I require a minimum of funding and your names shall be attached to an undertaking that will be spoken of centuries hence!

Montage, with much music. We see Vaucanson hard at work, e.g. filing gears, tearing down designs from the wall, crippled by bladder spasms. We then see projected a landscape, with a road stretching on. We hear bird whistle, and the lowing of cows

ABBE: How large is this strip of paper?

VAUCANSON: Yea long.

pause

ABBE: And you propose we should walk yet a mile further on this road in search of it?

VAUCANSON: Have we a choice? I can little believe that such ratios, so vital to this work, nay, essential to the completion of it, will not return to my possession.

long pause

ABBE: But Jacques, the odds....

VAUCANSON: Blast the odds! Odds are irrelevant! This duck was meant to be made!

ABBE: I say.... *(spying scrap of paper on ground)* Jacques! Jacques!

They dive for the scrap. Vaucanson reads scrap

VAUCANSON: *(disappointed)* No, it is not the ratios. It appears to be a strip torn from a love letter.

ABBE: Here on the king's highway?

VUACANSON: It was a blustery day on November 12th. Perhaps in a man's hand is pressed a letter from his Love just as he is taking his leave. In his carriage he reads with great anticipation, but finds that instead of cooing phrases, she is calling it off. "Enough," she writes."I wish it done." The man shreds the letter and scatters it to the wind, and here a scrap descended, to lie befouled....in a ditch....

ABBE: Well that's certainly one possibility. *(concerned by Vaucanson's narrative)* Jacques.... How fares Madame Chatelet?

VAUCANSON: I wouldn't know.

ABBE: You have not heard from her?

VAUCANSON: I have not. Nor have I thought of her. *(pause)* I never think of her.

Thunder rumbles. A Storm begins.

ABBE: *(hopeful that they can now go home)* Shall we give up?

Pause. The rain falls hard.

VAUCANSON: No!

Thunder claps. Montage continues. Much music. We see Vaucanson building the framework, studying the movements of makeshift wings, drinking turpentine, running over list of more materials needed

VAUCANSON: Read it back to me.

ABBE: *(reading)* "One worm gear with 112-toothed wheel and threaded cylinder, 2.8 inch diameter, 20 feet of copper wire 11 pound torque, and additional amounts for the cubitus of the right wing. Also feathers. Mallard.

VAUCANSON: Good.

ABBE: But you have not found the ratios?

VAUCANSON: I will have to reconstruct them.

ABBE: Do you have time?

VAUCANSON: Plenty. If I do not sleep.

Montage continues, with Vaucanson tearing down designs from the wall, crippled by bladder spasms, fighting sleep, finally falling asleep. Darkness. We then hear, softly, Chatelet singing the opening song. Lights up. Jacques, at table, head resting on palm, slowly awakes, and singing softly next to him, a 8-month pregnant Chatelet.

VAUCANSON: You?

CHATELET: You.

VAUCANSON: Am I awake?

CHATELET: I promise.

VAUCANSON: ...I dreamt... I don't even remember, except I stood naked with months of work for naught and a deadline in less than a day...

CHATELET: No, you have still nearly a month....And you will shape infinity into the dimensions of a duck...

VAUCANSON: But my dream, so vivid.... All that work... and no indication that they were all calculations in futility...

CHATELET: Dreams are for the dead.... You can dream... but you can do more than dream...

VAUCANSON: Yes, I can make the duck drink, play in the water with his bill, and unleash a gurgling noise like a real living duck, but with no assurance that I will not awake and find it was all yet again for naught....

CHATELET: Then awake and begin again, so long as you find yourself awake—strive! What more can you do?

VAUCANSON: With every atom of my being, I love you...I love you, and I know how all things move, yes, but what is it that moves them? What? And suddenly I am convinced that it is this love for you. For without you, all the world would seem lifeless and inanimate, I know it. But if I know the how and what, I still will never know why....why do all things move and why do I persist in loving you when you are clearly in love with someone else and carrying his child?

CHATELET: Jacques de Vaucanson.....Why do you think I've come to you? Because I have decided at long last to choose the man whose vision offers mankind a glimpse of things to come....

VUACANSON: *(looks around the room, then realizes—)* Me?

CHATELET: There are many who say what you are attempting cannot be done—

VAUCANSON: So many raspberries have been blown at me, the air is fragrant with fruit....

CHATELET: And yet you have faith..and I don't want to live with someone without it..the faith that all humanity tries as hard as it can, that we all mean well.....that History may prove us wrong, but we did what we thought best, with what we had—

VAUCANSON: Yes...Faith. It is slow but I know progress comes daily even though I cannot see it.... But how maddening in its pace...

CHATELET: Everything, from the wing of a dragonfly to the invention of the harpsichord, everything, everything, everything was built on trial and error.

VAUCANSON: yes, yes it's true....

CHATELET: from the powder in your peruke to Newton's First Law of Motion....

VAUCANSON: Yes.

CHATELET: The door hinge, and the pendulum clock.

VUACANSON: And domestic livestock breeding.

CHATELET: And soap-manufacturing—

VAUCANSON: —and knowledge of the lymphatic system—

by now a bit of intellectual/romantic play between them, which brings them closer

CHATELET: —and stained glass—

GREAT MEN OF SCIENCE, NOS. 21 & 22

VAUCANSON: —double-entry bookkeeping—

CHATELET: —and the Gregorian calendar.

VAUCANSON: The cultivation of the cabernet grape—

CHATELET: —intercolumniation

VUACANSON: —and the moldboard plough

CHATELET: —and the bagpipes.

VUACANSON: And dephlogisticated air.

CHATELET: Plus the banquet couch—

VUACANSON: —and belaying pins on ships.

CHATELET: And the parasol—

VUACANSON: The flintlock—

CHATELET: —bobbin lace

VUACANSON: —the crosstitch

CHATELET: —the mapping of Africa

VUACANSON: —and the shoemaker's awl for pegging shoes!

CHATELET: Yes.

VUACANSON: They all came about through struggle—

CHATELET: *(by now in embrace—)* —so Patience. Mankind is still in its infancy.

VAUCANSON: Yes—

CHATELET: I have faith in you...have patience with me and we will construct a life together—

VAUCANSON: *(beginning to feel giddy)* Upon trial and error—

CHATELET: Yes.

VAUCANSON: And you truly mean it.

CHATELET: Not only do I mean it, I'm quite o'erwhelmed by it—

VAUCANSON: *(beaming for first time in play)* You're quite o'erwhelmed? How...most...excellent good.

CHATELET: And Jacques perhaps, perhaps the child is yours...

VAUCANSON: No no no, it's not, it's not... but no matter.... I don't mind....

pause

CHATELET: Well... I should go...

VAUCANSON: I want to be with you.

CHATELET: No, I mustn't stand in your way... but such days ahead… *(they kiss)* ...I can taste them on my lips...

VAUCANSON: *(tears of happiness)* yes... yes...

CHATELET: *(nearly exiting, then turning around and saying matter-of-factly)* Oh, I nearly forgot. I found this scrap of paper in my bedroom. I don't know if its important. It appears to contain a number of different ratios....and its in your handwriting.... Have you been looking for it?

Jacques seizes scrap of paper. Montage with still grander music. Jacques in untucked shirt, wrench clenched in teeth, tearing down designs from the wall, bending duck prototype with pliers, etc. Musical coda, then a number of insistent knocks on the door. Vaucanson is deeply engrossed in hard thought and pained study and intense labor.

ABBE: *(through door)* Jacques...Jacques, it is I —

VAUCANSON: It's open.

ABBE: It's not open.

Pause. Then knock knock knock

VAUCANSON: It's open.

ABBE: Jacques it's locked.

VAUCANSON: It isn't. You have to push.

ABBE: I am. I am pushing.

VAUCANSON: No, push....push.

ABBE: I'm pushing.

VAUCANSON: Hold the handle and push.

ABBE: For God's sake, it is locked.

VAUCANSON: It is not locked. I was occasioned to unlock it an hour ago

Pause. More knocking. Pause.

ABBE: Jacques. The door is locked.

VAUCANSON: I'm telling you it's open, stop knocking and push.

ABBE: Jacques, we don't have much time—

VAUCANSON: *(half to self)* I know.... I know... in less than ninety-six hours I'm to present to the Academy a deterministic, dynamic model that yet will elucidate irregular, unpredictable behavior...

pause

ABBE: What? Jacques, I can't hear you.... Look, I have news of grave import that perhaps you have not heard, I beg of you, open the—

Vaucanson pulls on door, unfastens bolt, opens door.

VAUCANSON: Who continues to lock my door against my wishes?! Everywhere I turn, unexpected impediments!

The Abbe looks distraught, despite efforts to hide it. Though also clear that he is no longer the sot he was at beginning of play.

ABBE: You look terrible.

VAUCANSON: The work...The work involved!

ABBE: There's food outside the door—

VAUCANSON: Leave it outside.

ABBE: *(retrieving it)* You must try to eat a little.

VAUCANSON: I cannot.

33

ABBE: When was the last time you ate?

VAUCANSON: I don't remember. I can't even look at it.

ABBE: It is nourishment.

VAUCANSON: Put it out of sight.

ABBE: *(putting it behind screen)* If you want it, it's over here.

VAUCANSON: Fine.

ABBE: Do you see? Over here.

VAUCANSON: Fine! Now what is this about news of grave import...

ABBE: Yes... I will come to that. Jacques, How are you proceeding ....

VAUCANSON: I don't know if it's progress, or if I'm just going in circles. I have not left my rooms for weeks. So many different moving parts in such a small automaton...

ABBE: I'm worried about you, Jacques, sleep—there's such a thing as that....

VAUCANSON: Do you know where mankind would be if he always got a proper night's sleep? Still in the mud! We are the only creature who has said, "I am tired, but until I am finished, I will not sleep"—I will not sleep—

A knock on the door. The Abbe opens it to reveal Le Cat.

LE CAT: Abbe, you are here? So you have told him?

ABBE: No...I have not told him.

VAUCANSON: Told me what?

Silence. A pause long enough for Vaucanson, and perhaps audience too, to understand fully that Chatelet has died in childbirth.

VUACANSON: Oh god....

LE CAT: You could feed all the pigs in all the farms in France I'd wager from the trough containing nothing but our hard-won knowledge...And I think the pigs wouldn't notice a whit of difference between it and their usual fodder....

VAUCANSON: I disagree.

LE CAT: The ultimate cause of things has no more regard to good above ill than to heat above cold...

VAUCANSON: No, I disagree. But tell me Abbe, why was I not informed...

ABBE: I was summoned by Madame du Chatelet to be present, for she was enduring a labor long and difficult but your work she did not want to disturb.

VAUCANSON: How did Voltaire receive the news?

ABBE: He is in bed, having fallen down the stairs. His servant attests that he saw his master throw himself down on purpose....

VAUCANSON: The child?

ABBE: ...A girl...It struggled til morning, then it too....

LE CAT: And so we see our man's seed, hell-bent on producing life, has instead produced nothing but death....I once asserted that a trivial death had the most befitting irony...but a death in childbirth quite eclipses it.

VAUCANSON: You say these things out of fear Le Cat.

LE CAT: Cynicism. I have seen too much of the world to feel otherwise.

VAUCANSON: And that assertion is uttered out of naiveté...for contrary to your belief you have not seen enough to know...to know truly the way of things...

LE CAT: I have seen enough to know that life is little more than the momentary difficulty when swallowing your slaver.

VAUCANSON: No.

LE CAT: It gives one nothing but nausea to see you stand here and say that our lady's death was all part of God's shimmering plan—

VAUCANSON: (obviously struggling heroically with grief) Her death.... Madame du Chatelet's... death... so as her life... has and will continue to have generated incalculable consequences, and the world is altered irrevocably for her having lived in it, and died in it, just as the world had been influenced and adjusted step by step again and again before our time until it produced, as one of its near-innumerable effects, a child who would become Gabrielle-Emilie, patroness of the Sciences, and she might have perished when she was three, before anyone knew her or loved her, she might have succumbed to smallpox or consumption, or been run down by a carriage, or had her brains dashed out by a Hessian soldier when but a girl but it was not til now and it was this and so—

LE CAT: And so we will not find you throwing yourself down stairs?

VAUCANSON: No. Now If you will excuse me doctor, I have much work—

LE CAT: I should say you do.

> Le Cat turns round just as he is about to exit

LE CAT: Tell me.....What did you mean....that I said what I said out of fear?

VAUCANSON: What is your fear, Le Cat? The fear of striving for not a scrap of recompense...The fear that all the faithless share—that you will never find meaning in your loves and labours, so why even attempt...

LE CAT: (profoundly sobered) Yes... perhaps you are right... I am... moved by your vision, Jacques de Vaucanson, the magnitude of your undertaking... your fortitude.... You are a bulwark... a bulwark... and I thank you for it... I thank you for it....

> Le Cat exits

VAUCANSON: Abbe.... Was there much suffering?

ABBE: (lying) No. All in all she succumbed most peaceably.... But where then do you stand with the project, Jacques....Will you wash your hands of it?

VAUCANSON: Abandon the work?

ABBE: Perhaps you should give up.

VAUCANSON: No, no surely you understand the sincere necessity of completing it.

ABBE: I am relieved. Is there anything you need?

VAUCANSON: This is a list. The last.

ABBE: I'll go then. And Jacques... thank you...

VAUCANSON: Thank you?

ABBE: You, and who would have thought it, but you have replenished my faith in God. *(exiting)* May your endeavor be blessed my son.

VAUCANSON: Abbe.... Were there any last words...

ABBE: None to speak of. Madame du Chatelet's last words were regarding her child...

VAUCANSON: The daughter.

ABBE: Yes.

VAUCANSON: Abbe...was there much suffering?

ABBE: Yes. Much.

VAUCANSON: What were the words?

ABBE: She shook out of her delirium long enough to ask, "Et comment ça va mon petit canard?" She expired soon after.

VAUCANSON: Petit Canard... why canard? Why a duck?

ABBE: *(unaware of full significance)* Barely noticeable, but the child's toes were incompletely separated... lending an appearance of webbing.

> *Stirring music. In silhouette, we see a representation of Vaucanson's Duck, slowly moving. The duck sits atop a platform, underneath of which is a vast complex network of gears, levers, cylinders, etc.*

MEMBER OF ACADEMY: We will never fully know or comprehend the obstacles this great man has overcome to construct such a—

CITIZEN #2: It is an object of wonderment—

CITIZEN #3: That he will be made a full member of the Academy, that is certain!

CITIZEN #4: It must tour Europe—

CITIZEN #2: It will be the inspiration and awe of the continent—

CITIZEN #4: And England, birthplace of Isaac Newton—

CITIZEN #3: When once wound up, the machine performs all its different operations without being touched again—

ABBE: I will provide you an in-depth description of the movements of the duck, including the random stammer—

MEMBER OF ACADEMY: It is the Greatest Proof Yet Constructed that there is Wisdom and Design behind all Creation...

VAUCANSON: *(to self, still in shock)* Dreams are for the dead, and while you are awake... strive....

CITIZEN #4: *(with tears)* That is not merely a duck up on that pedestal, it is mankind, it is all of us, our lives....He has captured the very essence of

Human Existence...

VAUCANSON: (to self) Mankind is still in its infancy. We try, stumble, fall, fail, and try again, and we come ever closer in our toddling steps toward the open arms of our Maker...

MEMBER OF ACADEMY: Congratulations, Jacques de Vaucanson. You have done just as you said you would. Through months of labor, Employing Newton's laws of attraction by which the tides behave and the planets are known to rotate; Using calculations plotting the movement of the stars themselves across the heavens; Utilizing a system of springs and weights, gearwheels, cogs and escapements of your own construction fashioned in ratios of proven mathematical laws and proportion you have created a duck that flaps its wings, eats, and excretes...just like a duck.

Pause. Music builds. Vaucanson watches duck and then—

VAUCANSON: Yes.

Music building to end. Vaucanson watches the duck. Flap its wings, stretch its neck, and excrete. And repeat... Repeat... Repeat... Repeat... Repeat... Slightest change on Vaucanson's face as he watches the duck. A slightest indication for first time in play... of doubt. Stirring Music.

ACT II: A Frog He Would A Wooing Go...
The Story of Lazarro Spallanzani's Great Labour

CHARACTERS:
Housekeeper: Old woman. Italian accent.
Spallanzani: Near death, or so he believes. Italian accent.
Vaucanson: Elderly, near-senile.
Condorcet: Middle-aged. Preferably same actor as Abbe of Act I.

TIME: 1794.

Darkness. With candlestick and bowl, HOUSEKEEPER. Wind heard outside, whistling and banging the shutters. Distant bark of dog. Room dimly seen. Room clearly cold, dank, and draughty. Much clutter on desk. Preferably a bust of Reaumur, or portrait of Reaumur on wall. Housekeeper lights a candle with her candle. Sets down bowl of porridge. Faint croak of frogs. In candlelight, we see old man asleep with head on desk table. SPALLANZANI.

HOUSEKEEPER: Signore...?

pause

Signore.....?

She has in hand pail containing a few scraps of coal and a small shovel, having picked up these two articles by the grate, the small stove in the room. With shovel she bangs on pail. Or perhaps she bangs on the chamber pot. Great clatter either way. Lights should remain rather dim for first few pages of play.

SPALLANZANI: Don't wake me up, let me dream!

Clatter continues

Damn it, let me dream! Let me dream! The answer was there!

Clatter continues

Fine! Fine! All right Housekeeper, all right, enough with the banging.

Clatter ends.

HOUSEKEEPER: My pardons Signore. You are up?

SPALLANZANI: Yes.

HOUSEKEEPER: What did you dream? An answer?

SPALLANZANI: To hell with my dreams. Why don't you let in the light?

HOUSEKEEPER: The light?

SPALLANZANI: Yes, by all means, let in the light.

Housekeeper opens drapes. No light is let in for it is still dark.

HOUSEKEEPER: Look at that—completely dark. I don't see why you must awake so early.

SPALLANZANI: Experiments.

Housekeeper makes to exit

No, don't leave me alone until we are sure we have awoken.

Pause. Spallanzani and Housekeeper in dim light. Frog croak.

SPALLANZANI: All right, I'm up. Get out.

HOUSEKEEPER: Eat your breakfast while it is hot.

SPALLANZANI: I am eating it, I have been eating it. Now leave me alone.

Pause. Spallanzani, head propped in hand, closes eyes in thinking pose. Opens eyes.

SPALLANZANI: You linger?

HOUSEKEEPER: To be sure you do not return to sleep.

SPALLANZANI: How many times do I have to explain to you that I sometimes must think with eyes closed, but I'm not sleeping, now get out, I have much work!

HOUSEKEEPER: Yes, signore.

She exits. He closes eyes, forehead on palm. She enters.

HOUSEKEEPER: Signore?

We hear gentle snoring

Signore?

She again brings shovel to pail in a frightful banging

SPALLANZANI: Yes, I'm up, this time I'm up, enough with the banging. Enough with the banging! Do you want a beating?

HOUSEKEEPER: I am sorry Signore, I am only doing as you requested. I do not enjoy it.

> *She sets down chamberpot. Spallanzani has his morning vomit into the chamberpot.*

SPALLANZANI: Fine.

HOUSEKEEPER: You are very unreasonable in the morning.

SPALLANZANI: Fine.

HOUSEKEEPER: "Do you want a beating" indeed.

SPALLANZANI: When I say I am up I am up.

HOUSEKEEPER: But perhaps you will go back to sleep—

SPALLANZANI: I couldn't sleep now if I slit my wrists, the dreams I dreamed I'll never see again...

HOUSEKEEPER: What did you dream?

SPALLANZANI: Let me ask you a question about pants. You've sewn pants before, yes?

HOUSEKEEPER: Of course.

SPALLANZANI: *(indicating pants he wears)* Well take these pants for instance. If I were to count the number of parts—

HOUSEKEEPER: What sort of question is this?

SPALLANZANI: Just let me ask my question—

HOUSEKEEPER: It is too early for such questions.

SPALLANZANI: *(off behind screen to pass water)* It is never too early to learn. What time is it? Where's my watch?

HOUSEKEEPER: 4:30 o'clock.

SPALLANZANI: 4:30! No! Why did you let me sleep so long, it is nearly dawn!

HOUSEKEEPER: You did not go to bed til nearly two o clock.

SPALLANZANI: Yes.

HOUSEKEEPER: Sleep is necessary. Look! See! Completely dark.

SPALLANZANI: Dark now, but soon dawn will come, and even before the dawn, the dawn chorus—

HOUSEKEEPER: all the birds and their cheery songs—

SPALLANZANI: *(derisively)* Cheery songs... all the racket of the birds and who can concentrate with that? and then just when it has subsided, the street cries: the fresh fish and old chairs to mend. And kettles to mend. And sprats alive o! And knives to grind. What is a sprat? A kind of snail?

HOUSEKEEPER: A herring.

SPALLANZANI: *(derisively)* Sprats alive. And buy a bird cage, and have your boots cleaned. Buy a door mat. Onions fine onions. Broom, broom. Spring radishes. And just when this settles down—

HOUSEKEEPER: Not spring radishes.

SPALLANZANI: Yes, well they cry spring radishes. I hear it. And just when this settles down—

HOUSEKEEPER: Not spring radishes. Not until spring.

SPALLANZANI: Don't interrupt. It is nearly spring. No doubt there's an early batch to buy.

HOUSEKEEPER: This early, none worth buying.

SPALLANZANI: No of course none worth buying, they are never worth buying—

HOUSEKEEPER: Not to you, they play havoc with your stomach and intestines so I am not to buy them.

SPALLANZANI: Yes.

HOUSEKEEPER: They give you wind.

SPALLANZANI: No, it's not wind, how many times do I have to explain to you that it isn't wind, It's my fragile gizzard from years of scientific experiments. What would I care if radishes gave me a little wind, I live alone.

HOUSEKEEPER: I live with you.

SPALLANZANI: Yes you live with me. Technically. But you...what would you mind with a little wind.

HOUSEKEEPER: It is no hardship to avoid purchasing a radish if it means less wind.

SPALLANZANI: *(erupts)* It isn't the wind I'm talking about but ulcers and great vomiting upon these floors you clean with such diligence, feed me a radish and I'll vomit my life away. *(broods)* Why did you bring up radishes in the first place? It is always radishes. Why yet again are we talking about radishes? Where are you going, stay here. It is nearly five o'clock in the morning, do you understand, I don't want to talk about radishes, to hell with your radishes, soon the dawn chorus will begin, and then the street cries, and when that subsides, the horseclopping, the carriages on the cobbles to hell with your radishes and the rabble and all the rest of it and it won't be quiet again until it is quite dark!

beat

HOUSEKEEPER: And even then, the dogs.

SPALLANZANI: *(agreeing)* Oh yes, and the crickets.

HOUSEKEEPER: No, there are no crickets in the city.

SPALLANZANI: I hear them.

HOUSEKEEPER: Frogs, there are frogs in the city.

SPALLANZANI: The frogs are different.

HOUSEKEEPER: And frogs.

SPALLANZANI: Never you mind about the frogs.

HOUSEKEEPER: I do not like them.

SPALLANZANI: They are not here for you to like, they are here for an experiment that posterity will thank me for. Or not. To hell with posterity, I know at least its success will stick in the craw of our rival Reaumur.

HOUSEKEEPER: I do not like a hundred frogs in the house.

SPALLANZANI: Go away Housekeeper, you can take the porridge with you.

HOUSEKEEPER: You have not eaten.

SPALLANZANI: I am not hungry.

HOUSEKEEPER: It stinks in here.

SPALLANZANI: Fine.

HOUSEKEEPER: How long have you been wearing those clothes?

SPALLANZANI: These clothes? I just put them on.

HOUSEKEEPER: Oh did you.

SPALLANZANI: Will you please get out.

HOUSEKEEPER: What are you doing with the frogs.

SPALLANZANI: You wouldn't understand.

HOUSEKEEPER: Are you dissecting them?

SPALLANZANI: No.

HOUSEKEEPER: Why not?

SPALLANZANI: Would you like me to needlessly dissect my frogs?

HOUSEKEEPER: They would then be dead.

SPALLANZANI: Then by your leave, I shall first wheel the frogs past you in a cart for you to jeer at? All the innocent little frogs?

HOUSEKEEPER: *(a joke)* Some are innocent, but most are surely sympathizers to the crown.

SPALLANZANI: You have officially been in France too long.

HOUSEKEEPER: Yes. Yes I have.

SPALLANZANI: *(briefly sobered)* Yes... we have. You have seen the guillotine in action?

HOUSEKEEPER: Yes.

SPALLANZANI: *(broods)* Well at least it isn't a lingering death.... It's over quickly.

HOUSEKEEPER: Not with all the speeches that are made.

SPALLAZANI: Those poor pointless souls...

HOUSEKEEPER: They say it is only the elite they do in.

SPALLANZANI: The elite? Oh stay out of it all Housekeeper. The elite! Do you know who they're in for next? Half the members of the Academy! It seems we scientists have been "consistently singled out by the royalty for special treatment." Quite right! Anyone can see looking around here that I in particular have had special treatment.

HOUSEKEEPER: You are that piece of farmland that gets the extra dung.

41

SPALLANZANI: Yes, that must be me. Do you know what they've done with my friend Condorcet?

HOUSEKEEPER: Who?

SPALLANZANI: Condorcet!

HOUSEKEEPER: You have a friend?

SPALLANZANI: Yes! Though not for long. They've run him out. He's been hiding these last two months. And he! The secretary of the Academy no less! *(broods)* No, Housekeeper, the frogs in this experiment will not see death or dissection...

HOUSEKEEPER: Then what sort of experiment do you have in mind that involves a hundred frogs?

SPALLANZANI: You wouldn't understand.

HOUSEKEEPER: Does it concern semen?

SPALLANZANI: Yes, as a matter of fact, it does.

HOUSEKEEPER: All your life it is semen.

SPALLANZANI: All your life it is semen, all everyone's lives, it is semen, it is semen.

HOUSEKEEPER: It is no good.

SPALLANZANI: Were it not for semen, Housekeeper, it is well believed you would not exist.

HOUSEKEEPER: That is what I mean.

SPALLANZANI: Ho ho. Such sentiment. Wasn't it you going on about the birds and their pretty songs?

HOUSEKEEPER: What are you doing with the frogs and their semen?

SPALLANZANI: Nothing. I have spent a miserable week getting nowhere doing nothing on what could have been the most important series of experiments of my life. Perhaps. Perhaps not. But they are surely my last experiments.

HOUSEKEEPER: Why your last? Are you near death?

SPALLANZANI: *(quite serious)* Yes. I am near death. *(beat)* Oh no... Do you hear that.

HOUSEKEEPER: What.

SPALLANZANI: The peeping. It has begun.

> *Dawn chorus increases in intensity*

HOUSEKEEPER: So it has.

SPALLANZANI: The dawn is nigh and then it will be night and what have I to show for it.

HOUSEKEEPER: You have much to show for it.

SPALLANZANI: I have nothing to show for it. I have evacuated my life away.

HOUSEKEEPER: You are respected and admired in scientific circles.

SPALLANZANI: How should you know that.

HOUSEKEEPER: You told me.

SPALLANZANI: Get out. You have wasted the best part of the day. The part before the beginning.

HOUSEKEEPER: And the stove?

SPALLANZANI: Leave it.

HOUSEKEEPER: No coals?

SPALLANZANI: We are not made of coal.

HOUSEKEEPER: No we are not made of coal. But some of us are made of flint.

SPALLANZANI: What?

HOUSEKEEPER: Of flint.

SPALLANZANI: What is this?

HOUSEKEEPER: Before I take your leave, I will ask you one last time for permission to buy fabric.

SPALLANZANI: Thank God this is the last time.

HOUSEKEEPER: Your answer then still is no?

SPALLANZANI: I am not made of flint, and you are amply provided for.

HOUSEKEEPER: Flint, and I have petitioned humbly three times in as many months for—

> *From outside window: "Fresh Fish!" "Old Chairs to mend! Sprats alive! Sprats alive o!"*

SPALLANZANI: Didn't I tell you! Damn it to Hell! Close the window!

HOUSEKEEPER: It is already closed.

SPALLANZANI: Already closed! Well then we must seal the edges with wax—

HOUSEKEEPER: Why?

SPALLANZANI: To shut it out of course!

HOUSEKEEPER: You can't shut it out Signore.

SPALLANZANI: Can't I now.

HOUSEKEEPER: It is impossible. It seeps in.

SPALLANZANI: We'll see about that. A wall of cork perhaps.

HOUSEKEEPER: It is impossible.   43

> *Meanwhile, from outside window, we hear various street cries—*

STREET NOISES: Old chairs to mend!
Kettles to mend!
Buy a bird cage!
Knives to grind!
Have your boots cleaned!
Dust o! Dust o!
Buy a door mat!

Onions fine onions!
Broom, broom!
Spring radishes!

At "spring radishes" Spallanzani points to window triumphantly

HOUSEKEEPER: Ah. Spring radishes.

SPALLANZANI: You see! You see! And on the First of March.

HOUSEKEEPER: It is not the First of March. It is the Ninth of Wind.

SPALLANZANI: *(apoplectic)* Curse you woman, radishes do not give me wind!

HOUSEKEEPER: I am talking about the new calendar.

SPALLANZANI: What new calendar. What are you saying.

HOUSEKEEPER: It is the ninth of Wind. *(beat)* Ventose. *(beat)* Wind.

SPALLANZANI: *(impatient)* Yes wind. *(then realizing—)* Oh no...don't tell me the revolutionaries have done something to the calendar!

HOUSEKEEPER: They have revolutionized it, why have you not heard about these things.

SPALLANZANI: I have better occupations. And we are not French, we are exiles.

HOUSEKEEPER: I am French. "Liberty, Equality, Fraternity."

SPALLANZANI: Shut up.

HOUSEKEEPER: Wind is the sixth month. The first month is Vintage Month, the second is Fog, the third Sleet, then Snow, then Rain, now we are in Wind.

SPALLANZANI: And there are still 12 months?

HOUSEKEEPER: Yes. 30 days a month. But 10 days a week. Every 10th day a day of rest.

SPALLANZANI: Idiots. They say they are for the people, then institute less rest.

HOUSEKEEPER: I thought you would be in favor of less rest...

SPALLANZANI: What I do I do, but I would not impose a calendar of my habits upon the people.

HOUSEKEEPER: Oh you wouldn't?

SPALLANZANI: What?

HOUSKEEPER: There happen to be people in this very house.

SPALLANZANI: What are you talking about? What people? When was this calendar decided?

HOUSEKEEPER: In October. I mean, in Fog.

SPALLANZANI: In fog is right. Do they realize that they still cannot convince the earth from revolving around the sun in nothing less than 365 days and 30 days times 12 months is 360. What will they do with five extra days?

HOUSEKEEPER: Those will be feast days. They are named Virtue, Genius—

SPALLANZANI: I don't care about any of this. Get out. The Royal Academy in havoc, my good friend Condorcet in hiding and much abused, a

44

cantaloupe in the street turns out to be a severed head, my stomach's all atwist, leave, please...

HOUSEKEEPER: *(finding fabric)* What is this?

SPALLANZANI: Please leave.

HOUSEKEEPER: Signore!

SPALLANZANI: What? What does it look like!

HOUSEKEEPER: A bolt of taffeta.

SPALLANZANI: It is exactly a bolt of taffeta.

HOUSEKEEPER: How long have you had this.

SPALLANZANI: A miserable week.

HOUSEKEEPER: And you have not told me?

SPALLANZANI: Told you what?

HOUSEKEEPER: Signore, I don't understand.

SPALLANZANI: What.

HOUSEKEEPER: But thank you, it is very fine.

SPALLANZANI: Thank you? No, no, It is not for you.

HOUSEKEEPER: This is not for me?

SPALLANZANI: No it is not for you.

HOUSEKEEPER: It's not?

SPALLANZANI: No.

HOUSEKEEPER: Who is it for then?

SPALLANZANI: Who do you think it is for?

HOUSEKEEPER: There is a woman in your life?

SPALLANZANI: Unfortunately.

HOUSEKEEPER: *(clarifying)* Other than me there is a woman in your life?

SPALLANZANI: Please get out.

HOUSEKEEPER: I will not get out. Signore, I wish to register a grievance.

SPALLANZANI: Bah.

HOUSEKEEPER: I have petitioned humbly three times in as many months for fabric so that I can replace the timeworn and insupportable articles I now possess and each time you have said no no too expensive, too extravagant, no, no what do you need new dresses for—   45

SPALLANZANI: *(overlapping)* What do you need new dresses for? Who are you trying to impress.

HOUSEKEEPER: There is such a thing as decency.

SPALLANZANI: There is such a thing as economy.

HOUSEKEEPER: You can nearly see through the ones I have.

SPALLANZANI: No one cares, no one cares.

HOUSEKEEPER: They are very old.

SPALLANZANI: This is all very old. Do you know how little money I possess?

HOUSEKEEPER: Yes, and to think now a whole bolt for some woman I have not even seen, it is not right—

SPALLANZANI: Oh so now you must approve all my women?

HOUSEKEEPER: Yes, all your women.

SPALLANZANI: All the countesses and concubines slinking about here—

HOUSEKEEPER: Tell me who she is.

SPALLANZANI: There is no woman.

HOUSEKEEPER: Then who is the taffeta for?

SPALLANZANI: For me of course.

HOUSEKEEPER: For you?

SPALLANZANI: For me, for me.

HOUSEKEEPER: But look at this sheen! You will look embarrassing. You are too old to parade about in—

SPALLANZANI: *(interrupting)* I am not going to parade about—

HOUSEKEEPER: You will be that thing, a fop—

SPALLANZANI: Get out.

HOUSEKEEPER: They will see you and cut off your head. And you knew my situation, and you who profess to eschew all such fine things, and here.... Do not expect me to make any taffeta pants for you—

SPALLANZANI: I am worn out before dawn.

HOUSEKEEPER: I will not make pants for you to parade about after—

SPALLANZANI: Woman, the taffeta is not for me.

HOUSEKEEPER: Oh now it is not for you.

SPALLANZANI: It is for my experiments.

HOUSEKEEPER: Who is this woman.

SPALLANZANI: I am worn out before dawn!

HOUSEKEEPER: I demand an explanation!

SPALLANZANI: You demand?

HOUSEKEEPER: I don't see how you can use taffeta in an experiment.

SPALLANZANI: Oh so you don't believe me.

HOUSEKEEPER: No.

SPALLANZANI: Well I am.

HOUSEKEEPER: Then explain it then. *(pause)* Please. *(pause)* I would like to know.

SPALLANZANI: *(considers, then—)* It is very involved. You wouldn't understand. It is sci-en-tific.

HOUSEKEEPER: Then I will quit your service.

SPALLANZANI: Quit my service?

HOUSEKEEPER: Yes.

SPALLANZANI: After thirty...thirty—

HOUSEKEEPER: Yes, after thirty—

SPALLANZANI: No, forty—

HOUSEKEEPER: After forty one years of service, yes. With relief.

SPALLANZANI: And where will you go?

HOUSEKEEPER: Back to Pavia.

SPALLANZANI: What, Italy? It is under siege.

HOUSEKEEPER: I will go back to Pavia with pleasure and be done with you.

SPALLANZANI: But I am near death.

HOUSEKEEPER: I am sorry that I will miss the end.

SPALLANZANI: So go. You wouldn't understand, so why bother explaining.

HOUSEKEEPER: I have petitioned humbly three times in as many months for fabric—

SPALLANZANI: I know—

HOUSEKEEPER: —so that I can replace the timeworn and insupportable articles—

SPALLANZANI: I know—

HOUSEKEEPER: —I now possess and each time you have said—

SPALLANZANI: Yes, yes, I know what I have said.

HOUSEKEEPER: So to hell with you, goodbye.

She is at the door, holding the full chamberpot

SPALLANZANI: Leave then.

HOUSEKEEPER: I am sick of it.

SPALLANZANI: I can make my own porridge.

HOUSEKEEPER: I ask very little.

Housekeeper exits with chamberpot. Pause. Spallanzani sets to work. Loud frog croak. Cuts a swath of taffeta. Begins to pin a paper pattern to the taffeta, but pricks his finger.

SPALLANZANI: Bah!

Spallanzani impulsively crumples up paper pattern violently. Beat. Then begins to retch. Looks about for chamberpot. He cannot find it.

SPALLANZANI: You stole my chamberpot....

Opens door and calls out:

You stole my chamberpot! You stole my chamberpot! You stole my chamberpot!

Great amount of stomping, Housekeeper opens door, flings in now-empty chamberpot. Spallanzani grabs pot, waits for it, then vomits convulsively. Housekeeper lingers at door due to begrudging compassion. It can be seen that

47

she wears a traveling smock or is carrying a bag, though still empty.

SPALLANZANI: *(through retches)* How did you come to be.....How did you come to be....*(pause)* I'm asking you a question!

HOUSEKEEPER: Be what?

SPALLANZANI: Be what?

HOUSEKEEPER: You mean your Housekeeper?

SPALLANZANI: Human! I mean Human! This! You once were not, and now you're here....

HOUSEKEEPER: Yes I am here, but soon in Pavia.

SPALLANZANI: Do you have any idea how you came to be?

HOUSEKEEPER: You won't get me to say it.

SPALLANZANI: I'm not talking about sexual intercourse, I am talking about the mechanism behind sexual intercourse that creates life.

HOUSEKEEPER: I am leaving.

SPALLANZANI: I am trying to explain why I've been up every night in tears for over a week, I'm trying to explain why I purchased a bolt of fine taffeta, and you said you will quit my service if I do not—

HOUSEKEEPER: And you must drag sex into all of it?

SPALLANZANI: No, Sex drags us into all of it. And here we are. And I'll say it now—I'd rather each of us just split in two and have done with all this... coming together, but there's nothing to be done.

HOUSEKEEPER: But as the church says, "there is pleasure too, at coming together, which God in his mercy arranged for."

SPALLANZANI: Pleasure? To hell with pleasure! It only distracts us from what truly matters. How much better if God had made the act excruciating, so that each couple would have to pause in the middle of sex if only to ask, "why again are we doing this?" Why indeed! That is how it would be if I were God.

HOUSEKEEPER: You would be an unpopular God.

SPALLANZANI: So be it.

HOUSEKEEPER: I would not worship you.

SPALLANZANI: And why not?! When have you ever been with a man?

HOUSEKEEPER: If you do not explain to me what a bolt of taffeta has to do with this, I swear to you I will return to Pavia within the hour.

SPALLANZANI: *(derisively)* Within the hour.

HOUSEKEEPER: *(earnest to point of tears)* I mean it. I mean it. I mean it.

> Pause

SPALLANZANI: Come here..... *(Pause)* Come here!

> He holds up a vial.

This is a liquid, like water is a liquid, like wine is a liquid, like milk is a liquid. But this liquid, in the womb of a woman, creates life.

HOUSEKEEPER: Semen.

SPALLANZANI: Yes, And I want to discover exactly what it is in semen that initiates life, and where it is—in the watery part, or in the denser part containing the worms.

HOUSEKEEPER: Worms?

SPALLANZANI: *(with vial)* Believe it or not, there are thousands of spermatick worms swimming about in here.... Some even think these worms are essential to reproduction.

HOUSEKEEPER: But you don't?

SPALLANZANI: I don't Housekeeper, no. Parasites are found everywhere, in our blood, our intestines—these spermatick worms are merely parasites that have taken up home in my testes. It doesn't make sense that I would come from a worm.

HOUSEKEEPER: I think it makes much sense.

SPALLANZANI: But look—so many sperm are found in semen that it would mean an incredible waste of potential life, and it is not conceivable that a God would allow such waste.

HOUSEKEEPER: I think I've never heard anything more conceivable.

SPALLANZANI: You are very cynical, Housekeeper.

HOUSEKEEPER: And you, what are you?

SPALLANZANI: Don't change the subject. I'm working with frogs because I like frogs, and they're a damn sight easier to work with than humans. Not to mention that with frogs I can use artificial insemination. I can paint the semen onto the eggs directly! No one has thought of that before!

HOUSEKEEPER: Not even Reaumur?

SPALLANZANI: *(twisting face)* Reaumur? Reaumur's greatest scientific achievement will be when he discovers his own bottom…and shoves two fingers up it!

HOUSEKEEPER:And then he will publish his findings.

SPALLANZANI: *(amused with her joke)* Exactly!

HOUSEKEEPER: *(again impatient)* But what does this have to do with a bolt of taffeta.

SPALLANZANI: I'm telling you!

HOUSEKEEPER: You're not telling me!

SPALLANZANI: It comes down to this. There is no point in experimenting with frogs if I can't afterward apply what I've learned to humans. Right?

HOUSEKEEPER: But frogs are not humans.

SPALLANZANI: The difference is trivial!

HOUSEKEEPER: You think frogs and humans are the same, which I can't understand.

SPALLANZANI: No, you can, you can, stop pretending you're thick and just try...There are those who believe that unlike a human, a frog does not need semen to fertilize its egg. So If I'm going to work with frogs, and by god, I want to work with frogs, I first have to prove, once and for all, that semen is required, that the frogs can't go it alone...that they, in that, are like human beings...Now...how do I do that?

HOUSEKEEPER: How.

SPALLANZANI: Well this very issue came up at a party I went to—

HOUSEKEEPER: You?

SPALLANZANI: Yes. Don't interrupt. I was at a party...

HOUSEKEEPER: Where?

SPALLANZANI: It was a ball at a chateau.

HOUSEKEEPER: Really?

SPALLANZANI: Yes, there's no reason to be so surprised. I was at a party—

HOUSEKEEPER: When was this?

SPALLANZANI: Not long ago.

HOUSEKEEPER: How long?

SPALLANZANI: It was....fifty years ago..I was new to Paris, I barely knew the language, but yes, damn it, I was at a party.

HOUSEKEEPER: Fine.

SPALLANZANI: Fine! And I met a fellow scientist by the duck pond, and the frogs were quite loud and it was in casting back to events of that night...*(counts)* A scientist, a mishap involving a bodily function, and his damp clothing...that I had a revelation.

HOUSEKEEPER: I am ready.

SPALLANZANI: *(containing excitement)* All right... Housekeeper.... can you think of a situation in which a man and a woman has sexual intercourse... stay here, stay here... the man remains in the woman until he ejaculates... and yet they both can be utterly assured there will be no pregnancy?

> *pause*

HOUSEKEEPER: *(clearly uncomfortable)*When a man uses.... When the man's... semen... is contained.

SPALLANZANI: *(nearly embracing her, near tears)* Yes. Exactly! Exactly! And therefore none of the frog eggs should develop if the frogs mate while each male frog is wearing... a pair of tight-fitting taffeta pants! and that is why I am determined to make 29 pairs of tight-fitting taffeta pants as soon as possible, and that is why I have been up these miserable sleepless nights, being occupied in the unforseeably difficult task of constructing 29 very small pairs of tight-fitting taffeta pants, for frogs.

> *pause*

HOUSEKEEPER: Ah.

50

Pause. She turns to leave.

SPALLANZANI: Where are you going?

HOUSEKEEPER: Pavia!

SPALLANZANI: Good God, haven't I just done what you asked?!

HOUSEKEEPER: *(with fury)* So I am to come in every morning and be...and be mocked by these frogs fashionably dressed—

SPALLANZANI: This isn't about fashion, it's about Life, Life—

HOUSEKEEPER: It's about loyal service.

SPALLANZANI: Holy Christ you have not heard a word I've said—

HOUSEKEEPER: They will be wearing fabric meant for me—

SPALLANZANI: *(shrill)* It was never meant for you. It was never meant for you!

HOUSEKEEPER: This...is meant for you.

Housekeeper spits, exits, slamming the door.

SPALLANZANI: Just tell me, what's the trick for pinning taffeta together? Why is it so damned slippery!

The door is opened by the Housekeeper and slammed again. Spallanzani sets to work on pants. Sound of carriages on cobbles outside window. Frog croak. Exhalations and great curses of frustration. And outside the window:

STREET NOISES: Knives to grind!
   Buy a bird cage!
   Knives to grind!
   Have your boots cleaned!
   Dust o! Dust o!
   Buy a door mat!
   Onions fine onions!
   Sprats alive!
   Sprats alive o!

SPALLANZANI: *(derisively)* Sprats...

ThunderStorm. A miserable example of pants is completed. Holds it up for inspection. Pulls each end of waist to test durability. It splits down the middle. Lights begin to fade. Takes match to candle. He listens to church bells ring.

SPALLANZANI: And there's the day. Done. Damn it to Hell.   51

He shoves several of his materials off desk. Housekeeper enters.

SPALLANZANI: Why haven't you left yet.

HOUSEKEEPER: I have found a coach that will take me as far as Milan for a reasonable price. It leaves tomorrow morning.

SPALLANZANI: I have no traveling money for you.

HOUSEKEEPER: And I would be a fool to expect any. There is a man here who wants to see you.

SPALLANZANI: Where?

HOUSEKEEPER: At the front door.

SPALLANZANI: Why didn't you say so? Who is he?

> *Housekeeper shrugs.*

SPALLANZANI: What does he want?

HOUSEKEEPER: To see you.

SPALLANZANI: About what?

HOUSEKEEPER: *(shrugs)* He seems upset.

SPALLANZANI: Well I'm working.

HOUSEKEEPER: What should I tell him?

SPALLANZANI: That I'm busy.

HOUSEKEEPER: I will tell him you are busy with your pants and can't see anyone for a few days.

SPALLANZANI: Don't tell him that.

HOUSEKEEPER: I will tell him that.

SPALLANZANI: Fine. Fine! Send him in.

> *Pause. Condorcet, secretary of the Royal Academy rushes in, shuts door behind him, pale, panicked, wild-eyed, drenched, and wearing women's clothing. Gown, wig, makeup ill-applied. He is missing a shoe, his articles are in disarray. Heavy French accent.*

CONDORCET: Lazarro, thank God!

SPALLANZANI: What is this?

CONDORCET: Please, You must hide me! Immediately!

SPALLANZANI: Jean? Is that you?

CONDORCET: Yes, it is I, Jean Condorcet. Your friend.

SPALLANZANI: I thought you were in hiding.

CONDORCET: My hiding place has been discovered. Someone leaked. No matter. Praise be to God I made it here. I am nearly collapsed with exhaustion.

SPALLANZANI: *(calling out from door)* Housekeeper, get a drink for this man! A disguise, that was quick thinking.

CONDORCET: It was the work of panicked minutes, it is a most ill-fit.

SPALLANZANI: No, it is convincing.

CONDORCET: It is not too attractive, I trust. I do not wish to call any attention to myself if I am to escape the city.

SPALLANZANI: No, be assured, you are not too attractive.

CONDORCET: In the downpour, through Paris, first here then there, always one step ahead of the gendarmes, seeking asylum with old friends, but all my old friends—half have been arrested already, and the other half cast me back out on the street. *(angry at shoes)* These shoes make things impossible.

SPALLANZANI: But the gendarmes—they will not follow you here, will they?

CONDORCET: Yes, they might! That is why you must hide me, or they will arrest you too for harboring me.

SPALLANZANI: Arrest me? But I am Italian!

CONDORCET: Please, I fear for my life...

SPALLANZANI: But I have no place to hide you.

CONDORCET: Anywhere! I just need a few days. Don't you have a cellar?

SPALLANZANI: This is the cellar! I am very poor. But look, is it wise to even stay in the city?

CONDORCET: It's true, my only hope is to flee Paris, for if I am caught it is surely the guillotine which I will never allow, which is why I have this....

SPALLANZANI: What is it?

CONDORCET: Arsenic.

SPALLANZANI: *(looking into eyes)* No man... no....

CONDORCET: I won't suffer execution...

> *Pulling out of bosom a large bundle of papers tied with string*

but look, I'll leave Paris, but first a day of rest, and time to pass on this manuscript to some former member of the Academy sympathetic to the cause.

SPALLANZANI: What do you mean, "former member"?

CONDORCET: The National Convention has disbanded the Royal Academy of Sciences.

SPALLANZANI: They can't!

CONDORCET: Hah, can't they now. They have. "An elitist institution" they called it and snip snap. But we will go on, we must.

SPALLANZANI: What is the manuscript?

CONDORCET: Oh Lazarro, it is the culmination of my life's work! I completed it while in hiding. I was to hand the work off to a man tonight in fact, but I was flushed out before I could meet him.

SPALLANZANI: The topic, is it mathematics?

CONDORCET: No, it is a Sketch for a Historical Picture of the Progress of the Human Mind!

SPALLANZANI: *(agape)* You say there is progress?

CONDORCET: *(solemnly)* I know there is, Lazarro, I know there is. And you do too. In the 10th epoch, there will be equality among the classes and people will improve physically, intellectually, morally...

> *reads from work solemnly, much dignity in his muddied gown:*

"I picture posterity and how welcome is this picture of the human race, freed from all its chains—

SPALLANZANI: *(hearing a distant knock)* Ssh.

53

CONDORCET: —released from the domination of chance, advancing with a firm and sure step in the path of truth, virtue—

SPALLANZANI: Ssh!

Distant knock on front door.

CONDORCET: Did you hear that?

SPALLANZANI: Yes!

CONDORCET: It was a knock on the door!

SPALLANZANI: The gendarmes!

CONDORCET: Lazarro, what can I do?!

SPALLANZANI: Get out.

CONDORCET: I'll hide behind the drapes.

SPALLANZANI: No they'll see you.

CONDORCET: Then what can I do?

SPALLANZANI: You can get out. Try the window.

CONDORCET: It's too small. What about under your desk!

SPALLANZANI: No no, there are frogs underneath, they will be crushed—

Pause. Condorcet looks at the vial of poison in his hand. Looks at Spallanzani.

SPALLANZANI: No... no.... Put it away...

A knock on the door. Housekeeper enters.

HOUSEKEEPER: There is a man here who wants to see you.

SPALLANZANI: Just one?

HOUSEKEEPER: Yes.

SPALLANZANI: Did he say who he is?

HOUSEKEEPER: *(shrugs)* He is old.

SPALLANZANI: What does he want?

HOUSEKEEPER: To see you.

SPALLANZANI: About what?

HOUSEKEEPER: I couldn't care less.

SPALLANZANI: Housekeeper! Is he armed?

HOUSEKEEPER: I will send him in.

54

She exits

SPALLANZANI: No, wait!

An elderly man enters. Quite frail, appalling condition. Coughing wretchedly. It is Jacques de Vaucanson, scientist. Pronounced French accent. Approaching a senile parody of his Act I self.

VAUCANSON: Monsieur Spallanzani?

SPALLANZANI: Yes.

VAUCANSON: My pardons for disturbing you at such a late hour. I—Oh! And you have company...

> *Vaucanson winks and nudges knowingly for he has noticed a female form hiding not very well.*

CONDORCET: Jacques?

VUACANSON: *(flirting)* Do I know you?

CONDORCET: It is I!

VUACANSON: Madam?

CONDORCET: No!

VAUCANSON: *(amazement)* Jean?

SPALLANZANI: *(to Condorcet)* Is he one of us?

VAUCANSON: I have been all over Paris in search of you.

CONDORCET: *(to Spallanzani)* This is Jacques de Vaucanson, he is the man I was to give my manuscript to tonight.

VAUCANSON: *(to Condorcet)* Yes, but I heard you had to flee.

SPALLANZANI: *(calling out from door)* Housekeeper! A drink for this man! Monsieur Vaucanson, It is an honor to meet such an eminent scientist.

VAUCANSON: The honor is mine.

SPALLANZANI: I am no scientist, but... *(now truly noticing)*... but how old you are! I beg your pardon but was there no one better suited for such a grueling assignment?

VUACANSON: *(making an unwitting mockery of Act I)* I'm worn out, it's true. But we must push on. If we do not strive, then what can posterity hope for?!

SPALLANZANI: But how did you know to come here?

VAUCANSON: I received a tip from one of the gendarmes who knew Jean was headed in this general direction.

SPALLANZANI: *(panicked)* They knew?! Then they will wind up here, surely!

VAUCANSON: *(to Condorcet)* A disguise, that was quick thinking.

CONDORCET: It was the work of panicked minutes, and the rain made a shambles of it.

VAUCANSON: No, it looks fine.

CONDORCET: It is not too attractive, I hope.

SPALLANZANI: It's not.

VUACANSON: I am not so sure.

SPALLANZANI: You need to get out.

CONDORCET: For an attractive lady alone on the outskirts of the city might arouse suspicion. Ideally, I should appear past my prime.

VAUCANSON: Perhaps even a washerwoman.

CONDORCET: You must help me!

> *Housekeeper enters with water*

55

VAUCANSON: You can't be too careful. Perhaps you should swap clothing with his Housekeeper, her clothes seem more down-at-the-heels.

HOUSEKEEPER: (*indignant*) There is nothing wrong with them.

CONDORCET: (*to Vaucanson*) Yes, perhaps you are right. We will change immediately.

HOUSEKEEPER: Change?

SPALLANZANI: Yes, exchange dresses with the man.

HOUSEKEEPER: But I am not of a mind.

VAUCANSON: Give him your smock, quickly!

SPALLANZANI: Damn it woman, this is a great man! His life is on the line!

HOUSEKEEPER: Signore, you wish to take the very dress from my body. I am sorry but no, I cannot allow it. I am after all in your service no longer.

CONDORCET: (*desperate, near tears*) Please! Please!

HOUSEKEEPER: No. Jean-Marie Condorcet. Mathematician, philosopher, supporter of the Revolution and member of the revolutionary Legislative Assembly and Convention. Fleeing the city dressed as a woman, you will be discovered in a country inn outside of Paris and arrested. Two months later, at the age of 51, you will be found dead in your cell, officially from exhaustion, though more likely from your vial of poison.

    Housekeeper exits. Pause.

SPALLANZANI: (*having heard only the Housekeeper's "No."*) Well, so be it.

VAUCANSON: You look fine without the smock.

SPALLANZANI: This is the manuscript.

VAUCANSON: (*reading*) "Man will not always be corrupted by greed, fear and envy. He will one day be restored to the rights and dignity of his nature!"

CONDORCET: (*overlapping, reciting from memory*) "He will one day be restored to the rights and dignity of his nature!"

SPALLANZANI: You can't stay here.

CONDORCET: But friend, you are my last hope.

SPALLANZANI: But of course I'm not. At the very least, take a room in a country inn, you will surely be safer there than here. Go now, quickly, before they gain anymore ground.

CONDORCET: But—

SPALLANZANI: No, this is for the best, I'm thinking of you.

CONDORCET: If we but had your Housekeeper's smock—

SPALLANZANI: Forget the smock—

CONDORCET: But—

SPALLANZANI: Hang the smock! Here, drink this. Now you must go.

CONDORCET: Thank you. I should like to have stayed, I am very tired. (*pause*) But perhaps you are right.

SPALLANZANI: Good then. Farewell.

CONDORCET: I'm off.

VAUCANSON: Safe passage.

CONDORCET: Farewell.

SPALLANZANI: Godspeed.

CONDORCET: Thank you.

VAUCANSON: Good luck my friend.

CONDORCET: We'll meet again.

SPALLANZANI: Of course.

CONDORCET: Farewell!

VAUCANSON: Au revoir.

    beat

CONDORCET: I'm off.

SPALLANZANI: Au revoir.

VAUCANSON: Au revoir.

    Condorcet reluctantly exits. And as Vaucanson is about to exit:

SPALLANZANI: And you, Jacques de Vaucanson.

VAUCANSON: We have met before.

SPALLANZANI: Your clockwork duck will survive you.

VAUCANSON: Its parts were more durable than my own.

SPALLANZANI: It will be exhibited by Bontems, the famous maker of the mechanical singing birds. The duck will end up in the cabinet of curiosities of a certain Mr. Gassner of Karkov in the Ukraine. This cabinet, and the duck with it, will burn to ashes in 1879, the same year Albert Einstein was born, Cetewayo, king of the Zulus, was deposed, and Robert Louis Stevenson wrote *Travels with a Donkey*.

VAUCANSON: And you, Lazarro Spallanzani, will die of a urinary-tract infection in Pavia. Your corpse will fall into the hands of your rival, Reaumur, who will remove your penis and testicles out of maliciousness and put them on display in a jar at the university museum, where they will stay for over 200 years.

SPALLANZANI: That is most upsetting. God damn Reaumur.

VAUCANSON: Reaumur's corpse will be seized after his death by your colleagues, who will decapitate him and place his head in a jar, and for over 200 years his head will sit on a shelf next to your testicles.

SPALLANZANI: The result of our struggles is meaningless.

VAUCANSON: Yet the struggles themselves are noble—

SPALLANZANI: Life is a difficult movement of the bowels. If we persevere, it is because we haven't a choice. Call that noble.

57

VAUCANSON: And yet....

SPALLANZANI: *(conceding)* And yet....

VAUCANSON: *(decisively)* And yet.

SPALLANZANI: Yes. Yes.... Now get out. Out. Out.

> *Spallanzani kicks Vaucanson to the door, hurls him out door and he slams it shut. Gathers materials still on floor. Places them back on desk. Sits down. Shoves materials off of desk. Knock on door. Housekeeper enters with bowl.*

HOUSEKEEPER: They are all gone?

SPALLANZANI: We still might get a call from soldiers come to arrest me.....

HOUSEKEEPER: I will tell them you are busy with your pants.

SPALLANZANI: That man's dress was far nicer than yours. Why didn't you swap when you had the chance?

HOUSEKEEPER: It was not a dress for housekeeping.

SPALLANZANI: I thought you were done with housekeeping.

HOUSEKEEPER: I am done housekeeping for you, but the dress still is no good. I am not returning to Pavia for the balls and banquets, am I...

SPALLANZANI: You are returning to glimpse once more the Ticino River from the old town where you sat with your lover when you were young and comely.

HOUSEKEEPER: I couldn't give a curse for the foul Ticino.

SPALLANZANI: Perhaps you've never glimpsed it with a lover. *(pause)* Perhaps you never had a lover.

HOUSEKEEPER: Eat.

SPALLANZANI: Ah, porridge. I shall miss your cooking.

> *Housekeeper meanwhile picking up the materials lying on the floor, stifles a snicker*

SPALLANZANI: What was that?

HOUSEKEEPER: My pardons, Signore. A sneeze.

SPALLANZANI: A sneeze indeed. What is it? You did something to the porridge? As a last gesture you have spit in it.

HOUSEKEEPER: No. It is nothing.

SPALLANZANI: *(seeing her with materials in hand)* Or is it my patterns?

HOUSEKEEPER: No.

SPALLANZANI: Yes it is. I know that little smugness of yours.

HOUSEKEEPER: Have any of your frogs been fitted out yet in your pants?

SPALLANZANI: I have to make them first don't I.

HOUSEKEEPER: *(pointing to pattern)* How will you get their feet through so small a space at the bottom of the leg?

SPALLANZANI: Eh?

HOUSEKEEPER: Frogs have large feet.

SPALLANZANI: I know they have large feet.

HOUSEKEEPER: I suppose you'll just push.

SPALLANZANI: Yes, I'll just push, it won't be difficult. *(pause)* The pants must be tight!

HOUSEKEEPER: Good luck then.

SPALLANZANI: They must be tight!

HOUSEKEEPER: Fine.

SPALLANZANI: There can be no leakage! *(broods)* But I see your point. But I cannot contrive another way. A hook and eye perhaps?

> *Housekeeper stifles another snicker*

SPALLANZANI: *(fed up, pushes bowl off desk)* I am not hungry. Take this. Get out.

> *She picks up bowl and makes to leave*

I suppose you have a better way?

HOUSEKEEPER: No.

SPALLANZANI: You do.

HOUSEKEEPER: I can't think of anything.

SPALLANZANI: Well then stay out of it.

HOUSEKEEPER: A drawstring perhaps.

> *Housekeeper exits*

SPALLANZANI: A drawstring? Come back here! A drawstring you say?

HOUSEKEEPER: At the bottom of each leg. The pants legs can be quite baggy, but then pulled in at the ankle and kept there with a knot.

SPALLANZANI: But the string will fall off.

HOUSEKEEPER: Do you know nothing? You would keep it there by sewing it into a hem of course.

SPALLANZANI: A hem…

> *Pause. Blank face of Spallanzani. She hastily grabs fabric on desk and demonstrates—*

HOUSEKEEPER: You see, and you turn it over, with the string, then sew it shut, but leave an opening for the string to dangle out.

> *She makes to exit again*

SPALLANZANI: What sort of string? Thread would work, yes? I have strong thread.

HOUSEKEEPER: It stinks in here.

> *Housekeeper begins to exit*

SPALLANZANI: I am not using all the taffeta…..I won't be needing the entire bolt.

HOUSEKEEPER: Oh with the way you sew you will…

SPALLANZANI: There is a chance.

59

HOUSEKEEPER: What do I care?

SPALLANZANI: Help me, and you can have what is left.

HOUSEKEEPER: I will be in Pavia long before you are finished.

SPALLANZANI: If you assisted me, the pants could be completed sooner and you would have all that remained to take with you.

HOUSEKEEPER: Why are you in such a rush?

SPALLANZANI: I am near death.

HOUSEKEEPER: It stinks in here.

SPALLANZANI: Stop saying that. Will you or will you not? There's a good seven hours before dawn, 29 pairs of pants divided by two 14 and a half by 7 hours, a little more than 2 pairs an hour per person.

HOUSEKEEPER: It can't be done.

SPALLANZANI: It can!

HOUSEKEEPER: Why should I help you?

SPALLANZANI: I told you. For the taffeta.

HOUSEKEEPER: Do you think my life is ruled by fabric?

SPALLANZANI: *(agape)* Isn't it?

HOUSEKEEPER: *(with bit of relish)* But you need my help.

SPALLANZANI: Yes I need your help. And...more than that......

HOUSEKEEPER: I'm listening.

SPALLANZANI: Well I don't think you'll credit it but...it's true—

HOUSEKEEPER: Tell me...

SPALLANZANI: Well.....damn it...after forty-one years....you owe me.

HOUSEKEEPER: I owe you?!

SPALLANZANI: Well find your own reason then!

HOUSEKEEPER: I don't know why you bother at all!

SPALLANZANI: What do you mean? With what?

HOUSEKEEPER: This! Your work—

SPALLANZANI: *(exasperated)* Why? I told you why.

HOUSEKEEPER: Did you?

SPALLANZANI: Why does anyone do anything?!

HOUSEKEEPER: *(sincere)* Why does anyone do anything?

    long pause

SPALLANZANI: *(feebly)* ...why...

HOUSEKEEPER: Why have I persisted in cleaning your chamberpot every day for all these years.

SPALLANZANI: You have a nurturing personality. You could not live alone. You would shrivel.

HOUSEKEEPER: You would shrivel.

SPALLANZANI: I? No, no...I can live alone.

HOUSEKEEPER: I don't think so.

SPALLANZANI: Are you going to help me with my pants or not?

    Pause. And the Housekeeper at last relents and crosses to the table.

SPALLANZANI: There we are! The Great Nurturer.

HOUSEKEEPER: Enough of that.

SPALLANZANI: We can try at least.

    Pleased, Spallanzani shows her a seat. Housekeeper picks up needle and thread

HOUSEKEEPER: And all for semen.

SPALLANZANI: As soon as I acquired my first microscope sixty years ago, it was the first thing I examined, and it shall be my last...

HOUSEKEEPER: What did you do?

SPALLANZANI: What do you mean.

HOUSEKEEPER: When you first acquired your microscope. Where did you obtain the semen? Did you have frogs even then?

SPALLANZANI: You have so little imagination that you cannot construe where and how I might have obtained some semen?

HOUSEKEEPER: It's not sold in shops.

SPALLANZANI: Are you baiting me?

HOUSEKEEPER: I am sincere.

SPALLANZANI: I will tell you plainly then that I manipulated my own privatees in a fashion thereby obtaining a sample.

HOUSEKEEPER: *(shocked and intrigued)* Did you? What do you mean, "in a fashion"?

SPALLANZANI: Forget it.

HOUSEKEEPER: Does this have something to do with masturbation?

SPALLANZANI: *(impatiently)* Yes, it has everything to do with it.

HOUSEKEEPER: *(still more shocked and intrigued)* Really? And where did you commit this sin?

SPALLANZANI: Sin indeed.

HOUSEKEEPER: In Pavia?

SPALLANZANI: Yes in Pavia.

HOUSEKEEPER: Have you masturbated here in Paris?

SPALLANZANI: Enough of this.

HOUSEKEEPER: Have you masturbated in this room?

SPALLANZANI: I said enough.

HOUSEKEEPER: *(suddenly aware of the chair she is in)* Do you sit down when you do it?

SPALLANZANI: Good God woman, have you never done it?!

Housekeeper, without a word, puts down sewing materials and makes to exit

Where are you going?

HOUSEKEEPER: I am leaving.

SPALLANZANI: Are you making tea?

HOUSEKEEPER: No.

SPALLANZANI: You're coming back aren't you? *(realizing)* You're not pretending to have modesty!

HOUSEKEEPER: I do have modesty.

SPALLANZANI: Housekeeper, tell me truthfully, you've never had a lover, have you?

HOUSEKEEPER: *(lashing back)* You, the Great Fornicator, do what you will, but I have my beliefs—

SPALLANZANI: Who are you calling the Great Fornicator?

HOUSEKEEPER: You are the Great Fornicator.

SPALLANZANI: Oh I see!

HOUSEKEEPER: Intercourse before marriage is wrong—

SPALLANZANI: Yes—

HOUSEKEEPER: —and afterso its purpose is for making children! I am not ashamed of my virginity!

SPALLANZANI: But I've said the same thing all along!

Pause. Housekeeper intrigued.

HOUSEKEEPER: And yet you've never married...

Silence from Spallanzani.

You Signore have never been with a woman?

SPALLANZANI: No I have not.

HOUSEKEEPER: Not one?

SPALLANZANI: No.

HOUSEKEEPER: In all your life?

SPALLANZANI: Let's just drop it.

HOUSEKEEPER: So all these years—

SPALLANZANI: Yes.

HOUSEKEEPER: *(a statement)* So.

A brief moment between them.

SPALLANZANI: Yes. *(beat)* Yes.

HOUSEKEEPER: Why? Why no lover?

SPALLANZANI: I was busy.... Or because no one would have me... or no, I refused and I refuse to have sex for mere pleasure's sake, and I refuse to procreate if I don't know why I even exist....

HOUSEKEEPER: Were you never attracted to a woman?

SPALLANZANI: If I copulated out of blind attraction, if I didn't think about what it all meant I'd be no different and no better than Johann Carl Wilcke over there.

HOUSEKEEPER: Over where?

SPALLANZANI: There. That one.

HOUSEKEEPER: *(touched, actually)* You have named your frogs.

SPALLANZANI: Yes, after great men of our age.

HOUSEKEEPER: Who is Wilcke?

SPALLANZANI: He discovered the concept of specific heat—the amount of heat required to raise the temperature of a unit mass one degree.

HOUSEKEEPER: *(intrigued, pointing to another frog)* And who is that?

SPALLANZANI: That one with the spots is Antoine Lavoisier. Among other accomplishments, he revolutionized the language of chemistry.

HOUSEKEEPER: And that croaking one there?

SPALLANZANI: William Herschel. His was the largest reflecting telescope ever built and with it he discovered Uranus, the first planet to be revealed in over two thousand years. And this hopping bastard here is Francis Glisson, who explained how the gall bladder discharges bile only when it is needed. And there, Andreas Marggraaf, and there, Anders Celsius and Johannes Kepler and Joseph Black and Henry Cavendish and Allesandro Volta and Jan Ingen-Housz and Claude Berthollet. Each one has a story and we will make pants for them all!

HOUSEKEEPER: And Lazarro Spallanzani. You too deserve pants. For your work in casting doubt on the theory of spontaneous generation, and for your development of artificial insemination, you will be known as one of the great experimentalists of the 18th century. But due to elements you could not have foreseen, you will still conclude wrongly that spermatick worms are only worms and have no part in reproduction. You will never know that you got it wrong. You will not survive to see the year 1875, when Wilhelm Hertwig will be the first to observe the fecundation of an egg by sperm—that we are fertilized by what you call worms, just as worms turn us in our graves to dust.

63

finishing a pair of pants

There. That is one.

SPALLANZANI: Fine. Shall we have a fitting? Who shall it be?

HOUSEKEEPER: Who is this one?

SPALLANZANI: That is Francis Hauksbee, producer of a useful electrostatic generator.

HOUSEKEEPER: Are there any women?

SPALLANZANI: Have you not heard a word I've said? We are putting pants on male frogs—

HOUSEKEEPER: But you could still name one after a woman.

SPALLANZANI: No. That's too confusing. And no women scientists come to mind—

HOUSEKEEPER: You mentioned once a... Chamanet.

SPALLANZANI: Chatelet? Gabrielle du Chatelet?

HOUSEKEEPER: Yes, what about her?

SPALLANZANI: No. We're using Hauksbee. Get back to work.

A pronounced sigh of resignation from Housekeeper.

SPALLANZANI: I said no.

HOUSEKEEPER: Fine.

SPALLANZANI: All right, look, all the 29 female frogs, every one can be named Gabrielle du Chatelet. If I remember correctly, she died in childbirth. Now if our trousers fail, she'll give birth to 3,000 progeny.

HOUSEKEEPER: That's fine.

SPALLANZANI: *(having fitted pants)* Well, there's one fitted frog.

HOUSEKEEPER: So you will stay in Paris til you die?

SPALLANZANI: It is not a long wait.

HOUSEKEEPER: You should return to Pavia.

SPALLANZANI: With you? That's a horrible idea. But perhaps.

HOUSEKEEPER: There's no reason to stay.

SPALLANZANI: Sssh! Listen....

Cricket chirp

And you said there were no crickets in the city!

Cricket chirp and frog croak up to unnaturally high levels as lights dim. We hear birdsong. Spallanzani awakes.

SPALLANZANI: Birds?.... Those are birds... robins I think... *(realizing)* Oh christ, I fell asleep! Housekeeper?.... Housekeeper?!

We hear only a gentle, or actually rather pronounced, snoring from Housekeeper, who is asleep in chair

It will soon be dawn and what have I to show for it? Yes, go on, snooze on and abandon me....

He then notices a collection of small pants near her. He holds up pants and counts them as lights slowly rise. Birdsong heard.

One, two, three... eight, ten... one two three four... twenty... twenty-six, twenty-seven, twenty-eight, plus one on Hauksbee... twenty-nine... she did it, the old cow, twenty-nine pairs of tight-fitting taffeta pants....

Spallanzani finds an old blanket and gently drapes it over sleeping

Housekeeper. Tucks it to chin. Kisses her.

...dark now... dark now... but soon dawn will come, and even now, the dawn chorus... and then the street cries...the fresh fish and old chairs to mend. *(pause)* And kettles to mend. And sprats alive o!.. sprats alive... *(derisively)* Sprats....

(shrugging) Well... there is that at least... they are alive...

(relishing) Sprats... alive... o!..

(a trial run) ...Spallanzani alive o....

(shouting) Spallanzani alive o!

His shout however is cut short by a truly violent coughing fit. Housekeeper stirs in sleep. And he, resigned, exhausted, awed:

...Well let it. Let it begin then. Let it. Let the day become... beguile... bewilder... benumb... bedim... and then... beget... then beget... yet... another....

Music louder, and in growing light, Chatelet revealed

CHATELET: *(sung)* Awake my Paris...
   Stir from thy slumberings
   The worlds you now strive in
   Shall be snuffed and forgotten
   Come the dawn....
   Bid farewell and return
   To this one Dream we share....
   Paris.... Awake.... Awake.... Awake.... Awake....

Stirring music continues through curtain call.

65

YUSSEF EL GUINDI is a playwright living in Seattle. His most recent production was *Back of The Throat*, winner of the the 2004 Northwest Playwright's Competition. It was also nominated for the 2006 American Theater Critics Association's Steinberg/New Play Award, and was voted Best New Play of 2005 by the Seattle Times. It was first staged by San Francisco's Thick Description and Golden Thread Productions; then later presented by Theater Schmeater in Seattle; Manbites Dog Theater in Durham, North Carolina; the Cyrano Theater Company in Anchorage, Alaska; the Flea Theater in New York; the Furious Theatre Company in Pasadena; and Silk Road Theatre Project in Chicago. Silk Road Theatre Project produced another play of his in 2005, *Ten Acrobats in An Amazing Leap of Faith* (winner of Chicago's After Dark Award for Best New Play in 2006). His two-related one-acts, *Acts of Desire*, were staged by the Fountain Theatre in Los Angeles . Other recent productions: *Karima's City* (in San Francisco and as part of 2004's Cairo International Experimental Theater Festival, both presented by Golden Thread Productions), *Murder in the Mirror* (a radio play presented by Stage Shadows at the Museum of Television and Radio in New York), and *Men On Mars* (another radio play aired in 2004 by Shoestring Radio Theater in San Francisco). His adaptation of Chekhov's *A Marriage Proposal* into an Arab-American setting was staged by the Arab Theatrical Arts Guild in Dearborn, Michigan and was nominated for several PAGE awards including Outstanding achievement in Original Play or Adaptation. His short film, *Love Stalks*, won an award for best short narrative film at the Seattle Underground Film Festival and was aired on KTEH. His short stories *Habibi* (Seattle Review) and *Ohio* (Mizna) were recently published; and another short story, *Stage Directions for an Extended Conversation*, was published in Dinarzad's Children, an anthology of Arab-American Fiction. Yussef holds an MFA from Carnegie-Mellon University and was playwright-in-residence at Duke University.

Yussef El Guindi

Back of the Throat

CAST:
Khaled
Bartlett
Carl
Asfoor
Shelly
Beth
Jean

Note: Shelly, Beth and Jean can be played by the same actor

> *Khaled's studio. Futon on floor. Assorted objects, furniture. Bartlett stands opposite Khaled. Carl is flipping through a book. He will continue to methodically inspect other books, papers, as well as clothes.*

BARTLETT: We appreciate this.

KHALED: Whatever you need, please.

BARTLETT: This is informal, so—.

KHALED: I understand.

BARTLETT: Casual. As casual as a visit like this can be.

KHALED: Either way. Make it formal if you want. I want to help. I've been looking for a way to help.

BARTLETT: Thanks.

KHALED: Horrible.

BARTLETT: Yes.

KHALED: Horrible.

BARTLETT: Nice space.

KHALED: Yes.—A little claustrophobic. But it's cheap.

BARTLETT: Live simply they say.

KHALED: I'd live extravagantly if I could afford it.

BARTLETT: What's this say?

Bartlett picks up a picture frame from a table.

KHALED: A present from my mother.... It says, er, "God".

BARTLETT: "God"?

KHALED: Yes.

BARTLETT: It's pretty.

KHALED: It is.... I'm not religious myself.

BARTLETT: I've always been impressed with this... (*makes a motion over the writing with his finger.*)

KHALED: Calligraphy?

BARTLETT: Very artistic. Why the emphasis on—calligraphy? I see it all the time.

KHALED: Well—frankly—I'm not sure its—. I know in general that, the religion tends to favor abstraction to, er, human representation. The idea being to avoid worship, or, too much distraction with the, um, human form.... In truth I don't know a whole lot about it.

BARTLETT: No television?

KHALED: No. Too addictive. It's easier to remove the temptation.

BARTLETT: (*picking up a book*) You didn't see the images?

KHALED: Oh yes. God, yes. How could I not? I wish I hadn't.

We hear the tinkling of a tune. Khaled and Bartlett turn in the direction of Carl, who is standing holding a music box.

A beat as they all stand and listen to the tune.

CARL: "Oklahoma"?

KHALED: I've never been able to identify the tune.

BARTLETT: (*referring to the book*) And what's this about?

Carl closes the music box and places it next to another object he's selected. He resumes his search.

KHALED: It's the, um—Koran.

BARTLETT: Huh. So this is it.

KHALED: Another present from my mother. Her idea of a subtle hint.

BARTLETT: (*flips through book*) You're not religious, you say?

KHALED: No. She is.

BARTLETT: Didn't rub off.

KHALED: Unfortunately not.

BARTLETT: Why "unfortunately"?

KHALED: Well—because I hear it's a comfort.

BARTLETT: And if you had to sum up the message of this book in a couple of lines.

KHALED: Er. The usual. Be good. Or else.

BARTLETT: Sounds like good advice to me. How come you're not religious?

YUSSEF EL GUINDI

Khaled looks over at what Carl is rifling through.

KHALED: I was never comfortable with the "or else" part.

BARTLETT: Nobody likes the punishment part.

KHALED: I'd like to think God isn't as small-minded as we are.

BARTLETT: I guess the point is there are consequences for our actions. Funny, huh. How a book can have such an impact.

KHALED: Yes. I was just reading about Martin Luther and the Reformation and how the whole—

BARTLETT: *(interrupting)* Am I pronouncing that correctly? "Kaled"?

KHALED: Close enough. *(To Carl)* Is there anything in particular you're looking for?

BARTLETT: Don't mind him. He's just going to do his thing.

KHALED: But if there's anything—

BARTLETT: *(interrupting)* With your permission, if we still have that.

KHALED: Go ahead, but if there's something—

BARTLETT: *(interrupting)* "Kaled"?

KHALED: Er, Khaled.

BARTLETT: "Haled"?

KHALED: More Khaled.

BARTLETT: "Kaled".

KHALED: That's good.

BARTLETT: But not exactly.

KHALED: It doesn't matter.

CARL: Khaled.

KHALED: That's it.

BARTLETT: It's that back of the throat thing.

KHALED: Right.

BARTLETT: Carl spent some time in the Mid-East.

KHALED: Oh yes?

BARTLETT: So how do you stay informed then? With no TV. Newspapers? The internet?

KHALED: Both.

BARTLETT: And when you want to kick back, you...?

KHALED: *(not getting what he means)* When I...?

BARTLETT: How do you relax?

KHALED: Well...

BARTLETT: How do you spend your free time?

KHALED: Really?—That's relevant? *(Bartlett stares at him)* Er, sure, okay. I read, mostly.

BARTLETT: Uh-huh.

KHALED: That's my big thing, reading.

BARTLETT: And when you want to amuse yourself, you do what?

KHALED: *(referring to the books)* Actually I find that stuff amusing.

BARTLETT: *(holding up a periodical)* This stuff?

KHALED: Some of it.

BARTLETT: *(reading the cover)* "Wheat Production and the Politics of Hunger."?

KHALED: A real page-turner.

BARTLETT: *(pointing to the computer)* Can we look at that, by the way?

KHALED: It's kind of private. *(Slight beat)* It's—kind of private. *(Carl and Bartlett are looking at Khaled)* Will you be taking it away?

BARTLETT: I doubt we'll need to look at it.

KHALED: If you want to.

BARTLETT: I'm actually more curious about how you kick back. What you do when you want to relax. Break your routine. Spice things up.

KHALED: Can I ask how that helps you? Knowing how I amuse myself?

BARTLETT: The questions will seem a little intrusive, unfortunately. There's no avoiding that.

KHALED: I understand. I just don't have that exciting a life. Did I mention I'm a citizen, by the way? I can show you my—*(Carl holds up Khaled's passport.)* Right. Just so you know.

Carl puts it among two or three other items. This pile will gradually grow.

BARTLETT: Here's the thing. We know you're bending over backwards and I sense we're going to be out of your way shortly.

CARL: Be done in five.

BARTLETT: And we know you didn't have to let us do this.

KHALED: Are you looking for anything in particular? Maybe I can just point you to it.

BARTLETT: He's just going to poke around. It's a random thing.

KHALED: Are you sure? The strange thing is I was going to call you. A friend of mine said he would, which made me think I should too.

BARTLETT: Who?

KHALED: Er—a friend?

BARTLETT: Right; and that friend's name?

KHALED: *(hesitates)* Hisham. He wouldn't mind me telling you.

BARTLETT: Hisham what?

KHALED: Darmush. He was thinking of calling you too.

BARTLETT: I look forward to hearing from him.

KHALED: I thought maybe I should just to let you know I'm—here, you know. I am who I am and—just so you're not wondering—in case my name comes across your desk which it obviously has. I wish you'd tell me who gave you my name.

BARTLETT: Also know that anything you say here will be held in strict confidence.

KHALED: (*continuing*) Because then maybe I could address the concerns head on; so you don't waste your time. I imagine you're getting a lot of calls. People with scores to settle. Or skittish neighbors. Was it George? He seems a little too curious about where I'm from. He doesn't seem to understand my connections with my country of birth are long gone. Was it—Beth? We had a falling out. It's very strange not being able to address whatever accusations have been made against me. It's like battling ghosts.

BARTLETT: I didn't say anything about accusations.

KHALED: There haven't been? (*Bartlett stares at him; slight beat*) Er, amuse myself? Let's see, I go to movies, I read. I like eating out; I sit in cafes. I like to go for long walks. I feel like I'm writing a personals ad. I wish there was more to tell. You'll leave here thinking, gee, what a lame life this guy leads.

BARTLETT: That's the other thing: If you have nothing to worry about then you have nothing to worry about. I know a visit from us can be unsettling. It's an awkward part of this job that when we come around people aren't necessarily happy to see us. We've held meetings to see if we can't fix that, but I guess there's no avoiding the fact that this is what it is. I'm a government official, uninvited, and you've been yanked out of your routine.

KHALED: You're more than welcome, I assure you.

BARTLETT: And we appreciate that.

KHALED: I've wanted to help.

BARTLETT: What I'm saying is we know we've put you on the spot.

KHALED: Well—.

BARTLETT: (*continuing*) It would be natural to be ill at ease, regardless of whether you want us here or not.

KHALED: Sure.

BARTLETT: (*continuing*) Don't waste time trying to appear innocent if you are. If you're innocent you're innocent. You don't have to work at it.

CARL: (*turning around, to Khaled*) "Karafa".

KHALED: What?

BARTLETT: So relax.

KHALED: I'm trying.

BARTLETT: We're not here to get you for jaywalking. Don't worry about us finding small stuff. We all have small stuff we'd rather not have people see.

KHALED: Not even that. That's what I'm saying; I'm not even hiding any interesting, non-political stuff.

BARTLETT: Stuff like this. *(From under a pile of magazines, he picks out a porn magazine.)* Don't worry about this stuff.

KHALED: Okay. That.

BARTLETT: It's not a big deal.

KHALED: It's—sure.

BARTLETT: *(flipping through magazine)* Not a huge one anyway.

KHALED: It's legal.

BARTLETT: It's porn. Not good. But it's still okay.

KHALED: They haven't outlawed it yet.

BARTLETT: No, but that doesn't make it all right.

KHALED: It's—it's a debate, but sure.

BARTLETT: A debate?

KHALED: Er, yeah.

BARTLETT: A debate how?

KHALED: About—you know—the place of erotica in society.

BARTLETT: Uh-huh.... You think this is healthy? *(shows Khaled a picture)* With cows?

KHALED: I don't much care for the farm theme, no.

BARTLETT: You think this should have a place in society?

KHALED: It already does have a place in society.

BARTLETT: So does murder. Doesn't make it okay.

KHALED: I'm not sure I'd equate that with murder.

BARTLETT: You go for this stuff? On the kinky side?

KHALED: What's kinky? She's draped over a cow. It's actually meant to be an anti-leather kind of thing. If you read the blurb. A cow wearing a human. A reverse sort of—vegetarian's point of view of sex and fashion. It's a stretch. But someone in that magazine is obviously an animal rights person. Or is pretending to be for the sake of something different.

BARTLETT: The woman doesn't seem to fare too well.

KHALED: No, but—. What does this have to do with anything? It's one magazine?

Carl holds up four or five more porn magazines.

Yes. I'm allowed.

BARTLETT: Careful there. You don't want to get caught in little lies over nothing.

KHALED: What lie? I thought you didn't care about the small stuff.

BARTLETT: I don't. It's just a pet issue I have.

72

CARL: (to Khaled) "Hany-hany."

KHALED: I'm sorry: am I supposed to understand that?

BARTLETT: You don't speak Arabic?

KHALED: No. That's why I didn't call. I knew you were looking for Arabic speakers.

Carl holds up two books in Arabic.

Yes. I keep telling myself I should learn it. Look, I hope you're not going to pick apart every little thing because I'm sure you could come to all sorts of conclusions by what I have. As you would with anyone's home. Come to a bunch of false conclusions by what someone has. Which may mean nothing more than, you know, like a Rorschach test. Without taking anything away from your training; but still: a porn magazine; Arabic books? So what?

BARTLETT: Uh-huh.

KHALED: It's my business.—I don't have to apologize for it. Do I?

BARTLETT: No, you don't. Or any of these titles.

Carl hands him a few of the books he selected.

"Getting Your Government's Attention Through Unconventional Means", "A Manual for the Oppressed", "Theater of the Oppressed", "Covering Islam", "Militant Islam". (*Holds up a little red book*) "Quotations From Chairman Mao's Tsetung"?

KHALED: I'd heard so much about it.

BARTLETT: Do you feel that oppressed?

KHALED: I was a lit major; I read everything.

BARTLETT: And so on. (*he throws the rest of the titles on the futon*) It's not what we care about.

KHALED: Good because on the face of it I know —

BARTLETT: (*interrupting*) On the other hand a person is reflected by what he owns. It'd be silly to deny that. If you walked into my home, or Carl's, you'd find us. In what we did and didn't have. Just as you are here in all this.

KHALED: But—context is everything, isn't it? Otherwise, yes, some of this I know looks suspicious. I've played this game myself: Walked into my studio and wondered what it might say about me; seeing if something would make me out to be something I'm not.

BARTLETT: You're surrounded by the things that interest you.

KHALED: I have a book on assassins, what does that mean? I bet you've seen it and a red flag's gone up.

BARTLETT: What does it mean?

KHALED: Nothing. If I found that book in your home, what would that mean?

73

BARTLETT: It would mean in my line of work it would make sense to study the topic. What does it mean for you?

KHALED: I'm a writer; I read lots of things, for just in case—in case a plot line requires an assassin. I have a book on guns, which I'm sure you've selected. *(Seeing it)* Yes you have. I actually hate guns but finding that you might think gee, okay, here we go.

BARTLETT: Why do you have a book on guns?

KHALED: I told you, I'm a writer. I need any number of reference books on different subjects. That's the context.

BARTLETT: Okay. Now we know. That's why we have to ask. We have no way of knowing unless we ask. Which means throwing our net pretty wide. Please try not to get worked up in the process.

KHALED: I'm not.

BARTLETT: We're not here to unravel your personal life beyond what we need to know.

KHALED: It just feels this isn't as casual as you make it out to be. You're here for something specific, obviously, something brought you to my door. My name came across your desk and I wish you'd tell me why? If you allowed me to clear that up, maybe you could get on with finding the people you really want.

> *Bartlett and Carl stare at him.*

I mean I appreciate the effort you're making but I just sense something's being left unsaid and I would really like to address whatever that is. It's like this itch you've brought in that I wish I could just scratch, for all our sakes.

BARTLETT: Huh. Itch.

CARL: *(removes his coat)* Can I use your bathroom?

KHALED: It's right through there.

CARL: "Shukran."

> *Carl exits.*

BARTLETT: No, right, it's probably not as casual as I'd like it to be. Though we have begun training sessions on that very subject, strangely, even for old timers like me. "How to put people at ease." I didn't do too bad at it.

KHALED: No, you're—I am at ease.

BARTLETT: Thank you. In fact: *(takes out a form from his pocket)* If I can have you fill this out at the end of this, I'd appreciate it. It's an evaluation form. And then just mail it in. We're trying to get direct feedback from the public. Especially from our target audience.

KHALED: I'd be happy to.

BARTLETT: And if you could use a number 2 pencil.

KHALED: Sure.

BARTLETT: So yes, we try, but at the end of the day, there's no getting around the intrusiveness of all this: What am I doing here? A government official, in your home, going through your stuff and asking you questions.

KHALED: I'd love to know that myself.

BARTLETT: And that's what we'll find out. But in the meantime there's no avoiding the fact that that's who I am. Engaged in trying to find out who you are.

KHALED: I wish there was a way of showing you that I'm nobody interesting enough to have you waste your time.

BARTLETT: And you might not be.

KHALED: I'm not; how can I show you that?

BARTLETT: Well that's the thing. How can you show me that?

KHALED: Is there anything in particular you want to know?

BARTLETT: Is there anything you'd like to tell me?

KHALED: If you told me what brought you here—

BARTLETT: (interrupting) How about the computer? Anything I might want to see?

KHALED: No. Unless you want to look at a bunch of half-finished stories.

BARTLETT: Half-finished?

KHALED: Most of them.

BARTLETT: Why?

KHALED: "Why?"

BARTLETT: Writer's block?

KHALED: Sometimes.

BARTLETT: How come?

KHALED: It's an occupational hazard. It happens.

BARTLETT: Something going on to make you lose focus?

KHALED: Apart from the world going to hell?

BARTLETT: That inspires some people.

KHALED: Not me.

BARTLETT: It inspires me to do the best I can.

KHALED: Well, good.

BARTLETT: What inspires you, if I can ask?

KHALED: I never know ahead of time, that's why it's an inspiration.

BARTLETT: We know some of your interests, right, politics, sex.

KHALED: Not even that. But then, doesn't that cover most people's interests?

BARTLETT: I wouldn't say that. No. You wouldn't find these books in my house.

KHALED: Still, they're pretty basic, whether you have a direct interest in them or not.

BARTLETT: They're basic if you consider them important, otherwise they're not.

KHALED: To be an active, informed citizen? And to have a healthy interest in, in—sex; that's not normal?

BARTLETT: No. No, this isn't normal. I have to tell you, Khaled, none of this is normal. Right about now I would place you a few feet outside of that category.

Khaled looks dumbfounded.

To be honest, you are shaping up to be a very unnormal individual. I am frankly amazed at just how abnormal everything is in your apartment. I have actually been growing quite alarmed by what we've been finding. More: I'm getting that uncomfortable feeling that there's more to you than meets the eye and not in a good way. I wouldn't be surprised if we were to turn on that computer and find plans for tunneling under the White House. Or if Carl was to walk out that door having found something very incriminating indeed.

KHALED: You're—joking.

BARTLETT: I try not to joke before drawing a conclusion. It takes away from the gravity of the impression I'm trying to make.

The toilet flushes.

Carl. Are you done in there?

CARL: Just washing my hands.

BARTLETT: Can you hurry up, please?

CARL: I'll be right out.

KHALED: What happened to being casual?

BARTLETT: Oh, we're done with that. Could you turn on your computer, please?

KHALED: I—I think I'd like to, er...speak to a lawyer.

BARTLETT: Ah. Uh-huh.

KHALED: I—don't know what's going on anymore.

BARTLETT: I think you do is my hunch.

KHALED: Yuh. Okay. I think I'd like to speak to a lawyer if you don't mind.

BARTLETT: I do mind.

KHALED: I have the right.

BARTLETT: Not necessarily.

KHALED: Yes, I believe do.

BARTLETT: I'd have to disagree.

KHALED: I know my rights.

BARTLETT: What you do have is the right to cooperate with your intelligence and do the right thing and asking for a lawyer is a dumb move because it alerts me to a guilt you may be trying to hide. Which further suggests that I need to switch gears and become more forthright in my questioning; which usually means I become unpleasant. Which further irritates me because I'm a sensitive enough guy who doesn't like putting the screws on people and that makes me start to build up a resentment towards you for making me behave in ways I don't like....I am perhaps saying more than I should, but you should know where this is heading.

KHALED: (taken aback, trembling slightly) I'd...I'd like you to leave, please.

BARTLETT: I'm sorry you feel that way.

KHALED: I'm sorry too, but I—I think that's advisable. If there's something specific you want me to address, then fine. But. And in that case I would like to have a lawyer present. But I no longer wish to be subjected to this—whatever is going on here, so please. (He gestures towards the door) I'd appreciate it if you—and than if you want me to come in, I'll do so willingly with a lawyer.

BARTLETT: Er, Khaled, you can't have a lawyer.

KHALED: Yes, I can, I know my rights.

BARTLETT: No you don't, you've been misinformed. Could you switch on your computer please?

KHALED: I don't have to do that.

BARTLETT: Yes you do because I'm asking nicely.

KHALED: (moves towards the phone) I'm—I'm calling a lawyer.

BARTLETT: Is it smut you're trying to hide?

KHALED: No.

BARTLETT: Weird fantasies? Child porn?

KHALED: No!

BARTLETT: Child porn with domestic pets involved?

KHALED: What?

BARTLETT: So then it must be something to do with, what? Dicey politics? Military info; blueprints; communiqués with the wrong people?

KHALED: (overlapping) No. What are you—? None of that. No; that's—.

BARTLETT: I mean we've already established you're a left-leaning subversive with Maoist tendencies who has a thing for bestiality and militant Islam. Throw in your research on guns and assassins and I could have you inside a jail cell reading about yourself on the front page of every newspaper before the week is out.

KHALED: Is this—? What—? Are you trying to intimidate me?

    Bartlett stares at him.

    No.—Look, I—No. (goes to the phone and starts dialing) I don't know if this—if you're kidding me or—but. This isn't—

BARTLETT: Khaled.

KHALED: I don't know what's going on anymore. Something isn't...

BARTLETT: Put the phone down.

KHALED: I don't even know now if you're who you say you are. You could be a couple of con artists who walked off the street for all I know.

BARTLETT: Would you like to call our office instead?

KHALED: I would like you to leave.

BARTLETT: Okay but put the phone down first.

KHALED: I'm going to call my friend who'll know who I should—

BARTLETT: (interrupting) PUT THE PHONE DOWN!

Khaled puts the phone down. Slight beat.

KHALED: (quiet) I have rights. (slight beat) I do have rights. This is still—.... I don't have to show you anything if I don't want to unless you have a—.... Which doesn't mean I'm trying to hide anything, it just means I care enough about what makes this country—you know—to exercise the right to say no. There is nothing on that computer that would interest you, I promise you. And even if there were, I still have the right to—....

Bartlett continues to stare at him.

They're stories, okay, I told you. Still in progress. I'd rather not have people go poking around something that's still very private. It would be like opening a dark room while the photos are still developing. It would be a horrible violation for me. That may be—

BARTLETT: (interrupting, holds up his finger) Sorry: Khaled? Hold that thought. (goes to bathroom door) Carl. Could you stop whatever it is you're doing and come out please?

The door opens and CARL emerges wearing a different jacket and a baseball cap.

BARTLETT: Ah. Ah-ha.

CARL: I was searching the pipes.

BARTLETT: (re: the clothes) Well. There we go.

CARL: (re: the clothes) In the laundry basket, at the bottom.

BARTLETT: Really. Oh, well.

CARL: (holds up bottom of jacket) Evidence of nasty right here.

BARTLETT: (feels bottom of jacket) Yuck.

CARL: Smell it.

BARTLETT: I'll take your word for it.

CARL: Also: (takes out a swizzle stick)

BARTLETT: A swizzle stick.

CARL: And: (takes out a small piece of paper)

BARTLETT: A receipt. From. (reads it)

CARL: Guess where.

BARTLETT: Oh; wow.

CARL: Look at the date.

>Bartlett looks. Same date.

BARTLETT: Wow.

CARL: Proof positive.

BARTLETT: Looks like it.

CARL: He's our man.

BARTLETT: Uh-oh.

KHALED: What?

BARTLETT: Uh-oh.

KHALED: Why are you wearing that?

BARTLETT: You were where you shouldn't have been, Khaled; in a place you
shouldn't have gone to. Bad news. Very bad news.

KHALED: What is—? What does that—? *(re: the receipt)* I don't even remember
what that is?

>Khaled moves to look at it, but Bartlett gives the receipt to Carl, who pockets it.

BARTLETT: As we shift a little here *(he takes off his jacket)* I want to assure you
of a few things: we will not over step certain lines. We will not violate
you or your boundaries in any way. Though we might appear pissed off,
you are not to take it personally or feel this is directed at you per se. And
though we may resort to slurs and swear words, the aggression is not
focused on you so much as it an attempt to create an atmosphere where
you might feel more willing to offer up information.

>Over the above speech, Carl has taken a chair and placed it in various spots—
>as if to see where they might best place Khaled.

CARL: Here?

BARTLETT: Anywhere.

KHALED: What are you doing?

BARTLETT: *(to Khaled)* One more thing: at no time should you think this is
an ethnic thing. Your ethnicity has nothing to do with it other than the
fact that your background happens to be the place where most of this
crap is coming from. So naturally the focus is going to be on you. It's not
profiling, it's deduction. You're a Muslim and an Arab. Those are the bad
asses currently making life a living hell and so we'll gravitate towards
you and your ilk until other bad asses from other races make a nuisance
of themselves. Right? Yesterday the Irish and the Poles, today it's you.
Tomorrow it might be the Dutch.

KHALED: Okay.—Okay, look, look: You need to tell me what the hell is going on.

BARTLETT: We'll get to that. We're doing this as efficiently as we can.

KHALED: Because. I think. Actually, you know. *(moves to the door)* You need to

79

leave. I'm sorry, but—er. I don't have to do this. And I, er, yeah. You need to go. (opens door)

BARTLETT: Khaled.

KHALED: You need to go.

BARTLETT: Don't be a party pooper.

KHALED: I would be happy do this with a lawyer.

BARTLETT: Close the door.

> Carl moves towards Khaled and the door.

KHALED: You know what? I need to see your badges again because I'm not even sure anymore.

> Carl takes hold of the door and closes it.

Can I see your badges again please? Because. Whatever this is, this doesn't feel like it's, er, procedure. This is more like, you know, I mean, you're acting like a couple of, er, thugs, frankly. And I realize intimidation is part of the process, but this is—(a nervous laugh perhaps) speaking of boundaries.

BARTLETT: Anything you don't like, you write it down on the evaluation form.

CARL: You gave that to him already? (searches his pockets for his form)

BARTLETT: I understand your getting nervous. I don't care for this part myself. We're switching from being civil and congenial to being hard-nosed and focused. It will have the effect of taking away from your humanity and it doesn't do much for ours. Plus we're trying new approaches. It's all new territory for us. Which is why we're handing out these forms.

CARL: Here we go. (hands form to Khaled)

BARTLETT: You don't like something, write it down. Even if we haul you into permanent lock-up, we're still going to pay attention to your feedback. We might get things wrong in the short term, overdo things, with the interrogation, etc., but our image, honestly, how we come across, that can't be our main priority right now.

KHALED: Interrogate me about what?

BARTLETT: Our image can't be more important than questions of safety.

CARL: We don't give a rat's ass.

BARTLETT: We do give a rat's ass. But is it more important?

CARL: (half to himself) No, obviously we give a rat's ass.

BARTLETT: You care about this country? Yes? You want it safe?

KHALED: But I haven't done anything and you're acting like I have, what have I done?

BARTLETT: What is more important: Inconveniencing you with accusations of having broken the law or insuring the safety of everyone?

KHALED: But how am I a threat to that, I haven't broken the law!

BARTLETT: I'm speaking about in principle.

KHALED: Even in principle!

BARTLETT: I'm trying to be clear about this. I want the process to be transparent.

KHALED: I'm more confused than ever.

CARL: *(to Khaled)* You look like you need to sit down. You're beginning to wobble.

KHALED: What?

BARTLETT: Would you like a glass of water before we start?

KHALED: Am I under arrest? *(neither of them answer)* Am I under arrest? Because if I'm not and you're not taking me in, than you need to, this is over.

BARTLETT: Khaled.

KHALED: You need to go. *(Goes to door)* I know my rights. This is over. *(Opens door)*

BARTLETT: Khaled.

KHALED: You bet I'll fill in those forms. This is—this is way over the line. Acting like some—cutout pair of thugs playing tag to try and intimidate me. This is my country too, you know. This is my country! It's my fucking country!

BARTLETT: Khaled, the neighbors.

KHALED: I don't care if they hear it, let them hear it!

CARL: Not if you're guilty.

KHALED: I'm not guilty!

CARL: Then sit down and tell us about it.

KHALED: Tell you what?! You haven't told me what I've been accused of!

CARL: Shut the door and we'll tell you.

KHALED: I'm not going to tell you anything until I have a lawyer present! This is still America and I will not be treated this way!

> *Bartlett quickly walks over to Khaled, grabs him by the arm and drags him into a corner of the room—away from the door, which Carl shuts. Bartlett pushes Khaled into a corner and stands inches from him. While being dragged to the corner, Khaled says:*

What—? What are you doing? Let go of me. Let go of me.

BARTLETT: First thing: Shut up.

KHALED: No I—

BARTLETT: *(interrupting)* Second thing, shut up.

KHALED: No, I won't, I—

BARTLETT: (interrupting) If I have to tell you what the third thing is, I will shut you up myself.

> Khaled opens his mouth but is interrupted.

I will shut you up myself.

CARL: (walks over to them) Listen to the man.

BARTLETT: And if I hear you say, "This is still America" one more time I am going to throw up. I will open your mouth and hurl a projectile of my burger down your scrawny traitorous throat. Do you understand me?

KHALED: I'm not a traitor.

BARTLETT: Do you understand me?

CARL: Come on, man. Be cooperative.

> At certain points, with Khaled in the corner, Carl and Bartlett will completely block Khaled from the audience's view.

BARTLETT: (to Khaled) If I hear another immigrant spew back to me shit about rights, I will fucking vomit....You come here with shit, from shit countries, knowing nothing about anything and you have the nerve to quote the fucking law at me? Come at me with something you know nothing about?

CARL: (to Bartlett) Easy, man.

BARTLETT: It pisses me off!... "It's my country." This is your fucking country. Right here, right now, in this room with us. You left the U.S. when you crossed the line, you piece of shit.

CARL: (to Bartlett, quiet) Hey, hey.

BARTLETT: America is out there and it wants nothing to do with you.

CARL: Hey, Bart.

BARTLETT: It's galling.—Sticks in my craw. To hear these people who got here two hours ago quote back to me Thomas Jefferson and the founding fathers. They're not his fucking fathers.

CARL: They become his fathers. That's what makes this country special, man.

BARTLETT: I understand; but it's like they wave it at you like they're giving you the finger. (sing-song:) "You can't touch me, I have the constitution."

CARL: They do have the constitution.

BARTLETT: I know that, Carl. I'm just saying it's galling to hear it from people who don't give a shit about it.

KHALED: I do give a shit about it.

BARTLETT: No you don't.

KHALED: I do, very much.

BARTLETT: Don't lie to me.

KHALED: It's why I became a citizen.

BARTLETT: You became a citizen so you could indulge in your perverted little fantasies, you sick little prick. Come here, wrap the flag around you and whack off. *(He picks up a porn magazine)* Well I don't particularly want your cum over everything I hold dear!

CARL: Hey, Bart. *(Perhaps takes Bartlett aside)*

BARTLETT: *(to Carl)* I don't!

CARL: I know, it's okay.

BARTLETT: Jesus. God damn it.

CARL: I know.

BARTLETT: It's plain to see and we dance around it. We tiptoe and we apologize and we have to kiss their asses.

CARL: Don't blow it.

BARTLETT: I'm not; but sometimes it has to be said.

CARL: Okay, but let's stay on topic.

BARTLETT: This is the topic.

CARL: The point of the topic.

BARTLETT: *(to Khaled)* And I have nothing against immigrants. Let me make that clear.

CARL: *(takes porn mag from him)* Hear hear.

BARTLETT: The more the merrier. God bless immigrants. My great grandfather was an immigrant.

CARL: Mine too. Both sides.

> Carl will start leafing through the porn magazine.

BARTLETT: This country wouldn't be anything without them. God bless every fucking one of them. My family worked damn hard to make this country the place it is. And if you came here to do the same I will personally roll out the red carpet for you. But if you've come here to piss on us. To take from us. Pick all the good things this country has to offer and give nothing back and then dump on us?... then I don't think you're making a contribution, not at all.

KHALED: I am making a contribution.

BARTLETT: You're unemployed. You're on welfare.

KHALED: I have grants.

BARTLETT: That's taking.   83

KHALED: It's a prize.

BARTLETT: For what?

KHALED: For my stories.

BARTLETT: You haven't finished one.

KHALED: For past stories.

BARTLETT: You're blocked, you aren't writing, that means all you're doing is taking from the system.

CARL: *(still leafing through the magazine)* Leeching.

KHALED: I am writing, I'm just stressed out.

BARTLETT: You're involved in something you shouldn't be, that's why you're blocked. It's hard being creative when all you're thinking about is plotting destruction.

KHALED: I'm not, why are you saying that? What are you accusing me of?

CARL: *(throwing the magazine down)* The point is he doesn't have anything against immigrants. Let's be clear about that.

BARTLETT: *(to Khaled)* I'm dating an immigrant.

CARL: She gave you her number?

BARTLETT: *(to Khaled)* This is not why I'm pressing down on you. Apart from the reservations I just spoke about, the best thing going for you now is that you are fresh off the boat.

CARL: *(re: the girlfriend)* You lucky bastard.

BARTLETT: If it turns out you're not involved in any of this shit, I will personally apologize and invite you out somewhere. In the meantime, why don't you show Khaled why he's neck deep in doo-doo.

CARL: Love to.

KHALED: What?

CARL: *(reaches into his pockets; to Bartlett)* Hey, you know I met Miss September. *(gestures towards the porn magazine)*

BARTLETT: Who?

CARL: When I was helping the guys out on vice. *(Gesturing again)* Miss September. Just the nicest person. Devastated the attacks came on her month and ruined what could have been her big breakthrough. Was ready to quit until some guys wrote in saying how her body helped them through their darkest hours.

BARTLETT: *(not amused)* Great.

CARL: *(walks over to the bathroom, reaches in for his coat)* Now she only does spreads for special occasions. Usually to do with law enforcement.

BARTLETT: I don't really need to hear this.

CARL: *(reaching into his coat pocket)* I'm just saying, funny, huh? You never know what gets some people through the night. For some it's like, you know, the Church. For others—*(finds what he's looking for)* it's a place like this. *(he shows Khaled a photo)* Ever been to this strip club?

> Khaled tries to focus on the photo.

Well we know you did because here you are in this photo. *(shows him another photo)* Hidden in this hat and jacket I'm wearing, but: now that I'm wearing it we can pretty much say it's you. You can make out your jaw under the hat, and the earlobe is always a distinguishing feature. It's you, right?

Khaled looks but doesn't answer.

BARTLETT: Khaled.

CARL: Plus we have your receipt from the club and a bunch of other stuff that places you there.

KHALED: Why are you—? Why was this —?

CARL: So it is you.

Khaled hesitates.

I would acknowledge the obvious so you can quickly move ahead and establish your innocence, if that's the case. Which is not obvious.

BARTLETT: It's far from obvious.

CARL: I'd use this opportunity to clear up your name, if I was you.

Khaled is about to speak but is interrupted.

(*sotto voce:*) And look, man, don't be embarrassed about going to these joints. I've frequented these places myself. I'm not as hung up about this as Bart here is.

BARTLETT: I'm not hung up about them.

CARL: What I'm saying is someone in this room understands.

BARTLETT: I understand. It was the cow that put me off.

CARL: Personally, you can whack off all you want. You can take your johnson and do what you want with it, as long as it's legal. We're not here to judge you for what you do with your dick. What's that expression in Arabic they use? About a fool and his schlong? Anyway. If you're just embarrassed to admit you go to strip joints, don't be. I love a good lap dance myself. That ass waving in your face. The thighs working up a sweat. (*shows him the photo again*) You, right?

KHALED: Look I...I don't know where you're heading with this. I'm not going to incriminate myself when I don't even know what I'm being accused of. You asked if you had my permission to come in here and everything, well, you don't anymore, I'm sorry.

BARTLETT: We're so past that, my friend. Right now you're standing on our permission not to be disappeared into little atom-sized pieces of nothingness; and then shoved up the crack of the fat ass you'll be sharing a cell with. The best thing you can do for yourself is to identify yourself right now, and I mean right now.

Carl sticks the photo in front of Khaled's face.

KHALED: You can't tell anything. It's too dark. It's a silhouette for chrissakes.

BARTLETT: Then maybe we shed some light. Would that be helpful?

CARL: Shedding light is always a good idea.

BARTLETT: (*to Khaled*) This is going to be like pulling teeth, isn't it. Carl.

CARL: I'm ahead of you.

85

Carl goes over to the closet doors. At some point after this, he will take off his hat and jacket.

BARTLETT: Exhibit number one: *(shows Khaled another photo)* Have you seen this guy?

Carl slides open one of the doors, revealing Asfoor: erect, still. Perhaps a spotlight from within the closet is shone on him.

BARTLETT : Of course you have, he's been in all the papers. "Terribilis Carnifex", bringer of chaos, exemplar of horror and ghoulish behavior and very committed. And dead of course. Dying at the conclusion of his mad little goal. As a writer do you often wonder what might have been going through his mind at that instant he knew he'd accomplished his goal? Do you? I do. I wonder what he saw—just before he stopped seeing. What he thought, before he accomplished seizing everyone's mind and focusing it on him and his odious little ways. I admire him, you know. If I was an evil little shit, I'd want to be him. That's commitment for you. Dedication. *(to Asfoor)* What did you see, by the way?

ASFOOR: Nothing.

BARTLETT: What did you think?

ASFOOR: Nothing.

BARTLETT: Unfortunately, I can't get into his mind. But he did do a lot of typing.

Asfoor goes over to Khaled's computer. He will start typing

Quite the wordsmith. If a little cryptic. We've been able to trace most of his e-mails. Worked out of a library not too far from here. The librarian remembered him. Said he was like a dark cloud that changed the mood the moment he walked in. But said she felt sorry for him nonetheless. Reminded her of Pigpen, she said.

Carl slides open the other closet panel revealing SHELLY, wearing glasses.

SHELLY: Like in "Peanuts".

BARTLETT: Ah.

SHELLY: *(enters studio)* You know, the way he always had this cloud of dirt around him.

BARTLETT: I see.

SHELLY: That way. I thought it might be sadness at first, and felt the urge to say something to him. Cheer him up. *(to Asfoor)* It's a wonderful day. We haven't had this much sun in weeks.

Asfoor turns to her without saying anything.

Have a nice day. *(to Bartlett)* Didn't say much in return. No, I can't say he did. Barely smiled. His eyes were so... *(can't find the words)*.

BARTLETT: Yes?

SHELLY: Piercingly nondescript. As if I was looking at a description of a pair of eyes, and not the eyes themselves. Of course all these impressions may be hindsight.

BARTLETT: What do you mean?

SHELLY: You know, how new information about a person suddenly makes you see that person in a different light. I'm sure if you'd told me he'd saved the lives of a family from a burning house I'd be remembering him differently.—Though probably not.

BARTLETT: Anything else?

SHELLY: Well... *(hesitates)* He may have misread my attempts to be nice. Because one day he followed me into the room where we archive rare maps. And, well, made a pass at me. Didn't know he was there until I felt his hands. I screamed, of course. Pushed him away. I even had to use one of the rolled up maps to ward him off. I kept thinking, I hope it doesn't come to anything violent because this is the only existing map of a county in eighteenth century Pennsylvania.

BARTLETT: Why didn't you report the assault?

SHELLY: *(looking at Asfoor)* I don't know why I didn't.—I didn't want to give it—importance. Perhaps if I had you would've caught him and none of this would have happened. I'm sorry. How do you recognize evil?

BARTLETT: We appreciate the information you're giving now.

SHELLY: All I saw was an awful sadness. I had no idea his hurt had no end.

BARTLETT: Thank you, Ms. Shelly. If we have any follow-up questions we'll contact you.

SHELLY: I wish... *(to Asfoor)* I wish you hadn't done that. I wish there had been a way to get to you earlier, before things turned; before your mind went away. Because it has to go away to do that, doesn't it? Become so narrowed that nothing else matters.—I wish I could talk to you.—I would even let you...touch me, again. If it would open you up. If I could talk to you one more time; and find out more about you. Everyday I walk into a building filled with more knowledge than I could ever hope to digest. But none of the books can explain to me why you did what you did or who you are.... I wonder if you'd even be able to tell me?

BARTLETT: Thank you, Ms. Shelley. Carl will show you out.

> *With one last look at Asfoor, SHELLY heads for the front door. Carl opens the door and exits with her.*

87

I don't suppose you've ever seen this man up close? *(Bartlett briefly picks up a library book.)*

KHALED: Because we used the same library?

BARTLETT: Locked eyes across a library table?

KHALED: That's the connection? It's the only library for miles, everyone uses it.

BARTLETT: *(continuing)* Rubbed shoulders in the book shelves. Shared books? e-mails?

KHALED: (overlapping) That's what brought you here? You don't think I wouldn't have come forward if I'd seen him, if I'd have had any information about him.

BARTLETT: Perhaps you did and didn't know it; look at him again.

> Khaled's shown the photo. At this point, if not before, Asfoor is up on his feet.

KHALED: I know what he looks like. I would've remembered.

BARTLETT: Look at him again.

ASFOOR: Khaled.

KHALED: You're not going to pin this on me just because I went into the same building.

ASFOOR: I'm bleeding into you and there's nothing you can do about it.

BARTLETT: Pin what?

KHALED: Jesus Christ, I've been wanting to help.

BARTLETT: (overlapping) Pin what? You may have seen him, that's all.

KHALED: I wept for this country.

ASFOOR: So did I.

BARTLETT: I'm trying to jog your memory, you may have forgotten something, seen him at the computer.

KHALED: I know what you're doing and I'm not going to be screwed by something this flimsy. I will not be dragged in by association of having used the same space!

BARTLETT: Khaled: calm down; you aren't being accused of anything yet.

ASFOOR: We're all in this together.

BARTLETT: Perhaps you have some insight into this e-mail he sent; it's translated:

ASFOOR/BARTLETT: "Nothing the matter today. On Wednesday, I cut myself opening a can of tuna. Don't worry about that. Do you know Luxor? It's worth seeing."

BARTLETT: Or:

ASFOOR: "Tattoos, yes. Do it where the skin folds so you can hide it if you change your mind."

ASFOOR/BARTLETT: "I have a list for you."

BARTLETT: Is "Luxor" part of your e-mail address or how you sign off?

KHALED: No. "Luxor"? (pointing to the computer) Check it. This is like twenty degrees of separation. Then everyone in that library is a suspect. I use books, for chrissakes, I'm a writer.

BARTLETT: So you keep telling me.

ASFOOR: You're blocked, I can help.

BARTLETT: Ms. Shelly can't be definite she saw you two together, all the same she did say—

KHALED: (interrupting) How would she know who I am?

    Asfoor picks up a book.

BARTLETT: I showed her your photo.

KHALED: Where'd you get that?

BARTLETT: Your ex-girlfriend.

KHALED: (digests the information) How many people have you talked to exactly? What did Beth say?

BARTLETT: (consulting his notebook) But Ms. Shelly does think she saw him nearby when you came to ask for a book one time.

ASFOOR: (reads title of book) "Caravans of God and Commerce."

BARTLETT: Remembers it because you kicked up a fuss when they didn't have it.

ASFOOR: (reading from book) "The road to Mecca was perilous, and not only because of the dangers of the desert."

BARTLETT: Says he stood a few feet a way until you had finished and then followed you out.

ASFOOR: (reading from the book) "But also because of those who hid in them."

KHALED: What?

ASFOOR: (accent, to Khaled) Excuse me, sir.

KHALED: No.

BARTLETT: Said there may have been an exchange between you.

ASFOOR: (accent, to Khaled) I know book you want. I help you find it.

KHALED: That never happened. You don't think I would have remembered that? I'm a terrible liar. It would be obvious if I was lying.

    Asfoor has put down the book; Bartlett picks it up.

BARTLETT: I believe you. But you did find the book.

KHALED: In a book shop, I bought it.

BARTLETT: He never followed you out? Told you where you could find it?

KHALED: No.

BARTLETT: Perhaps the librarian did remember it wrong but if we speculated on this encounter that never took place, what might have happened?

KHALED: What kind of sense is that?

89

BARTLETT: He followed you out and:

KHALED: What am I supposed to speculate on?

BARTLETT: You're the writer, you tell me.

ASFOOR: Assalam alaykum.

KHALED: (disoriented) I can't remember what never happened.

ASFOOR: Assalam alaykum.

KHALED: (awkwardly) Alaykum salaam.

ASFOOR: (in Arabic) I know that book you want.

KHALED: I don't speak Arabic.

ASFOOR: (in Arabic) No?

KHALED: I'm sorry, I'm in a hurry.

ASFOOR: (accent) Please. A moment. I would like—my name is Gamal. Gamal Asfoor. Hello.

KHALED: Sorry but I have to go.

ASFOOR: I like to learn English. With you.

KHALED: I—no, I'm sorry.

ASFOOR: You teach me. I pay.

KHALED: I can't. I'm really busy right now.

ASFOOR: (hands him a piece of paper) My number here. I teach you Arabic. You Arab, yes? I watch you. I watch you in the library.

KHALED: No thanks. Thank you, no, goodbye.

ASFOOR: I know book you want. I get it for you.

KHALED: Really, I can't. (to Bartlett) That's ridiculous. There was no encounter. You're making stuff up.

BARTLETT: Well of course I am. You of all people should appreciate the importance of doing that. How that might lead you, stumbling, to a truth or two. Facts aren't the only game in town. Perhaps it never happened, then again, here are the Arabic books. In this story we're making up, maybe he gave them to you.

KHALED: What kind of deductive leap is that? That's worse than guessing.

 ASFOOR goes to sit at the computer.

BARTLETT: From his letters we know he shared similar interests with you: writing, poetry, Middle-Eastern stuff, politics, radical books, porn, didn't much like women. Said some nasty things about women in his letters.

ASFOOR: (at the computer) "Unclean."

BARTLETT: God knows what his childhood must have been like.

ASFOOR: "They corrupt. They diminish you. When I die, do not let them touch me."

KHALED: What on earth does that have to do with me?

BARTLETT: Well, Khaled, not knowing you; not really knowing much about you; just from meeting you and casual observance I would have to say your relation to the opposite sex seems to have a kink or two in it.

 Khaled looks at him dumbfounded.

Maybe you two commiserated and found solace in the same twisted images and depictions.

 Asfoor picks up a porn magazine and will glance at it for a while before returning to the computer.

KHALED: I don't know who you're talking about anymore; it's not me.

BARTLETT: I'm just saying.

KHALED: *(overlapping)* This is beyond making stuff up, this is Alice in Wonderland.

BARTLETT: Your girlfriend had a lot to say on the matter.

> *A knock on the door.*

KHALED: I knew it. She started this whole ball rolling, didn't she?

BARTLETT: I didn't say that, but she was helpful.

KHALED: She's the one who called you.

BARTLETT: The word "betrayal" came up a lot.

KHALED: *(continuing)* Something completely personal gets blown up because an ex holds a grudge. Great.

> *There's another knock on the door.*

BETH: *(off-stage)* I'm coming.

> *Beth enters from the bathroom in a bathrobe. She is drying her hair with a towel. Overlapping with this:*

KHALED: You're going to take the word of someone who's pissed off with me?

> *Beth has opened the door to Carl.*

CARL: *(shows her his badge)* Good morning. Ms. Granger?

KHALED: *(overlapping)* For something completely unrelated?

CARL: I wonder if we could talk with you a moment.

BETH: What is this about?

KHALED: Jesus, talk about the personal being political; now she gets to drive home that point and nail me with it.

BARTLETT: *(looking at his notebook)* She said some interesting things right off the bat.

BETH: So he was involved after all.

CARL: What makes you say that?

BETH: Was he like one of those cells that get activated?

KHALED: She said that?

BARTLETT: Why don't you let me finish first?

BETH: That would make sense. His whole life seemed to be one big lie. I don't think he has an honest bone in his body. What did he do exactly?

CARL: We're just trying to get a better idea of who he is at this point.

BETH: When you find out let me know. Because I sure as hell didn't. You spend two years with someone thinking you have a pretty good idea of who you're shacking up with, then boom, he pulls some shit that makes you wonder who you're sleeping with.

CARL: Like what exactly?

BETH: And I like to think of myself as an intelligent person.

CARL: What in particular made you—

BETH: *(interrupting)* Just everything. He never seemed to come clean about anything. Always keeping things close to his chest, like he had another life going on. It wouldn't surprise me if he was involved. Though I can't imagine he was high up in whatever structure they have. I could admire him if he was. But he's too weak for that. More like a wannabe. Like someone who would be quite willing to take instructions, if you know what I mean.

CARL: I don't; can you explain that?

BETH: Like he knew his life was for shit and something like this would give it meaning. He had that writerly thing of never feeling solid enough about anything. Of being woozy about most things. Of course when you imagine you're in love with someone, all their faults feel like unique traits that give them character. It's disgusting how love can dumb you down. Anyway, what else do you want to know? So like I said, it would just make sense. He never would tell me what he was working on or what he did when he went out. He just shut me out after a while. Could you turn around, please?

> *Beth has finished drying her hair and now selects a dress from the closet. She will proceed to put it on. Carl turns around.*

And then there was that quarrel we had soon after the attacks.

CARL: What quarrel would that be?

BETH: I almost flipped out because I thought he was actually gloating.

KHALED: That's enough, stop, stop, this is bullshit.

BARTLETT: *(consulting notebook)* That's the word she used: "Gloating."

KHALED: I never "gloated", that's insane.

BARTLETT: *(consulting notebook)* She went on to say that she felt you were almost—

BARTLETT/BETH: Defending them.

BETH: Praising them even.

KHALED: That's a lie.

CARL: Are you sure about that?

BETH: It sure sounded like that to me.

KHALED: She's twisting everything.

BETH: *(to Carl)* I don't think that would be an exaggeration.

KHALED: *(to Beth)* That's not what I meant.

BETH: *(to Khaled)* That's how it sounded.

> *If light changes have been accompanying the transitions of time/new characters, a light change would also signal the shift here.*

KHALED: I'm just saying we have to look for the "why"? Why did they do this?

BETH: Because they're evil assholes. Are you justifying this?

KHALED: Why are you so frightened of trying to figure this out?

BETH: Because if you go down that road then you're saying somewhere down the line there's a coherent argument for what they did. A legitimate reason. And there are some things that simply do not deserve the benefit of an explanation and being "enlightened" on an act like this would just be so fucking offensive. I don't want to know why they did this. I don't care.

KHALED: Don't you want to make sure it doesn't happen again?

At some point, Khaled moves to help Beth zip up her dress, but Beth jerks away, refusing his help. The exchange continues over this.

BETH: Next you'll tell me this is all our fault.

KHALED: Do you or do you not want to make sure this doesn't happen again?

BETH: And your solution is what, we should flagellate ourselves? It's not enough they fucked us over, now you want us to finish the job by beating ourselves up? Paralyze ourselves by examining our conscience?

KHALED: Our policies.

BETH: *(overlapping)* That's your idea of defense?

KHALED: We'll finish the job they started if we don't. You've always been able to see the bigger picture, why can't you see it now?

BETH: *(to Carl)* It was more than what he was saying. It was an attitude. The way he looked. And I used to think we shared the same politics.

KHALED: *(to Bartlett)* That is a complete—I wasn't justifying anything. I was saying let's get at the root causes so we can stop it once and for all. Where do you get "praising them" from that?

BETH: *(to Carl)* There was almost like a gleam in his eye. Like he was saying "it's just what you people deserve."

KHALED: *(to Beth)* No.

BETH: *(to Khaled)* You all but said it.

KHALED: Why aren't you hearing what I'm saying?

BETH: It was a rape, Khaled. It was a rape multiplied by a thousand. You don't go up to the woman who just got raped and say, you know what, I think you probably deserved that because you go around flaunting your ass so what do you expect. And if you want to make sure it doesn't happen again, then maybe you should go around in a fucking burqa.

93

KHALED: *(disbelief, then:)* The United States of America is not a woman who just got raped. The United States of America is the biggest, strongest eight hundred pound gorilla on the block.

Beth heads for the door.

You can't rape an eight hundred pound gorilla, even if you wanted to. Where are you going?

She doesn't answer.

Beth.

She starts to open the door but he shuts it.

Where are you going?

BETH: You have a nerve. Like you tell me.

KHALED: I just want to know.

BETH: Why? Are you afraid I might say something to someone?

KHALED: What are you talking about?—Beth: speak to me, you're freaking me out.

BETH: I followed you, you know.

KHALED: What?

BETH: Those times. When you went out. When you thought I was at work. *(to Carl)* I should also tell you that I thought he was having an affair. I'm still not sure he wasn't. I think he was doing personals, or a chat room or something. Or that's what I thought. He certainly was at the computer a lot. It must have been something steamy because every time I approached him he would do something to hide the screen.

Beth approaches Asfoor at the computer. Asfoor blocks the screen by turning around to face her. He smiles.

BETH: Or he would turn it off. I became convinced he'd hooked up with someone. Met someone on line. Our sex life... well never mind that. He denied it of course. We had blow ups about it. So...one day, I followed him. I wanted an answer once and for all. So I followed him. To the park, where he met up with this woman.... It was strange. It didn't last long. He talked. She gave him something, then left. When I asked later what he'd done he said he'd been in all day working. The second time I followed him was the day I was to leave on a business trip. Only this time the person he met was a guy.

Asfoor stands, goes to the closet, grabs a different hat and jacket, puts them on and waits at another point in the room.

Again, it only lasted minutes. And it kind of weirded me out. Later I thought that was because I was thinking, oh no, Khaled's bi and we've been living a bigger lie than I thought. But it didn't have that vibe. Khaled looked almost—frightened. Once again it was quick. Khaled left first, then the guy.

Asfoor exits through the front door.

I left for my trip and told myself I'd deal with it later. Then the attacks happened and none of that mattered for a while. But when I confronted him he freaked out.

KHALED: *(to Beth)* You've been what?

BETH: *(to Khaled)* I called. You were never at home when you said you were supposed to be.

KHALED: You followed me? How dare you?

BETH: Don't turn this around, I'm fucking supporting you while you're supposed to be writing.

KHALED: That doesn't mean you own me.

BETH: Who were they, Khaled?

KHALED: Fuck you, no, it's none of your business.

BETH: I thought you were having an affair; but now I'm not so sure. Now I'm actually worried. With the things you've said in the past, and now, and these meetings, and your secrecy. Yes, I know you don't like to talk about what you're working on, only you've been working on it for as long as I've known you and you have nothing to show for it. Are you having an affair? Either you're having an affair or you're up to something you shouldn't be. Either one makes you a slimy little shit. So which is it? Tell me or I swear to God I will tell someone what I'm thinking.

KHALED: You can't be serious.

BETH: I am, I'm really wondering.

KHALED: Beth. It's me.

BETH: Great, now tell me who that is.

KHALED: We're all freaked out by what's happened. Don't flip out on me.

BETH: Why couldn't you be up to something? Why not? I'm not sure I even know you.

KHALED: Okay, stop.

BETH: I'm not sure I've ever known you.

KHALED: You're flipping out, stop it.

BETH: No, tell me. You don't talk about your self or what you do. Your past is a fog. Suddenly you have material on subjects I had no idea you're interested in.

KHALED: What are you doing? This is like some 50's B movie, "I married a communist".

BETH: Are you fucking around on me?

KHALED: No!

BETH: Then you must be up to something you shouldn't be and I'm really starting to freak out.

KHALED: *(grabbing her)* Would you just shut up. You can't talk like that. Not now. Not even for a joke, people take this shit very seriously.

> *Beth just looks at him.*

Beth, Jesus Christ, wake up. I'm not a stranger.

BETH: *(to Carl, looking at Khaled)* It's funny how people change on you. I mean normally, when you don't think you might be staring at a murderer. How you can be so fascinated and in love with someone and then find all that fall away. And the person stands there naked and butt ugly and you get angry at yourself for ever having wanted this man. I really hope these attacks haven't permanently spoilt my views on love.

KHALED: *(to Bartlett)* It was a literary group.

BETH: *(to Carl)* Imagine; that's what he said.

KHALED: For writers; to exchange ideas.

BETH: It was like watching a man hide himself in one box after another; like those Russian dolls.

KHALED: *(still to Bartlett)* I'm not joking, that's what it was.

BETH: I gave up after that. A few days later I asked him to move out.

CARL: Would you still have a picture of him?

BETH: I don't know; I can check.

CARL: I'd appreciate that.

> *She exits. Carl makes notes.*

KHALED: Jesus. No wonder you beat a path to my door. For God's sake. She has an ax to grind. It was a list-serve for writers. We actually discussed plot lines and books. And yes there was some flirting going on, so what; my moral behavior is not on trial here. And the guy was a jerk because he passed himself off as a woman on line, and—he was just an asshole and I left. That's it. The sum total of my secrets. You could frame anything with enough menace and make it seem more than it is.

> *Slight beat.*

CARL: Bart.

BARTLETT: Yes, Carl.

CARL: Can I talk to you?

> *Bartlett and Carl move off to talk in private.*

BARTLETT: What?

CARL: Look: I'm thinking something.

BARTLETT: Go for it.

CARL: I don't think what we're doing now is getting us anywhere.

BARTLETT: Really? I feel like we're making headway.

CARL: Not—no.

BARTLETT: I think we've loosened his bowels and he's going to shit any second.

CARL: No, he's going to hold off because he's fixated on some idea of procedure. He thinks there's some script we're supposed to follow and that will protect him. He'll keep us a few facts shy of the truth and piss us off. The photo is too dark. And the clothes are generic. Important, but—.

BARTLETT: The receipt is pretty damning.

CARL: We need him to spill his guts.

BARTLETT: What are you suggesting?

CARL: There's an imbalance of authority right now and we need to correct that.

BARTLETT: I tried that already and you pulled me off.

CARL: Yes. But with all due respect, I think I know these people a little better. I've been there. I know how they think. There's some dark shit you have to know how to access.

BARTLETT: Carl—we're not allowed to do that.

CARL: (gets out a small guidebook) Actually, if we don't hit any vital organs, we can.

BARTLETT: No, I don't think so.

CARL: (reading) "Section eight, paragraph two. Willful damage is not permitted but a relaxed, consistent pressure on parts of the body that may be deemed sensitive is allowed. As long as the suspect remains conscious and doesn't scream longer than ten seconds at any one time. Some bruising is allowed."

BARTLETT: (looks at the guidebook) Huh. I need to re-read this. I completely missed that.

CARL: It has surprisingly useful tips. Especially on how to use simple appliances like microwaves.

BARTLETT: You're suggesting what?

CARL: To bring the full weight of our authority to bear on him. With the aim of making him adjust his expectations as to what options are available to him.

   Slight beat.

BARTLETT: Fine.... But gently.

CARL: Thanks.

   They turn to look at Khaled.

KHALED: What?

BARTLETT: (to Carl) I'm going to use the john.

CARL: Take your time.

BARTLETT: (to Khaled) Can I use your bathroom?—Thanks.

   Bartlett exits into the bathroom. Carl stares at Khaled.

KHALED: What's going on?

CARL: Khaled. (walks up to him) There's no easy way to segue into this. So I'm not going to try.

   Carl kicks Khaled in the groin. Khaled gasps, grabs his testicles, and collapses onto his knees.

First off: that has been coming since we got here, because of repeated references to an innocence that is not yours to claim. If you were innocent, why would I have kicked you? Something you've done has given me good cause to assume the worst. The responsibility for that kick lies with your unwillingness to assume responsibility for the part we know you played. We need to know what that was. It might have been a bit part, but never think that makes you a bit player.

Khaled doubles over and lets out a strangled cry.

Khaled.—Khaled.

Khaled topples over as he lets out a more sustained cry.

Don't overdo it. I didn't hit you that hard.— That's not pain you're feeling, it's shock. You're overwhelmed by the notion of pain—that more might follow—not what I actually did.

Khaled expresses more of his pain.

Enough with the dramatics or I'll give you something to really scream about.

Bartlett opens the bathroom door, looking concerned.

It's nothing. We're good.

BARTLETT: What happened?

CARL: He's faking it.

KHALED: *(strangled)* No.

CARL: It's shock. I was abrupt.

BARTLETT: Over ten seconds.

CARL: But he's conscious and it wasn't a sustained cry.

KHALED: What are you doing?

BARTLETT: *(worried)* Carl.

CARL: It's under control. Go finish what you were doing.

BARTLETT: Absolutely no bones.

CARL: One more kick and I'm done.

BARTLETT: This has to lead to something.

CARL: The info is in the bag.

KHALED: *(winded; to neighbors)* Help.

Bartlett gives Carl a worried look before going back into the bathroom. Khaled starts crawling towards the door.

Help me.

98 CARL: If you'd've kept your nose clean, then you wouldn't be here, would you, crawling on the ground, trying to get away from the next hit that's sure to come if you don't tell us what you and Gamal got up to.

KHALED: Please.

CARL: We know you talked with him.

KHALED: No.

CARL: You met up. In the strip joint.

KHALED: I'm not hiding anything. I swear to you.

CARL: We have the receipt. It's as good as a photo.

KHALED: I don't know what you're talking about.

CARL: You really give a bad name to immigrants, you know that? Because of you we have to pass tougher laws that stop people who might actually be good for us.

KHALED: I haven't done anything wrong!

Carl either kneels on Khaled's chest or else grabs him around the neck.

CARL: God: I know your type, so well. The smiling little Semite who gives you one face while trying to stab you with the other. You're pathetic, you know that. If you hate us, than just hate us. But you don't have the balls to do even that. You bitch and you moan and complain how overrun you are by us and all the time you can't wait to get here. You'd kill for a visa. That pisses me off. That's hypocrisy. Why not just come clean and own up that you hate everything this country stands for.

KHALED: *(winded/strangled)* No.

CARL: No, that's right, because you're too busy envying us.

KHALED: *(winded/strangled)* Get off me.

CARL: I could snap your neck just for that. What's the expression for "fuck-face" in Arabic? "Hitit khara?" "Sharmoot?"

KHALED: *(winded/strangled)* You're crushing me.

CARL: Just how crushed do you feel, Khaled? *(slight beat, then:)* Alright, I'm done.

He lets go and stands up. Beat.

Now do you want to tell me what you and Asfoor got up to in the strip club? Were you passing a message on to him? Were you the internet guy? The guy to help him get around? A carrier for something? What? What? Tell me, or I'll-

Carl pulls his foot back as if to kick him.

KHALED: *(flinching at threatened kick)* No!

CARL: *(continuing)* I will. I'll exercise my drop kick on your testicle sack and make you sing an Arabic song in a very unnatural key.

KHALED: I'm going to be sick.

CARL: You're going to be sick? I'm the one who's throwing up. Only I have the decency to do it quietly, inside, and not make a public spectacle of myself. *(perhaps grabbing Khaled by his lapels)* What did he want from you? What did he want? What fucked-up part did you play in all of this? What happened with you in there? What happened when you met up with Asfoor? What did he want?

Khaled opens his mouth as if he's about to vomit. Carl lets go as Khaled dry heaves. Beat.

You know what I really resent?.... What you force us to become. To protect ourselves. We are a decent bunch and do not want to be dragged down to your level. But no, you just have to drag us down, don't you. You have to gross us out with your level of crap. I personally hate this, you know that? I hate it when I have to beat the shit out of someone because then by an act of willful horror, whose effect on my soul I can only imagine, I have to shut out everything good about me to do my job to defend and protect. Here I am quickly devolving into a set of clichés I can barely stomach and you have the nerve to think you can vomit. No, it is I who am throwing up, sir, and if I see one scrap of food leave your mouth I will shove it back so far down your throat you'll be shitting it before you even know what you've swallowed again.

Beth enters dressed in a coat now. She carries a photo.

BETH: I found this.

Carl steps away from Khaled.

It's pretty crumpled, but. I threw most of them out.

CARL: Thank you. *(He looks at photo)* This will help.

BETH: Look—I...I just want to say.... I have no idea if he was involved in anything. I know I've said things to suggest he might've been. But I'm just telling you what I thought at the time, when we were all upset. Being a major disappointment and a shit doesn't make you a criminal.

CARL: Understood.

BETH: Okay.—Good.—Just so I don't feel I'm—you know.—This isn't about revenge.

CARL: Believe it or not, safeguarding the innocent is as important apprehending the bad guys.

BETH: Good. Okay. Well.... Bye.

CARL: Thank you.

She exits. As soon as the front door closes, the bathroom door opens and Bartlett enters. He walks over to Khaled, who is still prostrate on the ground.

BARTLETT: Anything?

CARL: He has a better idea of what's at stake.

BARTLETT: Anything solid?

CARL: Authority has been reestablished. That was important.

BARTLETT: Facts?

CARL: On the verge.

BARTLETT: Verge is where I left him.

CARL: Oh I think he's ready to talk. I think he knows we're not looking for sequential sentences that add up to poop; but details that fit in nicely with what we know happened at the club. Where you went to get a hard-on while plotting death and destruction.

BARTLETT: Can we get him off the floor? It looks bad.

Bartlett gets the chair as Carl moves to pick him up.

CARL: He's such a drama queen.

BARTLETT: *(helps Carl pick up Khaled)* The last piece of the puzzle fits, my friend. You were there. We had surveillance cameras. It wasn't your girlfriend who gave you away. It was your pecker.

> *They sit him down.*

You should have followed your religion's advice and avoided all depictions of the human form because that's what did you in.

CARL: Time for exhibit number four, I think.

BARTLETT: If we absolutely must.

CARL: You completely overlook her patriotism, you really do.

BARTLETT: I must have missed it. *(To Khaled)* We'll tell you what happened and you just stop us if we have it wrong, okay?

> *Throughout this next section, Khaled remains dazed, in shock. Carl slides open another closet door and sweeps the clothes on the hangars to one side.*

On a Tuesday night, August 21st, at around 10:05, you went to the "EyeFull Tower Club"; where a Ms. Jean Sommers, a.k.a, Kelly Cupid, "Dancer Extraordinaire and Stripper Artiste", as she calls herself, was performing.

> *With the clothes swept aside, a dancing pole is revealed. Light change in the closet to simulate club lighting. Perhaps a disco-ball effect and a couple of spot lights. Jean SOMMERS either enters or is already at the pole. She is dressed for the act: elements of a cowboy outfit, including two pistols slung on each hip. She might also be wearing a wig.*

The date on your receipt proves it and so does Ms. Sommers.

JEAN: I do. Anyway I can help, gentlemen.

CARL: Much appreciated.

JEAN: Will you want to see my act now?

BARTLETT: Is it relevant?

CARL: It might be. Clearly they met here for a reason. Your act may have been a signal of sorts. A series of unintended semaphores that spelt out a message to commence something. Why don't we have a look just to cover our bases?

JEAN: So you do want to see it?

CARL: You bet.

JEAN: You got it. Music.

> *Appropriate music starts and she performs her act. More burlesque and pole dancing than strip tease. After it ends, slight beat.*

BARTLETT: I don't see how they could have passed messages through that.

CARL: Maybe not, but it doesn't hurt to check.

JEAN: That was the shortened version.

BARTLETT: When did you first notice him?

JEAN: The first time he came or the second?

CARL: Are we talking dates, or?

JEAN: *(smiling)* Yeah, dates.

BARTLETT: The first.

JEAN: Hardly at all. Except he was nervous and sweaty. Which isn't unusual when I come on. And he had a couple of books. I thought maybe he was a college grad trying to cram for an exam.

BARTLETT: Hardly a place to study.

JEAN: You'd be surprised. I see more and more people with laptops. We've begun to offer plug outlets in our lap-dance area.

BARTLETT: Anything else, that first time?

JEAN: Not really. I give full attention to my act. I believe in giving your best regardless of what you're doing.

CARL: It shows.

JEAN: Others leave their body when they do this, I don't. To me my body is a celebration of who I am and I give it to others as a revelation. I try to be your average Joe's desire incarnate. With a little extra thrown in for the more discerning. Nobody leaves my act feeling short-changed.

CARL: Kudos.

JEAN: Thanks.

BARTLETT: Anything else at first glance?

JEAN: No, he was just a set of eyes. It was later. When he asked for a lap-dance that I had more time to observe him.

CARL: *(showing her Khaled's photo)* And you're sure it was this guy.

JEAN: Yeah, kinda. It was dark and he was wearing a baseball cap. But I'm pretty sure. And he was wearing this fatigue jacket.

Bartlett picks up the baseball cap and fatigue jacket to show to Khaled.

BARTLETT: Any chance you remember the book titles?

JEAN: Yes, as a matter of fact. I'm always curious what other people are reading so I looked. One was on tattoos, and the other had something something in the title—ending with God, which I thought was an odd combo. I plan on going back to college you know.

BARTLETT: So what happened next? When you went one on one?

JEAN: Well...

Jean moves towards Khaled. Appropriate music for a lap dance fades in quietly in the background.

I began my routine. The usual. I was feeling less than on that day. I had been groped earlier and was not feeling well disposed to the horny. But I do have a work ethic, like I said, and so I danced. I always give my best. *(she starts to sketch in some of her moves)* Even to people who turn out later to be scum who want to do us harm. Did I tell you my father was a marine?

CARL: No.

JEAN: Highly decorated. My outfit in many ways is a salute to him. That's what he was before he joined up. A cowboy, out west. At night, sometimes, he'd let me wear his medals.

BARTLETT: What can you tell us about Khaled?

JEAN: That's his name, huh?

BARTLETT: Yes.

JEAN: *(while dancing over a seated Khaled)* If I had him again...I know what I'd do with him. Coming here to do that to us.

BARTLETT: Well, we don't know for sure if he's—.

JEAN: *(interrupting)* I'd say touch me, Kaled, so the bouncers can come and smash your stupid face in. Coming here to get off on me while all the time wanting to do shit to us. Wrapping your women in black and then sneaking in here and getting your rocks off. I could pluck your eyes out. I could bend your dick round and fuck you up your own ass.

BARTLETT: Your sentiments are understandable. But if you could tell us what happened next.

JEAN: I should have known something was up. I thought he was extra sweaty because he was just too close to something he couldn't have. But it wasn't that. He was always looking around to check for something. It kinda pissed me off he wasn't giving me his full attention. At one time I stuck my boobs in his face and he actually moved his head, like I was blocking his view. I thought, what the hell are you doing here then? I take pride in what I do and expect some respect. Don't act like you're bored. I decided then and there to make him come. But then this guy shows up. Stands a few feet away and stares. Just stares. Like he'd paid for this show as well. "Do you mind?" I say to him.

BARTLETT: *(shows her Asfoor's photo)* This guy?

JEAN: Yeah. It was dark, but yeah. Both of them were Middle-Eastern, that I know. So I tell him to piss off but he just stands there and this Kaled is looking at him. Suddenly his attention is full on him. And he's changed. Like he's frozen or something. And this guy just stares and he's looking at Kaled and me. And I say again, "Do you mind?" And he looks at me and his eyes—they're like, I'm-going-to-get-you eyes. Only they're smiling and it's creepy. And then he leaves to the rest room. And Kaled starts to rise like he wants to follow. Only I push him back down. I'm really pissed off at this point, like I've been insulted. Like my skills have been called into question. So I did something I never usually do. I reached down and squeezed. *(She does so)* Just one time. And that did the trick. I finished him off. So easy....

103

Then he springs out of that chair and into the rest room.

The music stops; she moves away from Khaled.

And that would have been it; I would have moved on, onto the next customer, but something about them really annoyed me. So I looked for them to come out; to say something, like have some manners the next time, the both of you, and don't come back. But fifteen minutes later, they're still in there. And I say this to Stewart, one of the bouncers and he says let me check, and I say, no, let me do it. If I can embarrass these guys I will, so I go in.

She opens the bathroom door.

And… (*a laugh*) Damn if I don't see both of their legs under one of the stalls. And—they must have heard me, because Kaled comes shooting out and runs, just runs past me. And out saunters Mr. Creepy after him. Calm as can be, like he'd just been holding a meeting in his office. And I'm thinking—no, I actually say to him: "take that shit somewhere else." And he stares at me again, and this time it's scary. Real scary. Like he's telling me he could snuff my life out with his pinkie if he wanted to. So I get out of there and tell Stewart about it, only they're both gone when he goes round to check.... And that's my story.

BARTLETT: Did you get a sense of what they might have been doing in the stall?

JEAN: Not a clue. Might have been sucking each other off for all I know. Or shooting up. Who knows? At least one of them's dead. Have you got the other one yet?

CARL: We're working on it.

JEAN: I wouldn't mind getting him in that chair again. Give him a good thwack from me if you find him, care of Kelly Cupid.

CARL: Will do.

JEAN: Anything else I can do for you?

CARL: Not at the moment.

JEAN: Well...I'd better get ready for my act then.

CARL: Maybe we'll come back to check out the longer version.

JEAN: I'd like that. I'd hate to think my routine was being used for a nasty purpose.

Jean smiles at Carl, then exits. Bartlett and Carl turn to Khaled. Bartlett drags a chair and sits opposite Khaled. Carl either sits on the edge of the table, next to Khaled, or stands over him. Khaled looks at them.

Beat.

KHALED: She's lying.

BARTLETT: Here's where I have to pry a little more than I like to. Can we— look at your pecker? Please? Very briefly. To clear something up. 'Cause this thing about tattoos keeps coming up.

Khaled makes to bolt out of his chair but Carl pins him down, wrapping his arms around his chest, immobilizing his arms. Bartlett puts on a latex glove.

I'm sure it's nothing. I bet it's nothing. But it sure does make me wonder.

Bartlett starts to undo Khaled's trousers. Khaled writhes in his chair in protest. This can be done with most of Khaled's back to the audience.

KHALED: No.—No.

BARTLETT: *(overlapping)* What with that e-mail he sent about tattoos, and the book, and doing it where the skin folds, where you can hide it.

KHALED: *(half in tears)* Stop it. No.—No.

BARTLETT: *(overlapping)* Was there like some secret mark you each showed yourselves? To ascertain something? Membership? Commitment? What were you doing in there for fifteen minutes? Excuse me. This is embarrassing for me too.

He has yanked Khaled's pants down far enough for him to look.

What's that? Is that a birthmark? Or?

Carl also looks.

What is that?

CARL: Liver-spot?

BARTLETT: *(still looking; slight beat)* Yeah.... Yeah. It's what it looks like.... That couldn't be a tattoo, could it?.... I wish we'd bought our camera with us.... Next time. *(he continues to peer, then: a light slap on the thigh to indicate he's finished)* Alright. *(he stands)* Thank you. Apologies for that. Not a part of my job that I like.

Carl lets go, Khaled covers himself with his hands, and starts to pull up his trousers but Bartlett prevents him from doing so by placing his foot on his trousers.

But it still leaves us wondering what you did all that time in the bathroom with one of the more hideous individuals we've come across. Now would be the time to fess up to any deviant sexual inclinations. It might get you off.

Slight beat.

KHALED: *(quiet)* I was never there.

BARTLETT: *(slight beat)* Alright.... We're going to leave you to think about it. Come back later, tomorrow. We'll take a few things with us now.

He nods to Carl to take the laptop.

Look them over. Assess what we have. What needs filling in.—What might have occurred to you overnight? *(he picks up books from the pile)* And then talk some more. You're not taking any long-distance trips, are you? *(looks at KHALED, then moves to the door)* Here're your choices, Khaled, that you can think about. Either you're innocent. In which case proving that might be difficult. Or you're guilty, in which case telling us now would score you points because we'll find out soon enough. Or: you're innocent

105

of being guilty. You didn't know what you were getting into. Stumbled into it. Through deception. Other people's. Your own stupidity. And that would be okay too. We can work with that. We can work with you to make that seem plausible.

At the door now. Carl carries the laptop.

Think about it. And about those evaluation forms: they're no joke. It's your chance to respond. That's what this is all about. At the end of the day, we're fighting to safeguard that right. It sounds counter-intuitive. But that's the struggle for freedom for you. It's never as straight-forward as you'd like it to be.

Slight beat.

CARL: *(to Khaled)* "Ma'salamma."

BARTLETT: *(turns to Carl)* What does that mean?

CARL: Peace be with you.

BARTLETT: I can go with that. *(to Khaled)* Peace be with you.

They take one last look at Khaled who remains slightly bent over, covering his crotch. They exit and close the door behind them.

Beat.

Khaled pulls up his trousers. Beat. The closet door slides open revealing Asfoor. He enters the room.

ASFOOR: *(accent)* You... you help me, yes? You and me, private class. I have...I have need to—to learn. Quickly. Yes?... When first I come to this country—I not know how to speak. How...even to say anything. How one word best is placed with what word next. Yes? But in my head? It is a river of beautiful speech. Like in Arabic. Arabic is.... It is the way into my heart. But everywhere, when I open ears, first thing, everywhere now, is English. You not get away from it. Even back home, before I come, I hear it more and more in people who do not speak it. I say, I must learn language that is everywhere. Language that has fallen on our heads and made us like—like children again. What is this power? What if I know it? I say to them, send me there so I learn this. I want to learn. And in my heart, I say I want to write. I want to write a book. In English. That is goal, yes? And one day, I say...

While accent is maintained, the broken English gradually starts dropping.

I might even teach it.... I will teach language back. I will make them speak their own language differently. I will have them speak words they never spoke before. I will make them like children too, speaking words over and over to make sure they understand it. And soon my language will also fall on their heads. Like theirs falls on ours. Exploding in our brains till we can't even dream in peace.

Slight beat.

And so they sent me.... They send me.

Asfoor draws closer to Khaled. Khaled does not look at him.

And now...my tongue...it wants to rise. Soar. As it used to. It wants to take off in this new language and conjure up brilliant words. It wants to do things in English that seemed so impossible for so long. I can help you find your voice too.... You're stuck. I know you are. You've lost your way. I can feel it. I can help. Most of all...above all else, Khaled...I know how to inspire.... I know how to inspire.

Beat. Blackout.

107

BRET FETZER & JULIET WALLER PRUZAN Bret Fetzer and Juliet Waller Pruzan have been collaborating as Poisonous Toy Theater since 1998. Their plays—including their Natural Disaster series—have been performed at On the Boards (Seattle) and Impact Theatre (Berkeley), and toured through the King County Performance Network (Washington). *Tornado* was first published in The Rendezvous Reader: Northwest Writing, published in 2002. *Avalanche* was first published in Fall 2006 edition of The Kenyon Review. Bret Fetzer's solo plays include *Planet Janet* and *Mars is a star who defies observation*. Juliet Waller Pruzan's first solo play is *Told You Once (told you a hundred times)*.

Juliet Waller Pruzan & Bret Fetzer

TORNADO

CHARACTERS
Windy Green, age 7
Buster Green, her father
Flora Bell Canford, her mother

Note: All other characters [Windy's teacher, the students, the delivery plane pilots] are portrayed by an articulated sound that indicates intention but has no recognizable words; sort of like the voices of adults in Peanuts *t.v. specials. This is indicated by the word 'hubbub'.*

> *Windy Green stands alone on stage beside a doll house of enormous proportions; ideally, both she and the doll house would be around five feet tall.*
>
> *Student hubbub. Windy's teacher addresses Windy with hubbub.*

WINDY: Certainly, Miss Johnson. I am merely waiting for the class to come to attention.

> *Teacher hubbub, followed by a beat of silence.*

Ahem. How My Parents Met, a presentation by Windy Green, age 7, of Spacious Skies Elementary. My story begins eight years ago. This is my father, Buster Green, age 32.

> *She presents a doll, possibly a Ken doll or a GI Joe, possibly simply a paper cut-out.*

Buster was a maritime clown. He entertained the troops on battleships and submarines with his funny acrobatics. I am unable to demonstrate his comic powers with the means at my disposal, so you will have to trust me when I say he was a very successful clown. "Ho ho ho, Buster you are so funny we'd like to give you a medal for hilarity." Like that. One day, as he was on an aircraft carrier in the middle of the Atlantic Ocean—the second-largest ocean in the world with an estimated area of almost 32 million square miles—while Buster juggled and did pratfalls and pretended to be drunk in a very amusing manner, a tornado swept through our town and tore Buster's house straight off its foundations. This is Buster's house.

She indicates the enormous doll house beside her.

Student hubbub.

Yes, you are correct, this is not actually my father's house, just as this is not actually my father. A real house would not fit inside our classroom. These things represent these real-life persons and objects for the purposes of my dramatic narrative. I hope that clarifies matters.

She opens the front of the house to reveal the interior.

This is Buster's house. Like nearly every house in our lovely town of Amber Waves, Kansas, latitude 39 degrees 50 minutes north, longitude 98 degrees 35 minutes west, it is a two story townhouse with three bedrooms, two bathrooms, a dining room, a living room, a kitchen with refrigerator and electric stove, and a den. All of our houses are alike because Amber Waves is a planned community, which means that it did not spring naturally from a hardy and honest pioneering spirit, but was artificially foisted on the countryside to support corporate interests.

Teacher hubbub.

I'm sorry, Miss Johnson, I did not intend to be perceived that way. I will refrain from socio-political commentary from now on. The foundation of Buster's house, like the all other houses in Amber Waves, contains a basement, to be used as a storm shelter in case of tornadoes, which are a recurring natural hazard in the American Midwest. Because of his absence, Buster's basement was unused; however, with a precision and delicacy that suggests divine intervention—

Teacher hubbub.

I'm sorry, Miss Johnson, I will refrain from religious intimations from now on. With a precision and delicacy that can only be described as "unusual," the tornado set Buster's house down upon another foundation, the basement of which was in use, by Miss Flora Bell Canford, age 29. This is Flora Bell Canford.

Windy displays another doll.

You are no doubt wondering what happened to Flora Bell's house, which was similarly ripped from its foundations by the tornado. This will be revealed later in the story.

Windy begins to move Flora Bell through the house.

When Flora Bell came up from the basement, she did not at first realize this was no longer her house.

At this point, another actor appears who plays Flora. She is visible to the audience and performs the actions that Windy makes the doll do, but the actor does not have any of the physical objects referred to; Windy has miniature versions which she makes her doll manipulate. The actor speaks Flora's lines.

FLORA: Well, I'm glad that's over with. My book, where did I put—goodness, the wind must have swept into the house and knocked everything around. My glass of water was right here and now—well, here's a glass of water over here, but I could have sworn I had a different glass—maybe it was me who got knocked around by the storm! I'd better go upstairs and lie down, it's been a difficult day. Goodness, when did I get those sheets? Are those the ones my Aunt Lydia left me? And when did I put them on the bed? A little sleep will do me a world of good.

She lies down on the bed.

Oh, I feel better already. Say, that's an interesting picture I've got hanging above my dresser. I have no idea who's in that picture. In fact, I'm sure I've never seen it before. If that man was one of my ancestors, I don't think I'd be who I am at all.

She rises and goes to the closet.

I do not wear baggy pants and polka-dotted cummerbunds. Or do I? Maybe I have been knocked about and don't even know my own name. I think I'm Flora Bell Canford at 724 Ginger Rogers Street, but maybe I'm wrong. Maybe I'm really Harriet Smith at 137 Jimmy Cagney Place or Juniper Withrow at 15 Veronica Lake Lane or—

She picks up a piece of mail.

Mr. Buster Green at 854 Fred Astaire Avenue. Goodness!

She drops the letter. She looks down at it and then looks at her own body.

Now, I may be confused about many things but I am certainly not Mr. Buster Green. Which means...and that...or even...oh my.

WINDY: With that, Flora Bell jumped into her car—which was still parked on the street outside because tornadoes are amazingly particular—and she drove to 854 Fred Astaire Avenue where she found an empty lot, even though there was a sidewalk in front and a swimming pool in back and a barbecue and everything. Flora Bell was very conscientious, so she left a note for Mr. Buster Green on his front steps, which used to lead to his porch but did no longer.

FLORA: Dear Mr. Buster Green: I am not a thief. It is by no act of my own that your house is now on my property and I do not know where my own house is. Please come to 724 Ginger Rogers Street if you wish to claim your house. Cordially yours, Flora Bell Canford.

WINDY: Then she went home, that wasn't home any longer, or rather was and wasn't home at the same time. For a few days she cooked with Buster Green's groceries, read Buster Green's books, and made a lovely dress from Buster Green's bedsheets because of course her own clothes were nowhere to be found. Then, one day:

Windy knocks on the side of the doll house. Flora opens the door. Buster stands on the other side. As with Flora Bell, the actor speaks and behaves as Buster, but does not have any of the props referred to.

FLORA: Yes?

BUSTER: Flora Bell Canford?

FLORA: Yes?

BUSTER: I understand you have my house.

FLORA: Yes. Yes, I do.

WINDY: Buster and Flora Bell investigated the situation and learned—from a young boy named Arthur who'd chained himself to a mailbox so he could watch the tornado firsthand, a technique I do not endorse though I admit it has intriguing possibilities—that Flora Bell's house had been dropped about a mile north into Purple Mountain Lake. Arthur knew because he heard the splash. There was no way to bring it back up, and they couldn't afford to move Buster's house back to his own property, so Buster and Flora Bell made a deal.

Buster flips a coin.

BUSTER: Call it!

FLORA: Heads!

BUSTER: Heads it is.

WINDY: Flora Bell would live on the top floor, Buster would live on the ground floor, and the kitchen would be mutual territory.

BUSTER: I'm afraid, Miss Canford, I'm going to need my bed.

FLORA: Well, of course. And I wouldn't feel right sleeping in someone else's bed, at least, not now that I know who that someone is. I'll just, well, I'll just sleep on the floor, if I could borrow some sofa cushions—

BUSTER: Miss Canford, I don't know if you know this about me—

FLORA: Are you sure I need to know—

BUSTER: To entertain sailors on submarines, I learned how to scuba dive. It would be my honor, Miss Canford, to escort you to the bottom of Purple Mountain Lake to retrieve your important belongings.

FLORA: Escort? Scuba dive? Me? Oh!

WINDY: And so they did.

Windy turns on small fans under the house that blow green streamers up from the floors, like underwater plants. She may also dangle small plastic fish from the ceilings. As she makes the dolls scuba dive through the house—using miniature scuba gear—Buster and Flora mime the same actions, perhaps while wearing scuba masks. They wander through the house, collecting this and that. At one point, they open the refrigerator, and light shines out of it.

And as they swam through Flora Bell's rooms, finding her most intimate belongings and rescuing them from a watery grave, Flora Bell fell in love.

At this point, the story's forward progress must stop so that you can learn some very important facts about Flora Bell Canford, and that is that she is a literary topiarist. She trimmed garden hedges into the form of poems of her own devising. This is an unusual profession. In fact, Flora Bell Canford was the only professional literary topiarist in all of the United States, because she had been hired by America's Beautiful Appliances, Incorporated, the company that founded our town of Amber Waves, a company based in Yokohama, Japan—

Teacher hubbub.

I'm sorry Miss Johnson, I did not realize that statements of economic fact were a form of socio-political commentary. America's Beautiful Appliances hired Flora Bell to make topiary poems because they had a very small airfield, and the airplanes of the Fruited Plain Delivery Company, who delivered America's Beautiful Appliances to the world at large, often had to circle above for half an hour or more, and the pilots found this very boring. Flora Bell's poems could be read from a height of 700 feet or more, and this kept the pilots alert and entertained. At first, Flora Bell wrote haiku, because haiku are very short.

Windy flies plastic planes over the house as Flora Bell recites.

FLORA: A sly winking eye;
Close the door and the light goes out:
Refrigerator.

WINDY: The pilots of Fruited Plain slowly banked to the left, making wide sloping circles, and these haiku filled them with purpose.

FLORA: So many uses:
Baking or suicide.
It's a gas oven.

WINDY: Some poems were more effective than others. As she gained experience, Flora Bell's poems grew more ambitious.

FLORA: I offer up my floured palm
For a life of easy calm;
The alchemy so swift it's almost tender,
This is the essence of my blender.

Pilot hubbub goes on quietly under the first paragraph of Windy's following lines:

WINDY: Pilots began to demand longer holding patterns so that they could contemplate Flora Bell's verses at greater length. They held discussion groups and seminars over their radios. And America's Beautiful Appliances was very satisfied.

This was the state of Flora Bell's life when the tornado came to town. We will now return to our story, at the very same moment we paused.

As they swam through the rooms of her aquatic house, communicating only in gestures and signs, watching their breath fly up to the surface in bubble form, Flora Bell fell in love. But because her love was born in the cool, blue, submarine silence, when they took off their scuba gear, she found herself unable to speak of the feelings in her breast. Instead, she put her love for Buster into topiary form.

FLORA: I baked a cake, I baked it long
    Inside my toaster oven;
    My cake for you, who are so strong,
    Just like my toaster oven.
    My cake is fluffy, soft, and light,
    And fills my toaster oven;
    Aromas fill the day and night,
    All from my toaster oven.
    Oh will you come and take my arm,
    Beside my toaster oven,
    And keep me warm and safe from harm
    Just like my toaster oven?

WINDY: And the pilots, reading this and other poems, fell in love with Flora Bell.

Pilot hubbub, which continues in the background of the following poem.

FLORA: Such joy that I no longer
    Have to stay in strange cafes—
    In my own home I utter
    My own victory hurrays!
    I no longer rely on my whispery cry
    Of "Waiter, oh waiter, please waiter!"
    I now sit and sigh and press buttons on my
    Coffee percolator.
    Will you sit and help me spoon?
    Sit and sip beneath the moon?
    Oh please come to me soon!
    And our fingers will touch
    As we brew—thanks so much!
    And we drink it with sugar and such.

WINDY: Desperate to express their love, yet never on the ground long enough to go to her house, the pilots began to drop presents on her house and gardens.

Windy begins dropping miniature kitchen items on parachutes over the house.

Buster and Flora Bell look up at the items floating down.

BUSTER: There's a broiling pan.

FLORA: And a blender.

BUSTER: Another mixing bowl.

FLORA: Can't have too many of those.

BUSTER: Some measuring cups.

FLORA: Goodness. The company is so generous with their bonuses.

WINDY: You see, though the pilots were brave in the air, flying enormous airplanes, laughing at danger and whistling at disaster, when it came to

114

their hearts, they were shy and afraid to be hurt. So they never signed any of the gifts they sent.

BUSTER: Watch out for that dishwasher.

FLORA: Mr. Green, may I offer you an egg timer? I think I have three.

BUSTER: Miss Canford, that's mighty generous of you. Can I offer you anything? I have an exploding cigar, or a flower that squirts ink.

FLORA: No, thank you, that's very kind.

WINDY: And Buster, though brave in the sea and staunch on the land, was afraid to fly, and so didn't read these poems meant only for him. He came and went as his work demanded, and Flora Bell waved to him as he drove his car down Ginger Rogers Street, and then smiled at him when he came driving back. All the way to the ocean from Kansas. You may wonder why Buster lived in Kansas, of all places, so far from his place of work. I can't tell you. I don't know. You may wonder how Buster could have lived in the same house as Flora Bell, seeing her almost every day, saying good morning and good night and good afternoon in between, never noticing when she looked at him a little too long or turned away a little too soon, never seeing that she was in love with him. You may wonder, but I can't tell you. I don't know.

Teacher hubbub.

Miss Johnson, I have timed my presentation to end precisely before the lunch bell. If your interruptions make me unable to keep to my schedule, I do not wish to be held responsible.

Ahem. It's said that lightning never strikes twice in the same place, but this isn't true for tornadoes. Two years after the first, a second tornado came roaring through Amber Waves, Kansas, just as Buster Green was driving back from the Pacific Ocean. It plucked him right out of his convertible but left the car on the ground—again demonstrating the discriminating powers of our atmospheric disturbances—and tossed him hundreds of feet into the air.

Buster is twisted and twirled by the wind.

Then—and only then—did Buster Green read the poems that were written for his eyes alone.

BUSTER: My heart is like a freezer door
All crystalline and cold.
All vacuum-sealed inside is stored
Such feelings so untold.
But if you pulled the handle wide
If you and I both felt
A longing that it hurts to hide
At last my heart could melt.

WINDY: And then, on the brink of death, held far above the earth by winds that can reach the speed of 300 miles per hour, Buster Green fell in love.

BUSTER: Flora Bell...you're so wonderful...I always thought so but I didn't know half of how wonderful you are...

WINDY: By the kind of luck that defies belief, a circus train was passing near Amber Waves at that very moment. The tornado set him down on the topmost chair of a ferris wheel as it rolled through the Kansas wheat fields, all the golden grains whirling like a dance contest under the tornado's influence. I don't know how he got back to Amber Waves when the train dropped him off, but he did.

BUSTER: Miss Canford?

FLORA: Mr. Green?

BUSTER: May I call you Flora Bell?

FLORA: You may. May I call you Buster?

BUSTER: You may—

FLORA: Buster, would you marry me?

BUSTER: Flora Bell, I would be most happy to do so.

WINDY: Flora Bell could tell by the look in Buster's eyes that everything was different now, and suddenly she could say what she'd wanted to say for so long. Buster and Flora Bell were married, and Flora Bell's poems only grew all the more passionate.

FLORA: Who would have thought a tumbling dryer
Such heated yearnings could inspire?
For in that whirling windowed space,
We see our underthings embrace!
Watch my girdle—and your t-shirt—
I blush, the way they touch and flirt!
Your union suit—it makes me gasp—
Holds my panties in its grasp!
And as they fling themselves around,
You hear a bumping, thumping sound,
And fear that something's come apart—
Be soft, my love—you hear my heart.

WINDY: And the pilots' hearts about burst with longing.

Pilot hubbub, of a particularly yearning and sighing nature.

And nine months later, I, Windy Canford Green, was born. And to commemorate my birth, my mother made a topiary birth announcement.

And for the first time, the Fruited Plain Delivery Company pilots discovered that they had been betrayed.

Angry pilot hubbub.

And they had it in their power to take their revenge.

Controlling the fall, Windy slowly drops a proportionally sized refrigerator onto the dolls of Buster and Flora Bell.

Lights go down on the actors playing Buster and Flora Bell.

Teacher hubbub.

But I am an orphan, Miss Johnson. The ending will explain who signs my report cards—

A school bell rings. Teacher hubbub. Classroom noise.

But—it will just take a moment, I have new parents—please—

But everyone has left.

Windy follows her classmates outside, disappointed.

An airplane is heard passing overhead. Windy waves to it.

A lunchbox, stamped "Fruited Plain Delivery," on a parachute falls beside her. Windy picks it up, opens it, and removes a peanut-butter sandwich.

She eats, and her natural resilience returns.

The end.

Avalanche

CHARACTERS
Albert, a bartender
Henrick, a depressive
Carla, a mountain climber
Dagmar, a librarian
Assorted Townspeople

Scene 1: Customs

The border Guard steps out. A Hiker pauses appropriately.

GUARD: What have you got?

The Hiker presents a pair of snow shoes.

On your way.

The Baker steps up and pauses, holding a box.

Open up.

The Baker opens the box, revealing pastries. The Guard looks at them hungrily.

BAKER: Have one. On me.

The Guard takes one and eats it. With a full mouth, he gestures to the Baker to be on his way. Albert steps up and pauses appropriately.

GUARD: Open up.

Albert opens his package. The Guard sorts through it.

Whiskey...vodka...

He pulls out the mouthpiece to a tuba.

What's this?

ALBERT: Washing machine part.

GUARD: What does it do?

ALBERT: Well it...a bit complicated, actually...you know that part that goes whirr whirr, churning back and forth?

GUARD: Depends on the washer.

ALBERT: Too true! Well, this fits over the axle on which the whirr whirr part turns—in that kind of washer. Fits against some ball bearings, and there you are.

GUARD: Hmm.

He tosses the mouthpiece back into the package.

On your way.

Scene 2: Henrik's complaint

Henrik addresses the audience.

HENRIK: The first thing to go was my right kidney. I drank twenty-four cups of coffee every day, black, really hardcore African blends, you'd think your whole insides would rot out but it takes a lot of work! I put in that work and the fruits of my labors were starting to ripen: My right kidney gave up the ghost and what should happen but my next door neighbor gives me his.

NEIGHBOR: So young, to be so troubled! It was the least I could do.

HENRIK: Like I wanted his nasty old kidney. Thought it would give up under the brunt of some serious Colombian roasted thirty cups a day, but the thing keeps processing like a hand-tooled Maserati. By now I'm also drinking white Russians and sidecar cocktails like water, and with due diligence, my liver started to sputter and cough. In steps my grocer, who decides she can get by with half a liver and donates the rest of it.

GROCER: We live in a miraculous age, when such a thing is even possible!

HENRIK: Then, out of the blue, my appendix bursts! As the searing pain stabbed into my belly, I thought I was rescued at last. Then my history teacher gives me his!

TEACHER: Oh, I wasn't using it.

TEACHER'S WIFE: Ask him if he'd like my tonsils!

TEACHER: You see, in our small town of Bodenlos, we believe that everyone should do as they please. No one's dreams go unsupported here! If young Henrik wishes to lead a dissolute life of decadent pleasures, then the community will support him—for in our isolated Alpine valley, every person is precious. All around us loom high, snow-capped peaks; at any moment, disaster could thunder down around our heads. Trust, care, and help each other out: These are our bywords. As replacement organs could never come quickly enough through the mail—it comes once a week by dog-cart, dragged by a sturdy St. Bernard—everyone in town will give of themselves to provide Henrik the life he wishes to lead.

HENRIK: There's no telling them 'no'—if I cut my legs off, they'd insist on sewing someone else's on!

Scene 3: An Alpine tour

Carla addresses a tour group, the Lost Altitude Club. She carries a clipboard.

CARLA: Welcome to Bodenlos, and the glorious mountains surrounding it! I am Carla, your guide. Though I myself am new to this village, I hope I will capture its spirit and introduce you to the majesty of the Swiss Alps.

She gestures to a broadly drawn map of the area.

We are here, at the foot of Mt. Vertraumt, and we are going to end up here, at the peak. Do not be frightened by the distance or the altitude, though they are fierce and intimidating. These mountains demand respect—and without it they will crush you like an insect under a bootheel—but if you are humble and recognize their power and glory, you will be rewarded with visions of almost mystical beauty. Are there any questions?

Member 1 raises her hand. Carla calls on her.

Yes, you.

MEMBER 1: Where are you from? I find your accent quite intriguing.

CARLA: I am from Paraguay. Next question?

MEMBER 2: Where is Paraguay? I've never heard of it.

CARLA: Paraguay is in South America, very far away from here. Yes?

MEMBER 3: Is that one of those countries where Nazis are hidden? I've read quite a few books about that.

CARLA: There are no Nazis in Paraguay. Perhaps in Argentina. Are there any questions about the tour?

MEMBER 1: I detect just a hint of Deutsch in your accent, along with that exotic Sud American inflection.

CARLA: I am a mountain climber, and we are going to climb this mountain now. No more questions; please put on your goggles and muffs.

119

Scene 4: Bodenlos Public Library

Dagmar sits at her desk. Enter Albert. All library conversations are held in whispers.

ALBERT: Dagmar, has—

DAGMAR: Hello, Albert. I've set aside a special book for you.

She pulls out a book and hands it to him.

ALBERT: *The Poems and Songs of Tavern Keepers' Local #357 of Kansas City, Missouri.* What is this?

DAGMAR: It's a collection of poems about beer, whiskey, and barstools.

ALBERT: This is not what I asked for. I don't read poetry.

DAGMAR: But you're a bartender.

ALBERT: That's like saying a fireman who doesn't like cookies will like a cookie if it's shaped like a hydrant.

DAGMAR: But everyone likes cookies.

ALBERT: This is very thoughtful of you, I'd like to return it now.

DAGMAR: You can't.

ALBERT: Why not?

DAGMAR: It's not a library book, it's a gift. I bought it.

ALBERT: I would like to donate this wonderful and touching collection of poems to the library. You may put a plaque with my name on it inside the front cover.

> *Albert starts to exit, leaving the book behind. He runs into Henrik, who is smoking.*

HENRIK: Hi Albert.

> *He coughs.*

Thanks for the lung.

ALBERT: At least try to take care of it, Henrik.

> *Albert exits.*

HENRIK: Fascist!

> *Dagmar sadly picks the book up and polishes the cover absentmindedly.*
>
> *Henrik approaches Dagmar.*

Did my request come in?

DAGMAR: Here you are. *A History of Ether.*

HENRIK: Thank you.

> *Turns to the audience and reads from* A History of Ether:

Both elixir and toxin, it calms the soul and tears the flesh. One's throat turns ragged, one's mind sets sail on an ocean of bliss. Well named it is after the fictional medium of electromagnetic waves, called luminiferous... *(entranced by the word:)* Luminiferous.

...considered to be present yet askew from the physical world, so similarly do those who breathe ether feel present yet askew. Sadly, when one returns from this sacred journey, one's brain aches as though bruised, as though purpling and sallow from savage ill use...

> *Henrik exits. Carla enters the library. She sits beside Dagmar.*

DAGMAR: Can I help you?

CARLA: There is no church in Bodenlos.

DAGMAR: We feel that organized religion interferes with the rights of the individual.

CARLA: But what if the individual wishes to pray?

DAGMAR: We have a book about home altars with many instructive illustrations—

CARLA: What if the individual needs to confess?

DAGMAR: Well—the police station is three blocks south—

CARLA: I refer not to crimes, but to sins.

DAGMAR: I'm not comfortable with that distinction. One either obeys one's desires without hurting others, or one violates the social contract.

CARLA: My soul is burdened.

DAGMAR: While it would be inappropriate for me to argue with what you say about yourself, I'd prefer you not use such inflammatory language in my library.

CARLA: Your library is the closest thing to a sacred place in all of Bodenlos. The hush within its walls creates a space in which I can hear my own thoughts, hear my own heart beating, hear the yearning of my spirit. I would like to make this my church. Will you hear my confession?

DAGMAR: I...I...

CARLA: Your townspeople speak often of the need to support the dreams of your fellows.

DAGMAR: Yes, but—

CARLA: It is my dream to unburden my soul.

DAGMAR: Fine. Fine. Go ahead. Don't mind me if I continue doing my job while you unburden.

CARLA: I am only recently come to Bodenlos.

DAGMAR: (*puttering around*) Yes, yes, I'm listening.

CARLA: I did not come here of my own free will.

    Against her will, Dagmar is intrigued.

DAGMAR: Go on.

CARLA: My heart, which should be my soul's ally in our struggle through life, has betrayed me again and again. Whenever I hear the sound of a trumpet, or a trombone, or even a euphonium—

DAGMAR: Those would all be members of the brass family of instruments, noted for their loud, blaring sound, from which the word "brassy" has sprung.

    Pause. Carla is appalled that her confession has been interrupted.

I'm sorry, you were speaking.

CARLA: I'll come back.

    Dagmar is mortified that she's been rude.

DAGMAR: I'm sorry.

CARLA: *(softly)* I'll come back.

> *Carla exits. Dagmar looks after her, confused.*

Scene 5: Customs 2

> *The border Guard steps out. The Grocer pauses appropriately.*

GUARD: Open up.

> *The Grocer opens his package. The Guard wrinkles his nose.*

What is it?

GROCER: Oysters and clams.

GUARD: How long have they been in transit?

GROCER: Not too long. Have one.

GUARD: *(hurriedly)* On your way.

> *The Grocer exits, a trifle insulted. Albert pauses appropriately.*

Open up.

> *Albert opens his package. The Guard sorts through it.*

Brandy...vermouth...

> *He pulls out the stops of a tuba.*

What's this?

ALBERT: Spare typewriters keys. For a manual typewriter.

GUARD: You have a typewriter?

ALBERT: I'm nostalgic.

GUARD: There's no letters on them.

ALBERT: You have those engraved, once you know what you need. You never know what letters will wear out first.

GUARD: E.

ALBERT: Or S, or T. A. Or I. You never know.

GUARD: I bet you E. Twenty marks.

ALBERT: Okay.

GUARD: You'll tell me, right?

ALBERT: Absolutely. My word of honor.

GUARD: What's this part?

ALBERT: Just, sort of, a cartridge. So you don't lose the keys.

GUARD: Hmm.

> *He tosses the stops back in the package.*

On your way.

Scene 6: Bodenlos Public Library 2

Carla enters and sits beside Dagmar, who tries to seem busy but listens intently.

CARLA: Whenever I hear music played on a brass instrument, my heart stirs. My body feels warm, and my loins—that most unruly and disobedient organ—seem to catch fire. Many a musician has used this accursed weakness to seduce me.

DAGMAR: *(gasps)* The bastards!

CARLA: With their lips, broad and bruised from the rigors of their instrument, pressed against mine, I was in paradise. When the loud and blaring music of our lovemaking came to an end, I was tossed into a burning pit of loss and shame. And so I fled my native Paraguay, hoping to keep my strange passion a secret in foreign lands—but as I walked down a night-shrouded street in Paris, jazz would spill from a café window, or a symphony would play on the Barcelona radio, or a marching band would parade past my place of work in Amsterdam, sending me into an orgasmic swoon. This can't be hidden. I clutch the nearest man to my bosom and rut like an inflamed lioness, my hands digging hungrily into their backsides, my throat moaning with desperate, animal need.

Dagmar feels compelled to fan herself quietly.

Then I heard of Bodenlos, a town so threatened with overhanging snow that all brass instruments are forbidden, lest their trumpeting sound set off an avalanche.

DAGMAR: This was instituted in 1347, after the concert hall collapsed under 50 feet of snow.

CARLA: And here the snow never melts, so there is never a reprieve.

DAGMAR: No other instrument troubles us; even kettle-drums and cymbals are harmless. Only the brittle, metallic vibrations of the brass family threaten us with doom.

CARLA: So you see, you and I are kin, for we share the same enemy. A cruel enemy who steals our free wills.

DAGMAR: Sister! Let me embrace you!

But Carla holds her at arm's length.

CARLA: Please: You are my confessor. We are intimates, but not friends.

DAGMAR: I understand. I don't understand, actually, but I'll read up on it.

CARLA: Thank you. My soul feels clear and pure once again. I will come back.

Carla exits. Dagmar looks after her with a sigh.

Scene 7: The Bodenlos Alehouse

Albert is polishing a glass. The Border Guard enters.

GUARD: Albert! I have five minutes for a little pick-me-up!

ALBERT: How about a Ticklish Spinster?

GUARD: What's in it?

ALBERT: If I told you, it would ruin the whole experience.

GUARD: I'll have one.

> *Albert mixes the drink and hands it to the Guard.*
>
> *The Guard slams it back. Dazed, he starts searching for his wallet.*

ALBERT: On me.

GUARD: Thanks.

> *The Guard exits in a daze, almost knocking over Dagmar, who enters reading a book:* Zelda Fitzgerald's Guide to Cuisine.

DAGMAR: Hello, Albert.

ALBERT: Dagmar.

DAGMAR: On May 17, 1923, Zelda Fitzgerald had a glass of champagne with bitters and a small onion. What is today?

ALBERT: May 17?

DAGMAR: I would like a glass of champagne with bitters and a small onion.

> *Albert begins to create the cocktail.*

ALBERT: Have you finished *The Dinners and Drinks of Emily Brontë* already?

DAGMAR: I have. Albert, what would you be if you weren't a bartender?

ALBERT: *(He thinks for a moment.)* A butcher.

DAGMAR: Do you like meat?

ALBERT: Not particularly—

DAGMAR: Then why—

ALBERT: —that's why I became a bartender.

DAGMAR: Oh.

ALBERT: Here's your cocktail.

DAGMAR: Do you have any hobbies?

ALBERT: I collect beetles.

DAGMAR: But there's only one species at this altitude.

ALBERT: I like to be thorough. It's very satisfying.

DAGMAR: Are you a patron of the arts?

ALBERT: I'm starting to like music.

DAGMAR: Oh—I have the book you requested—*How To Be a One-Man Band.*

> *Eagerly, Albert reaches for it, but Dagmar starts to flip through it.*

It's very interesting. The harmonica and accordion are very complex, while the bass drum is simple enough, depending on what you want to do with it, of course. Then there's the bugle, not much use for these instructions. Look, he plays the cymbals on his head!

ALBERT: Does that seem comical?

DAGMAR: What?

ALBERT: Are you mocking my interest in music?

DAGMAR: No, I—

ALBERT: It's none of your business what I do with my own time.

DAGMAR: What did I say—?

ALBERT: Dagmar, I think you should leave.

DAGMAR: But...

> *Albert stares at her. Dagmar, embarrassed, turns to go.*

Excuse me...

ALBERT: Leave the book, please. I requested it.

DAGMAR: Of course.

> *She leaves the book on the bar and exits.*

Scene 8: Henrik's survey

> *Henrik accosts a Dentist and his Hygienist on the street.*

HENRIK: I'm conducting a survey. How would you like to die?

DENTIST: With a full set of gleaming teeth, still strong and impermeable, with well-shaped crowns and a firm gum-line.

HENRIK: *(with remarkable restraint)* I haven't finished my question.

DENTIST: *(abashed)* I'm so sorry.

HENRIK: Would you rather, A, be bludgeoned to death in your sleep, or B, accidentally fall down an empty elevator shaft?

> *The Dentist and Hygienist reflect momentarily.*

DENTIST: These are our only options?

HENRIK: Yes.

DENTIST: I'm afraid I must object to this arbitrary restriction of choice.

HYGIENIST: But Henrik has asked us, and so must need to know our answer for his own reasons, which he need not express. We must be generous with our imaginations.

DENTIST: *(with an adoring smile)* I adore your logic.

HYGIENIST: *(pleased but concerned that he will reveal their affair)* Klaus...

HENRIK: *(impatient)* Would you rather, A—

DENTIST: May I offer the option of dying in bed, surrounded by my loved ones?

HENRIK: No.

HYGIENIST: If you were bludgeoned in your sleep, it would be messy, but you wouldn't know what had happened.

HENRIK: If you select A, you should also know that you would awaken after the first blow, which was nonetheless powerful enough to damage all motor control, and so you could be conscious but helpless as the following blows crushed your skull and spattered your brain matter all over your pillow, blankets, and the nearby wall.

DENTIST: If you fell down an elevator shaft, there would be those distressing moments—mere seconds, but I'm sure they'd feel eternal—between losing your balance and hitting the bottom.

HYGIENIST: But if it were dark enough, you wouldn't know when you were going to hit, and I understand that the state of free fall is simultaneously terrifying and exhilarating. Is the shaft perfectly dark?

DENTIST: And how deep is it? Will you build up a good velocity before you hit, or is there the danger of merely being maimed and suffering extensively?

HENRIK: Thank you, that's enough, go away.

HYGIENIST: Glad to be of service!

They exit. A Policeperson enters.

HENRIK: Hey, you. Would you rather be boiled in hot oil or flattened by a steam roller?

POLICEPERSON: I would like to be lying on a green hillside, with blue and yellow flowers in full bloom all around me, the air pregnant with their rich scent, with a horse pressing his head between my legs, his rough tongue licking me into a state of orgasmic bliss as I have a stroke and suddenly, painlessly, my brain ceases to function.

HENRIK: I appreciate your specificity. Go away.

The Policeperson exits. Carla enters.

Would you rather be slowly devoured by flesh-eating bacteria or slip in the shower, knock yourself unconscious, and drown in an inch of water?

CARLA: Something inside prevents me from even contemplating this question.

HENRIK: It's just a hypothetical survey! Have you no capacity for speculation?! Why does everyone have such a stick up their collective ass?!

CARLA: Something inside me insists I go on every day, tells me every morning that it is possible to find happiness despite all evidence to the contrary, that the world can be enjoyed despite its chaos and callousness, and if I am not happy and joyful now, I can be, and will be, when I am able.

HENRIK: That is the most appalling thing I've ever heard.

CARLA: It is?

HENRIK: If there's one thing I appreciate about my life, it's that I can end it.

CARLA: You can?

HENRIK: I can and I will.

CARLA: But why?

HENRIK: The proper question—always—is why not?

Henrik exits. Carla looks after him with a sudden pang.

Scene 9: Bodenlos Public Library 3

Dagmar gestures to a patron, a Beekeeper, to her desk.

BEEKEEPER: I'm sorry—My outfit does rustle loudly, I apologize—

DAGMAR: No, no. Could I ask a favor of you?

BEEKEEPER: You can ask.

DAGMAR: Would you sit here for a moment?

She indicates her own chair.

BEEKEEPER: I...don't have the necessary skills to manage your library.

DAGMAR: No, no. You don't need to do anything. Just sit here.

BEEKEEPER: Just sit?

DAGMAR: Just sit.

The Beekeeper shrugs and sits in Dagmar's chair. Dagmar sits in the chair Carla sat in before. She hesitates.

BEEKEEPER: For how long?

DAGMAR: Not long, not long.

She takes a deep breath.

I'm afraid that I don't know what I want.

The Beekeeper is startled.

That the things I think I want—the things that spark my fantasies, that I think would be good for me, or that I think would be bad for me but in a very, very exciting way—these aren't the things that actually...how do I describe this...these aren't the things that actually happen.

BEEKEEPER: It's everyone's civic duty to discern their desires to the best of their ability and act on them appropriately.

Dagmar stares at the Beekeeper for a moment, now understanding why Carla was appalled when Dagmar interrupted her before.

DAGMAR: Thank you. Thank you very much for sitting there.

BEEKEEPER: That's it?

DAGMAR: Yes, that's—that's it.

BEEKEEPER: That was easy. I could sit here longer.

DAGMAR: No, no. I need to sit there now. But thank you.

BEEKEEPER: Do I rustle too much?

DAGMAR: No, but if, just for the moment, you could rustle somewhere else, I would appreciate it.

BEEKEEPER: Oh. Oh. Of course.

The Beekeeper exits.

127

Scene 10: Customs 3

The border Guard steps out. Albert pauses appropriately.

GUARD: Open up.

Albert opens his package. The Guard sorts through it.

Gin...tequila...

He pulls out the horn of a tuba. He looks at Albert.

ALBERT: Ear trumpet for a deaf elephant.

GUARD: There are no elephants in Bodenlos.

ALBERT: I'm hoping to get some.

Pause.

GUARD: I can trust you, can't I, Albert?

ALBERT: Of course.

The Guard puts the horn back in the package.

GUARD: On your way.

Scene 11: Carla's survey

Carla stops assorted Passers-By. She writes their responses on paper on a clipboard.

CARLA: Excuse me. I am going to ask you a question. You needn't answer, but if you refuse you will be smothering my private dreams in their swaddling clothes. Question: Why do you stay alive?

PASSER-BY 1: Receiving mail.

CARLA: Not sending it?

PASSER-BY 1: No. I'm ashamed to admit that. But getting a letter is the most wonderful thing in the world.

CARLA: You—what makes life worth living?

PASSER-BY 2: Hollandaise sauce. With a lemon tang, and it can't be mayonaissey. Mmmm.

CARLA: What keeps you alive?

PASSER-BY 3: Sleep. Naps, really.

128 CARLA: Why naps?

PASSER-BY 3: Lying there, drifting to sleep, in the middle of the day—that's how I know I'm living the life I desire, when I have the freedom to nap.

CARLA: Why are you alive?

PASSER-BY 4: Persimmons.

CARLA: But they're only available for such a short time.

PASSER-BY 4: I can wait.

CARLA: And you, why do you live?

PASSER-BY 5: For the end of some things, and the beginning of others.

CARLA: Thank you.

> *Henrik enters.*

You! How perfect. Here.

> *She hands him her results.*

HENRIK: What's this?

CARLA: A list of reasons to live.

HENRIK: According to who?

CARLA: Whom.

HENRIK: Despot.

CARLA: According to everyone. All sorts of people. Surely one of these reasons will speak to you.

HENRIK: Why are you giving this to me?

CARLA: No reason.

HENRIK: It's a violation of my privacy. I rebuke your foreign ways.

CARLA: I—I thought you might like it.

HENRIK: I don't.

CARLA: Oh.

HENRIK: It appalls me.

CARLA: Oh.

HENRIK: The hypocrisy of it.

CARLA: Oh.

HENRIK: Even your survey for life can be an instrument of death!

> *He tries to slash his wrists with the edge of the paper. Carla watches, stunned and horrified. Henrik cuts himself.*

Ow.

> *He sucks at his wrist.*

CARLA: What if...what if my dearest wish is that you stay alive?

HENRIK: I don't have to accept that.

CARLA: I wish you would.

HENRIK: I don't have to! I don't! I won't! I refuse! I'm running away!

> *But he hasn't yet moved.*

CARLA: Goodbye.

HENRIK: I'm running away now!

> *Henrik flees. Carla slowly exits in the opposite direction.*

129

Scene 12: Bodenlos Public Library 4

Henrik enters the library and approaches Dagmar's desk.

HENRIK: *Has Knots: A Guide for Boys* come in yet? I am in desperate need!

Dagmar looks up at Henrik and sees a new possibility.

DAGMAR: Henrik, sit here.

HENRIK: Why?

DAGMAR: Please.

Curious, Henrik sits in Dagmar's chair. Dagmar sits in the chair for patrons. She takes a deep breath.

I always thought I liked hands. A man's strong hands, rough from work or smooth from leisure, stubby gravedigger's fingers or the long, slender digits of an oil painter—all kinds of hands, but distinctive hands—they were what I thought was truly erotic. But when I saw such hands, a particular pair of exciting hands, my fantasies were paralyzing. I couldn't say hello, I couldn't meet his eyes, I couldn't casually touch him in such a way as to say, implicitly, "Look at me as you look at no one else."

HENRIK: What—

DAGMAR: Shhh.

Dagmar puts her finger against Henrik's lips.

So it was inevitable: The man who didn't interest me at all, a man with dull, mundane hands, a man for whom my very absence of attraction created a vacuum, and love rushed in to fill it.

HENRIK: Can—

DAGMAR: No. As trumpets are to Carla, boredom is to me. Am I dull? Am I boring?

HENRIK: Who—

DAGMAR: I don't think so. My inner life is fierce and stirring. My body may sit at this desk, but my mind spelunks in Carlsbad, swims the Amazon, rides the Trans-Europe Express!

Pause.

HENRIK: Is that all?

DAGMAR: I'm not sure yet.

Pause.

Yes. Thank you. I'll take my seat back.

HENRIK: Who's Carla?

DAGMAR: Carla is this unfortunate woman who is sent into spasms of erotic passion by the sound of any brass instrument.

She catches herself.

I think that that's a secret.

HENRIK: But I asked! Secrets are immoral! Life should be an open book!

DAGMAR: Why do you destroy yourself, Henrik?

HENRIK: I don't know.

DAGMAR: You don't know, or you don't want to tell me?

HENRIK: I don't know. I have a right to be ignorant.

DAGMAR: Henrik, I think you're keeping a secret from yourself.

Henrik is so outraged he cannot speak; in protest, he leaves.

Scene 13: The Bodenlos Alehouse 2

Albert is behind the bar. Henrik enters in a panic.

HENRIK: Albert! I need a drink.

ALBERT: Because your liver feels too good this morning?

HENRIK: Because women are falling in love with me.

ALBERT: How terrible! Like who?

HENRIK: This woman I met on the street! She asked me to live for her! And the librarian is in love with me too!

ALBERT: What makes you think that?

HENRIK: She's behaving very strangely.

ALBERT: She needn't be in love to do that.

HENRIK: But she talked about love. To me. I don't even know her name, it's unfair.

ALBERT: Are you in love with her?

HENRIK: No. Not at all. Not in the slightest.

ALBERT: You could try.

HENRIK: No! Love is a complete compromise of the individual! Like a petty, jealous god, it demands sacrifices and obligations, it pretends to bring joy but smuggles in pain. The poets speak of wild abandon, but reality leads to the most awful domesticity—lovers are neutered, like housepets.

ALBERT: Henrik, I have always known you are a bad citizen, but I have not until now known how truly bad you are. The Russians are a romantic people: See if this vodka will loosen your heart.

He hands Henrik a bottle.

Her name is Dagmar.

HENRIK: Who is Carla?

ALBERT: Carla?

HENRIK: The librarian—

ALBERT: Dagmar.

HENRIK: Dagmar—spoke of Carla.

ALBERT: Carla is a dream. If starving men dream of bread, I dream of her; if

131

men at sea dream of land, she is my new world. The space by my side is her absence. Though I have seen her at the bakery, at the post office, at the drugstore, at two different streetcorners, and—

He mentally assesses the right number.

—four times at the concert hall, she and I have not yet met, mutually, because I want that moment to be perfect, and I don't yet know what that perfection could even be. But if it isn't—if that moment doesn't change my life—

Pause.

Then I will join you in your sad, hollow, loveless world.

Henrik is nonplused.

HENRIK: Is this the same woman?

ALBERT: There is only one Carla in all of Bodenlos. She is from Paraguay.

HENRIK: And is she aroused by trumpets?

Albert looks at Henrik for a moment.

ALBERT: What?

Scene 14: Albert betrays his principles

Albert addresses the audience.

ALBERT: And so I telephoned McCorkle & Crew in London, Fine Brass for Over 40 Years, and requested a trumpet. They were out of trumpets. I requested a saxophone. They said saxophones are woodwinds. What do you have, I asked. We have tubas. Only one left. I'll take it, I said. But it had to be smuggled in, so I bought it one piece at a time. It took three months. And now I have it all assembled. I place it in a bag, and I take it to the foot of Mt. Streben.

Carla waits patiently for a tour group, holding her clipboard. Albert arrives with a backpack containing his tuba.

CARLA: Are you part of the—

She flips through her papers.

—the Alpine Romance Club?

ALBERT: Yes.

CARLA: That's a very large backpack.

ALBERT: I like to be prepared.

CARLA: It looks very heavy.

ALBERT: I like the challenge.

Carla shrugs.

CARLA: As soon as the others have arrived, we will begin.

ALBERT: No one else could make it.

CARLA: No one?

ALBERT: Bad shellfish.

CARLA: So far from the ocean, what fool would order shellfish?

ALBERT: My exact words, but they wouldn't listen.

CARLA: Do you still want to climb?

> *Pause.*

ALBERT: More than anything in the world.

Scene 15: Carla's last climb

> *Carla addresses the audience.*

CARLA: After putting on our goggles and muffs, we begin to climb. The weather is crisp and glorious; the entire world seems to glow with a cold but luminiferous passion. Rigorously we scaled the mountain, hiking up slopes, clambering up rocks, making our way handhold by handhold up vertiginous cliff faces. Up. Up. It is my favorite word. Up. Until we came to rest on a ledge, 7000 feet above sea level, still two thousand feet from the crest of Mt. Streben. Streben: To strive. This mountain is my life. I will not rest. I will not give up. And as I am thinking this, this man I've never met before, to whom I have been tied by a thin nylon line for the past three hours, opens up his backpack.

> *Albert unzips his backpack.*

What are you doing?

> *Albert pulls out the tuba.*

What have you done?

ALBERT: I'm in love with you.

CARLA: I don't even know you.

ALBERT: I know. I'm sorry. This isn't perfect. But it's as close as I can imagine.

> *Carla braces herself in agony as Albert takes a breath and tries to blow into the tuba, but he can't muster up enough air. He tries again. No success. He tries a third time, fails, then collapses in exhaustion.*

I only have one lung. Henrik has crushed my dream without even meaning to.

CARLA: How dare you. You have learned my secret and want to use it against me—you, a citizen of Bodenlos! You disgust me.

ALBERT: Henrik convinced me. He told me love mattered more than freedom, more than truth, that it was truth and it was freedom, the truth of who you are and the freedom to act as you truly must. I told him this contradicted what he'd said before about love. He called me a tyrant. And I ordered a tuba. Carla, I love you.

CARLA: Who is this Henrik?

ALBERT: Henrik is trying to kill himself, but he doesn't know how. Carla, I love you.

133

CARLA: Does Henrik have a small scar down his bottom lip, right here?

ALBERT: He was trying to knock himself out with a toilet seat so he would drown in the bowl. Carla, I love you.

CARLA: He didn't succeed.

ALBERT: No. He never does. Carla, I love you.

CARLA: And Henrik told you to do this. He told you.

ALBERT: Yes. He did. Carla—

CARLA: Give me the tuba.

Confused, Albert does so.

What's your name?

ALBERT: Albert.

CARLA: Albert, in a moment, I will fulfill your deepest wish.

She takes a deep breath to blow in the tuba.

Scene 16: Dagmar says goodbye.

Dagmar addresses the audience.

DAGMAR: I heard the sound as I was shelving Confessional Etiquette, by Father Pigro Sognatore, in which I'd sought solace but found only chiding. The sound reverberated from one majestic crest to another, slowly flying over our town like a monstrous bird, the great expanse of its wings cutting off the sun and leaving us in darkness. I had never heard this sound before in my life, but I knew what it was instantaneously. It was the last page, the signature, the period. It was the end.

A Library Patron leaps to his feet. A low rumble builds underneath the following exchange, or perhaps a mounting vibration that shakes the audience.

PATRON: Everyone, run for your lives!

DAGMAR: We're the only ones here.

PATRON: The clarion of doom! The fanfare of armageddon! The trumpet of Ragnarok!

DAGMAR: It's all right. There's nothing we can do.

PATRON: My life is unfinished! I still don't have my own apartment! I haven't yet learned how to foxtrot!

DAGMAR: No one can do everything they want to.

PATRON: Why not? Why not? Why not?

DAGMAR: I don't know.

She embraces the Patron, who bursts into tears. The rumble continues to mount.

134

Scene 17: Henrik's heart attack

Henrik addresses the audience. The rumble continues to mount.

HENRIK: I'd been lying naked in snowbanks all morning, hoping to catch pneumonia. But not even a sniffle. The torment of good health! A stroke was the only solution: If they transplanted someone else's brain into my skull, then someone else could face my agonizing life! But I don't know what causes strokes. Apparently no one does. Blood just clots in the brain for no apparent reason. And then I hear it. And I can't believe he's actually done it. Sure, I'd encouraged him, but it was so long ago. And now! It's happening! That terrifying sound! And I am so happy, I have a heart attack. Everything I've ever wanted, all at once. I'm in heaven.

The rumble crescendos during this next speech.

And then the snow came crashing down. It picked me up and threw me through the air and caught me again. I was crunched between two gigantic waves of white, crystalline snow, my body packed in on all sides by bone-chilling cold.

Silence, except for Henrik's voice.

I could feel my body slowing down. Wait, I said, I'm supposed to die. Now. Right now. I'm going to die. Now. Don't make me wait. But there was nothing I could do. In ten...or twenty...or fifty years, they'll unfreeze me. They'll fix my heart. No. Stop. My blood was slowing down. My organs were slowing down. Even my thoughts were turning sluggish.

He speaks more and more slowly.

It's not going to happen. I'm not going to die. I'm just going to slowly, slowly, start to die, without actually dying. Without actually going away. I'm still here. I'm. Still. Here. Hello. I'm. Still.

Blackout.

SUNG RNO'S plays include *wAve, Behind the Masq, Weather, Yi Sang Counts to Thirteen, Gravity Falls From Trees, New World, Drizzle and Other Stories, Cleveland Raining,* and *Infinitude.* His work has been produced by East West Players, Thick Description, Asian American Theater Company, North West Asian American Theater, San Diego Asian American Rep, Dance Theater Workshop, Immigrants' Theater Project, Seoul International Theater Festival, New York Fringe Festival, Sanctuary, and Ma-Yi Theater Company. Honors include an NEA/TCG playwriting fellowship in residence with Ma-Yi Theater Company, the Whitfield Cook Prize (for *wAve*), a New York Fringe Festival Best Overall Production Award (for *Yi Sang Counts to Thirteen,* directed by the author), a Van Lier/New Dramatists playwriting fellowship, a Van Lier/New York Theater Workshop playwriting fellowship, and first prize in the Seattle Multicultural Playwrights' Festival. His plays and poetry are anthologized in *But Still, Like Air, I'll Rise; Premonitions; Echoes Upon Echoes* and *The Nuyorasian Anthology.* He has received commissions from Second Stage/ Time Warner, EST/Sloan, The Public Theater, Mark Taper Forum, Dance Theater Workshop, Ma-Yi Theater Company, and was a resident artist of Mabou Mines. He holds a BA in creative writing from Harvard, an MFA in creative writing from Brown, and is a fifth year resident of New Dramatists.

Sung Rno

CLEVELAND RAINING

A play in two acts,
with a prologue and epilogue

He cannot see her happiness,
hidden in a thicket of blanket
and shining hair.
On the grass beside their straw mat,
a black umbrella,
blooming like an ancient flower,
betrays their recent arrival.
Suspicious of so much sunshine,
they keep expecting rain.
— *Cathy Song,* Magic Island

We must talk now. Fear
Is fear. But we abandon one another.
— *George Oppen,* Leviathan

CHARACTERS

Jimmy "Rodin" Kim, a Korean-American man in his late 20's. A failed artist.
   Walks with a noticeable limp.
Mari Kim, his younger sister, a medical student in her early 20's. A healer.
Mick, a mechanic of sorts, late 20's. A native Ohioan, non-Asian.
Storm, a woman involved in a motorcycle accident, late 20's. An Asian American
   woman who rejects everything "Asian".

SETTING

The Kim family lives in a country house in Ohio, about a hundred miles south
of Cleveland. The action is divided around the Kim's garage (a converted barn)
and their front porch. The Volkswagen in the garage should be the most real
object on stage. Everything else should fluid, ephemeral, barely real.

TIME

An apocalyptic time.

PROLOGUE

Scene 1

JIMMY: Fork.
   Spoon.
   Knife.
   Brush.
   Bread.
   Water.
   Paint.
   Brush.
   Mother.
   Pencil.
   Brushfork.
   Forkbrush.
   Mother.
   Motherbrush.
   Paper.
   Knifepencil.
   Knifer.
   Forker.
   Fuck.

     Pause.

   Eatdrinkshit.
   Chew...chew.
   Eatdrinkshit.
   Chew...chew.
   Brush.
   Dripping.
   knifeshitdrink.
   Dripping.
   Pencil. Mother.

MARI: When I was a baby
   my *Ahppah* had to
   feed me by himself
   Uhmmah wasn't around so he
   would come home early
   from the clinic to make
   me lunch and at first he
   had trouble making
   the rice because he
   had to make it soft
   like porridge for me
   I would stare up at
   the reflection of me in
   his glasses and he would
   never look at me, but
   stare at the pot as the
   rice got cooked,
   sometimes I caught him
   looking at me and I—

     Pause.

   would smile at him he
   would tell me that I
   looked just like *Uhmmah*
   he wished we were
   still in Korea he
   wouldn't say it he just think
   it but I didn't
   figure all of this out
   until later, much later.

Scene 2

Mari, alone in the light.

MARI: My mother, my *Uhmmah*, my painter, she painted a still life of a bowl
of cherries and she captured the color just right. I could stare at that
painting for hours. She had caught them at that exact instant when it
would only be a matter of hours before they would start smelling too
sweet, like wine. If I stared at that painting my body would move...the
inside would a little left of the outer...like when the earth shakes slightly,
you feel disoriented. Then one day I couldn't stand just looking at the
picture anymore and I had to lick the surface with my tongue to taste the

138

cherries, but the taste wasn't there. My tongue got cut, there was the taste of blood. And still, the taste wasn't there.

ACT ONE

Scene 1

Late morning—the garage, a converted barn. Tools, used car-parts are scattered on the floor. To the left is a Volkswagen bug, battered and rusty, resting on blocks. Beyond the wall are cornfields and trees in the distant horizon. Lights come up on Jimmy sleeping in the Volkswagen. Mari sits next to him, slowly wrapping a bandage around her arm. Jimmy tosses and turns. Mari stops wrapping the bandage, stares at her brother.

Long silence.

MARI: *Oppah.*

> *Pause.*

Jimmy.

> *Pause.*

Rodin.

JIMMY: *(Waking.)* What?

MARI: Help me.

> *He gives her his finger. She ties the bandage. He gets up and starts putting on clothes, shaving, etc.*

> *Pause.*

I couldn't find him.

JIMMY: Yeah?

MARI: I went driving for an hour.

JIMMY: He'll come back.

MARI: You think?

> *He doesn't answer.*

While I was driving I saw this accident on the road. This woman riding a motorcycle hit this pickup truck. I got out of my car to help, but she wouldn't let me touch her. She's screaming at me like I was the one who hit her. Tries to tear my hair out. She wants to kill the driver in the pickup, but she can't move, so she starts throwing parts of her bike at me. She hits me with this– *(She points to an exhaust pipe on the ground.)* Finally the ambulance came and took them both away.

JIMMY: Women shouldn't be out on the road. *(He cuts himself shaving.)* Shit! *(He puts tissue paper on the cut.)*

MARI: I saw her face so clearly as she flew over her bike. Like I've known her my whole life. And this is the crazy thing she hit her own grandmother.

JIMMY: Weirder things have happened.

139

MARI: Like what?

JIMMY: She could have hit her lover. Or her boss. Her minister. See, the possibilities are endless. I'm hungry.

Jimmy looks at Mari expectantly.

I thought maybe you had fixed something.

MARI: Think again.

Jimmy pulls out a jar of kimchee out from the car and a bottle of beer. He opens the jar and starts eating with a pair of chopsticks.

JIMMY: You want some?

MARI: No thanks. I'll never understand how you can eat kimchee on an empty stomach.

JIMMY: Kimchee is the one distinctive dish that Koreans have. There is no other dish in the world that comes close to it.

MARI: Sauerkraut.

JIMMY: Sauerkraut is for a baseball game, on top of a hotdog. Kimchee is more...spiritual.

MARI: And that's why you eat it?

JIMMY: I eat it because I'm lazy.

MARI: Shouldn't you be at work?

JIMMY: Oh...I was meaning to tell you...I quit. Don't look at me like that. Look, I'm unpacking a crate of tomatoes. I'm being the model worker. Then this lady comes up to me. Asks me where the bananas are. Bananas.

MARI: So what?

JIMMY: She was calling me a racial slur.

MARI: Chink is a slur. Gook is a slur. Banana is...a fruit.

JIMMY: What does it mean to you?

MARI: It means white on the inside, yellow on the outside.

JIMMY: It means assimilated. That's a fucking slur, if I've ever heard one.

MARI: You were in the fruit section.

JIMMY: It was her tone. She didn't just ask me for the bananas. She asked me for the bananas. You see? So I just get real quiet with her, just stare her in the eyes, and I say, "I don't know, ma'am, we don't serve people like you," and I throw a tomato in her face. Right in the eye.

MARI: You got fired.

JIMMY: Fired, quit—it's semantics.

MARI: Bullshit.

JIMMY: The only bullshit around here is that a big flood is about to come and no one seems to be aware of it.

MARI: The flood.

JIMMY: For a whole year I've been dreaming about the same thing, this Volkswagen.

MARI: I know.

JIMMY: It was in my head, every night—I couldn't get rid of it. It scared me at first, but then I saw the power of it. This dream was a vision of some kind. Instead of resisting it, I opened myself up to it. And then—

MARI: I bet you expect me to bring in the money.

JIMMY: And then, I walk into this junkyard and I see it. It's the exact one that showed up in my dreams, sky blue, rust in all the right places. So I have to buy it, now don't I? But in these dreams I'm floating. You and I are floating. In this car, this very Volkswagen right here. There's enough kimchee and beer to last us forever. It's raining and raining. Everything gets covered up. Ohio becomes one big lake.

MARI: One big lake.

JIMMY: That's right. You have no imagination, that's your problem.

MARI: It's always an escape for you. You have to be running.

JIMMY: I'm not the one who blew out of this house. I'm still here.

MARI: You don't ever worry about him?

JIMMY: Of course I do. But I don't have to see him in front of me sipping his tea, reading his newspaper to know what's happening with him.

MARI: That's a cop-out.

JIMMY: You believe what you want to believe. I just don't see how driving all over the interstate changes anything. He's probably not even in the area. Maybe he left us so that we could be free. Free to concentrate on more important things. The rain. The flood.

MARI: Why do you keep talking about this flood?

JIMMY: It's going to happen. I can feel it.

MARI: What you're feeling is all that kimchee you ate.

JIMMY: It'll be a mission of mercy. I'll take people in need. For instance, those two women in the accident.

MARI: You're not a prophet. You're a fired stockboy. You're someone whose names himself after a sculptor and then...

JIMMY: Then what?

MARI: (Beat.) And you don't even care that he's been gone for almost a week now—no trace, nothing, zip, nada, zero. Why do I have to be the one who looks for him?

JIMMY: No one told you to look for him.

MARI: No one told you to dream about Volkswagens.

JIMMY: I'm happy about my Volkswagen. Are you happy about what you do?

MARI: I'm not supposed to be happy. The unwritten law of all Korean families the youngest sibling takes care of everyone else's shit.

JIMMY: You exaggerate.

Mari exits, bumping into Mick as he enters. Mick is awkward and pushy at the same time. He wears overalls with his name "Mick" written into the fabric over his chest. He stands in the doorway for a moment.

MICK: Hello.

JIMMY: Yes.

MICK: Are you Jimmy Roadin?

JIMMY: Rodín.

MICK: I hope I didn't come at a bad time.

JIMMY: No. That's just my sister.

MICK: What seems to be the problem?

JIMMY: She doesn't understand me.

MICK: I meant about the car.

JIMMY: Right. I need some work on the engine.

MICK: This VW here? Well, it's a beaut alright. Want to make it bigger? More power?

JIMMY: That wouldn't hurt, for what I need it for. But I need more than that.

MICK: More?

JIMMY: It has to be waterproof.

MICK: Uh-huh.

JIMMY: I need it to float actually.

MICK: Why, you taking it out onto Lake Erie or something? Ha-ha...

JIMMY: Yes.

MICK: Oh yeah? What the hell for?

JIMMY: For the big flood that's coming.

MICK: I'm sorry, am I at the right place?

JIMMY: I don't know, are you?

MICK: *(Checking his notebook.)* Yes, I am. Now let me get this straight. You want to make a boat out of a Volkswagen? What the hell for? And why a Volkswagen?

JIMMY: It was a vision, a vision that I've been dreaming about for a year.

MICK: Like a ghost.

JIMMY: Don't you know what I'm talking about? When you're a kid, you just wish things, like—

MICK: Like wishing the world was made of ice cream.

JIMMY: Yeah, or you think—

MICK: You're trapped on a island with some gorgeous, stacked babe—

JIMMY: But then you wake up and it's not there anymore—

142

MICK: Your sheet's soaking wet. (*Beat.*) You're talking about all those ideas you have when you're a little kid. I don't have those no more. But I understand where you're comin' from. Where do you want to go with this thing?

JIMMY: We'll have to see when the rains come. Maybe up north.

MICK: You mean, Cleveland?

JIMMY: If we have to.

MICK: Now I know you're crazy. And how long you figure to be on this thing?

JIMMY: A few months maybe.

MICK: You have a sail?

JIMMY: No.

MICK: Should never trust a machine without having a backup. That's why we got two hands, two legs. In case you lose one, you got an extra. What kind of fuel you using?

JIMMY: I'd like to build a fusion device. That way we can use the water as fuel.

MICK: What do you know about fusion?

JIMMY: I have some books.

MICK: A book don't tell you jack.

JIMMY: My father was a doctor. He taught us things.

MICK: So it's in your blood.

JIMMY: You're a mechanic, right?

MICK: And a damned good one. Don't get me wrong. I want to help you. I just don't work like you do. I block things out of my head. But I like the idea of making a VW float. What'd you say, we were gonna float over Lake Ohio ?

JIMMY: Why not?

MICK: I like that. Yes, very much. You're payin' me, right?

JIMMY: Are you scared?

MICK: Scared? There ain't too much in this world that I'm scared of. Except a few things. Certain vegetables mainly. But why are you doing this?

JIMMY: Think of those people who climbed Mount Everest. Why do they go to all that trouble? People want to know how it feels to be on top of that damned thing.

MICK: I don't like heights. Shit, if I want to be on top of something, it's not going to be some damned rock.

JIMMY: If you were to climb a mountain, why would you do it?

MICK: But I wouldn't.

JIMMY: What if there was a mountain in front of you and you absolutely had no choice? What if you had no choice about it? Answer the question.

MICK: I told you, I don't know.

JIMMY: Use your imagination.

MICK: Like we used to do in nursery school? Like that?

JIMMY: Yes. Like that.

> *Mick sits down. He closes his eyes.*

MICK: Alright...Imagine it. Jesus. Okay...I can see the mountain...a big mountain...a tall mountain. Trees on it, the whole nine yards. And birds, they're shitting on me and everything. Are you satisfied?

JIMMY: Walk towards it.

MICK: I'm walking...

JIMMY: What do you see?

MICK: Corn...lots of corn.

JIMMY: What else?

MICK: Cows. *(Sniffs.)* Manure. I'm still walking towards it, there it is, I mean, it's miles away, you want me to start flapping my arms? *(He stops.)* Jesus. *(He opens his eyes.)* What are you doing to me?

JIMMY: Nothing.

MICK: You were leading me into the corn.

JIMMY: So what?

MICK: I don't like corn. Do you?

JIMMY: I don't know...I eat it.

MICK: Yeah, but do you go crazy about it? Do you hang out with it?

JIMMY: Corn tastes good. It's a vegetable. It doesn't hurt anybody.

MICK: But man, I hate it. I hate corn. The sight of it makes me nauseous.

JIMMY: So don't eat it.

MICK: It sticks in me. It doesn't come out when I eat it. So everytime I see it I feel like I'm eating it again.

JIMMY: It's just a plant, man. Ignore it.

MICK: You can't ignore it out here! It's like ignoring an ocean when you're swimming in it! It's a fact of life, it's there every day, every morning you wake up, staring you in the eyes. So when I closed my eyes, you know what I saw? The stalks of corn—they started breeding, like fish—they started swimming and then there was like a school of them—and they were breeding like faster than you could even count—until there was like a whole fucking ocean of corn, a whole fucking country of corn—and I can't stand corn! I've just been fooling myself. I thought I could condition myself, you know to like, or at least to get along with it. But it doesn't work that way. Shit. The world just isn't the way we want it, is it?

JIMMY: No.

MICK: It's a sign. I can see that. A sign for change. When do we leave?

Scene 2

Mari is reading a thick medical book while sitting on the porch. Mick sits a small distance away from her. He wipes his face with a dirty rag. Silence, then...

MICK: You don't mind me sitting here, do you?

MARI: No.

MICK: That's good. Because this is a mighty nice spot to be sitting. I can understand why you like it.

MARI: I'm glad.

MICK: Your brother's a little strange, ain't he?

MARI: Strange?

MICK: He's building an ark. Out of a Volkswagen.

MARI: He likes to keep busy.

MICK: Well, he's no Noah. *(Beat.)* Maybe you're weird too, what do you do?

MARI: I'm studying to be a doctor.

MICK: You've got the temperament of a doctor.

MARI: What do you mean by that?

MICK: By what?

MARI: "You have the temperament of a doctor." What the hell is that supposed to mean? I'm not just a cold, heartless scientist.

MICK: I never said you were.

MARI: You insinuated it.

MICK: Sorry.

MARI: You know, I used to play the piano. But then...my hands...didn't behave the way they used to. So I stopped playing.

MICK: What happened to your hands?

MARI: I had...an accident.

MICK: I don't generally like doctors. But you're different somehow.

MARI: Because I'm a woman? An Asian woman?

MICK: I can tell you really don't even like it. I don't like what doctors do. They open you up. They stick things into your body. *(Beat.)* So are you coming too?

MARI: Where?

MICK: To Cleveland.

MARI: Who's going to Cleveland?

MICK: Your brother.

MARI: I don't travel with my brother.

MICK: Why not?

MARI: That car isn't going anywhere.

MICK: You're a sceptic.

MARI: Skeptic?

MICK: Yeah.

MARI: I'm a realist.

MICK: But life isn't real, you know. It just doesn't work that way. For instance, my truck fell on me once. I was under it and the jack slipped. By the time the tow truck came I felt like me and the truck had fused, like I had melted with that engine and that steering column. They lifted all that metal off of me and part of me was still trapped in my old Ford.

MARI: Why are you telling me this?

MICK: To show you the possibilities out there.

MARI: Look. There's not a cloud in the sky.

MICK: You have beautiful eyes. Has anyone ever told you that?

Scene 3

On the porch. Mari begins to read from her book.

MARI: *(Opening the book and reading.)* "The cadaver should not be mistaken for a real live person. A cadaver is only a receptacle, a tool, a construction that houses something else, something once living. It is something similar to an empty house. The people who once lived there have all moved somewhere else to another city, another country. The cadaver is an empty space, four walls, a ceiling and silence. There should be no attachment to the house itself, not even to the people who have left."

She closes the book, pulls out her diary. She scribbles for a few moments, then turns back to her previous entry. She reads, the lights and sounds "reliving" this dream.

This was my dream last night. I'm driving down the interstate and it's overcast. I can see the highway stretching over the plains for miles, but I look to my right and I see a farm, cows grazing, but past all of this I see trees stretched out across the sky, the stalks of wheat are like porridge like hair like someone's belly and then it seems like I can see even further, that past the fields, past the farms, I see...water...and waves and I can smell the salt the heat the taste of that sea. I feel like turning the car into that wetness, that abyss. Only there's the shoulder, there's the guardrail, so I ignore it, I keep driving, I keep my eyes on the road. But I can't stop looking over there, into that invisible lake in the side of my vision, so finally...I do it...I turn I take a sharp turn I'm turning and— Then I'm flipping...through the air...flying and flipping...over the barrier, up and over, there's the totally pure moment of silence, and then it's all noise concrete, glass, the car the air the metal breaking, all of it breaking, and I'm bleeding, I'm in pain, I'm hurt, but I can't tell you, I can't tell you how happy I feel.

Lights come up on Jimmy and Mick working on the engine. Mari walks around them and talks; they do not acknowledge her.

146

All this dreaming. It upsets me. First my brother, now me. This dreaming. I fear the car because maybe...he's right. Maybe there's no hope. Maybe it all has to come down...the house, the memories, the keepsakes ...maybe, maybe, it all has to go. I can't believe that. *(Addressing Jimmy.)* Our father, fast becoming a memory. I try to keep him alive. I put hundreds, thousands of miles on my car trying to find some trace of him. I write letters to distant relatives. But no. Nothing. Explanation? Is that what I seek. No. Something different. Something more than the facts. *(To Mick.)* And these strangers that come into our lives. What to do with them? What way of expressing ourselves can be sufficient? How to make it into a neat appetizer to serve on a dish? So silly. So stupid.

> *Lights fade on the garage as—Storm walks up to the "porch" area. Dressed in motorcycle gear, one of Storm's legs is bleeding noticeably. She has the dazed look of a survivor. Mari crosses over to porch, sits down as she was before.*

STORM: Hi.

MARI: Hi. Can I help you?

STORM: What?

MARI: I said, can I help you?

STORM: Do you think you can help me?

MARI: It depends on what your problem is. Wait. This morning. You were in the accident. You were on the bike.

STORM: Bike? My bike's back home isn't it?

> *Parenthetical statements are as if to her Grandmother:*

(All safe and sound, like nothing ever happened to it!)

MARI: Of course...it is.

STORM: No, there's nothing wrong with my bike. (Lay off! Just for a moment!)

MARI: Excuse me?

STORM: *(Picking up Mari's book.)* What's this? Gray's Anatomy. Studying to be a doctor are you? Well, I've always admired doctors. (Hey I'm about to ask her, don't worry.)

MARI: Who do you keep talking to?

STORM: Oh, just my Granny. She's telling me that I should quit beating around the bush. (No thank you! No! I said no!)

MARI: Granny?

STORM: My Grandmother. She's just asking me if I want a whiskey shot and I said no. She's bugging me, because it seems that my bike isn't safe and sound at home. You haven't seen it around here have you?

MARI: No, I'm afraid I haven't.

STORM: (I tried, okay? She said she hasn't seen it!) Well, thanks for the chit-chat. I best be going.

MARI: You shouldn't be walking around like that. Your leg...

STORM: It's just a scratch.

MARI: I think I should take you to the hospital.

STORM: I need to find my bike first. See, I just kind of lost it.

Storm loses her balance, Mari holds her.

MARI: Maybe you should just rest inside for a little while.

STORM: No, I don't like being inside of things. Hospitals, houses, buildings, you name it...relationships...I can't stand them. Let me just sit here for a little bit, then I'll be on my way. *(She sits in Mari's chair.)* (I know it's not polite, but it's only for a moment.) Jesus, she can be such a pain in the ass sometimes.

MARI: I really think you should be in a hospital.

STORM: I don't believe in them. Like I said, I admire doctors, but hospitals they're like tombs. Big fluorescent tombs. *(She inhales the air.)* What's that smell?

MARI: My brother likes to eat kimchee.

STORM: Kimchee?

MARI: You don't know what that is?

STORM: No.

MARI: You're Asian aren't you?

STORM: I'm what?

MARI: Asian.

STORM: You mean, like a boat person? No, I'm American.

MARI: But your parents must have been Asian...

STORM: You've got a lot of nerve assuming all that. I never knew my parents, okay? I've lived with Granny all my life. She's not really my Granny, she just likes people to call her that. No, it wasn't kimchee I was smelling, it was some WD-40. My favorite machine lubricant.

MARI: My brother's working on his car.

STORM: What about your parents?

MARI: They don't live here anymore.

STORM: (Hey! I'm just talking here alright?) She's very weird about guests. She thinks if a guest comes you have to treat them like royalty. And if you go over to someone else's house, forget it, you'd better behave like you're in a museum.

MARI: You always talk to her like that?

STORM: We're very close. Well, it was nice meeting you. Hope you find someone who does know what kimchee is. *(She gets up, her leg can't support her weight and she sits back down again.)* Do you mind if I rest here for just a little bit?

MARI: Why don't you just stay for awhile? I can put you in my brother's old room.

148

STORM: No, this is fine. I like being outdoors.

MARI: But what if it rains?

STORM: It's not going to rain for a long time.

MARI: I like you already.

STORM: Is it okay if I call you Doc?

MARI: Just don't treat me like one. And what should I call you?

STORM: My name is Storm.

Scene 4

Nightime, garage. Mick is sleeping near the car. A lone spot on Jimmy, who speaks as if trying to explain something to himself.

JIMMY: Didn't always get these things in my head. Used to follow the rules. Listened to my father, did most of what he said. He gave me medical books to read. We got along fine. Then I decided to take up hunting. I went out on a day when it was wet. The sky grey, almost black. I kept walking even though I was getting lost. The rain starts coming down. It rolls down my face and it feels like I'm crying. Then I am crying. I can't really tell. It's all mixed together. I lean against a tree and I look up and this is crazy, there's this huge pencil in the sky. It's huge, monstrous. Big and yellow, the size of a tree. It's coming straight towards me, the eraser side down. Like it wants to rub me out. I said, this fucking pencil is not going to get me and I point my gun at it, only it's slippery and I feel it slipping. I hear it go off. I'm standing in a puddle. I look down and the rain is red. I'm not crying anymore. My foot's sinking deeper and deeper into this puddle. Can't move. Can't think. The rain comes down harder. I try to yell out. I can't hear myself. I'm drowned out by the wind. And I'm just this tree in a storm, the bark all stripped away. Just a naked piece of wood. That's when I changed my name from Kim to Rodin. Kim means gold in Korean, but doesn't mean a damn thing in English. It's abstract, a word like "algebra" or "mutation". I wanted a name that meant something to me. Now Rodin was perfect, I thought. Jimmy R. Had a gangster ring to it. Someone who lived by his wits. And I had a battle wound to back it up. No one was going to mess with me.

A light comes up on Mari, who approaches Jimmy slowly. She is meant to be a figure of his imagination, his conscience.

MARI: And who was messing with you big brother?

JIMMY: Who let you in here?

MARI: I live here, don't I? Answer the question. Who was messing with you?

JIMMY: Everyone. The kids at school, my teachers. My father.

MARI: And so you took on the name of Rodin. The French sculptor. Silly, don't you think?

JIMMY: I did what I could.

MARI: Because...as I remember it, you were never an artist. You failed at it. I have a vivid memory of you coming back from school, angry about how no one understood you, how life was just shit...and then you went up into the attic and started getting Mom's old painting things.

JIMMY: Do we have to go through this?

MARI: And you were wearing this oversized painting shirt and you had an easel set up, you looked just like a painter should look I guess, although I've never met a real live painter, I mean, there was Mom, but I never knew her. And you tried and tried and tried to paint something, anything, but then what did you?

JIMMY: I burned it all.

MARI: Even Ummah's things.

JIMMY: Yes.

MARI: And then what did you do?

JIMMY: I don't remember.

MARI: And then what did you do?

JIMMY: I told you, I don't...

MARI: *(Emphatically.)* What?

JIMMY: I stepped on your fingers.

> *Mari stares at him with a look of victory. He bows his head. Light out on Mari. Jimmy holds his head in his hands. Mick stirs in his sleep, wakes up.*

MICK: Jimmy R? You alright?

JIMMY: I'm fine.

> *Pause.*

MICK: I want to ask you something. Why do you live in this barn?

JIMMY: Convenience. And I don't want to drive my sister insane.

MICK: You guys could just live apart.

JIMMY: No, we need to be together. But a little apart.

MICK: I've been thinking. About Noah. Now the reason that old guy got on his boat was that the world was too corrupt and sinful, right? After the flood, then Noah and God should have had a clean slate to work with. Things should have gotten better. And they might have, for just a short time. But then the same old shit started happening the same greed, the same corruption. The harlots...

JIMMY: Harlots?

MICK: Yeah, all of that shit. So my question is why go to all that trouble when you end up at the very same place that you started from?

JIMMY: I look at it like motor oil. You have to change it constantly. Does the engine get any better? No. It's maintenance. Having a flood every now and then is a form of maintenance.

MICK: Jimmy R, you don't have to put everything into car talk for me to understand. *(Pause.)* Are you going to take animals?

JIMMY: Animals?

MICK: Like Noah did. Two of every kind two rabbits, two sparrows, two pigs, two cattle...

JIMMY: We don't have to be like Noah.

MICK: We might get lonely, you know? My leg hurts. I can't sleep when my leg hurts. A good sign, though. My leg only acts up when it rains.

JIMMY: What happened to your leg?

MICK: I was under this pick-up truck and it fell on me. Fucked my leg up really bad. I was lucky it didn't kill me. I actually didn't feel that much pain. I kind of liked being under that truck. You want to know a secret? *(Beat.)* I got...kind of turned on being under that truck.

JIMMY: Turned on?

MICK: Yeah, like...I got hard. I've never told anyone that before.

JIMMY: I don't know what to say. Did you come?

MICK: No! Jesus, that's sick.

JIMMY: Sorry.

MICK: I cared very deeply for that truck. When it's wet, my leg acts up. Probably the metal in there feeling like it has to rust. It has a mind of its own.

JIMMY: I have something like that too. With my foot. It happened a long time ago. A hunting accident.

MICK: You don't look like a hunter.

JIMMY: It was dark. This flash storm. It started raining. The gun was wet, it just slipped in my hands. That's all it did, really. Just slipped in my hands. You know, metal and water, they just don't mix.

MICK: And then what happened?

JIMMY: My sister came out. I think that's the day she realized she could be a great doctor. Because you see, there was no one else in the house. My father...he was gone. He was away at the clinic.

MICK: It was bad?

JIMMY: There was some blood. It didn't hurt though. That always surprised me.

Scene 5

On the porch, night. Storm is sleeping on a makeshift "bed", made from a lawnchair. Mari sits next to her, watching over her. She opens her diary again.

MARI: *(Reading while writing.)* Someone's sticking their face into the crib. I'm sleeping. I feel someone's lips. Soft. Warm. There's that smell that I remember but I don't know from where. I open my eyes, my baby eyes and I see my brother's face. He looks sad, he looks scared. Why are you scared, *Oppah*? Someone's shouting in the other room. Someone's crying. I'm crying. *(Stops writing.)* If that someone is me, then who is the other someone? *(To Storm.)* Can you tell me? A simple sign would do. I've been driving for over a week now. Still no sign of him. Driving so much my callouses have callouses. I dream in interstate miles, in state highways that bump and jerk through my head while I try to sleep. And still no sign. Memory is my only weapon, my only hope. My friends tell me to move on, to leave this place. They don't understand. Escape doesn't always solve things. You can't just leave the pieces behind and expect everything to be fine. The past finds you. What you've done before, comes to your door today and tomorrow. Look at my mother and father. They leave their country, Korea, they come here, they make a better place. They think that they can just pick up where they left off. Just lift the needle off that record player, put another disc on, let the needle drop back down again. But see, the music has changed. You need different ears here. In this corn country, this state where flat is a color, and grey is a song. Are you getting all of this? Because I see you Storm. You look like me. We have the same hair, the same eyes. Similar, not that different. Then I think I know you. I don't really of course. But I think I do. And that gives me a strange kind of hope, a feeling that I can stay.

Jimmy appears (not at all dreamlike), in his pajamas, his hair a mess. He and Mari stare at each other for a moment. Jimmy looks at Storm.

JIMMY: Who's this?

MARI: The motorcycle woman.

JIMMY: This isn't a hospital.

MARI: It's not a garage either.

JIMMY: What's her name?

MARI: Storm.

JIMMY: She almost looks Korean.

MARI: She's not.

JIMMY: How do you know?

MARI: A name like "Storm"?

JIMMY: You never know these days. I mean, she could be our mother for all we know.

MARI: That's not funny. Why are you up, anyway?

JIMMY: Mick just kept telling me his crazy stories. He fucks trucks.

MARI: He's definitely not normal.

JIMMY: Well, who is these days? *(Pause.)* When you go driving...what do you see?

MARI: Sometimes...when there's no one else around...I close my eyes, I swear, I can feel him.

JIMMY: That's dangerous. You could get yourself killed.

MARI: I even take my hands off the steering wheel. Then the car seems like it's floating. And I slow down. I can feel him right there. And knowing this keeps me warm for the next few hours as I drive and drive.

JIMMY: (*Agitatedly.*) Nothing I've done even approaches that. How can you just sit there and tell me a story like that? So calm. It doesn't even affect me...

MARI: But it does affect me. That's why I told you.

> *Jimmy leaves. Lights dim for a second, Mari falls asleep, then the lights brighten morning, a new day. Storm opens her eyes. She wakes Mari.*

STORM: I'm not Korean. Did you hear me?

MARI: You were eavesdropping?

STORM: I can't help my ears from hearing things. Just leave me out of all this ethnic bullshit. Any word about my bike?

MARI: It's in the shop.

STORM: You gave my bike to mechanics? Who the hell gave you permission to do that? Mechanics are the worst! They're worse than dentists. At least a dentist doesn't have the radio on, playing for-shit-music, some blonde bimbo up on the wall, while he's got a drill stuck in your mouth. A dentist would never do that. How come you know so much about the crash? You ain't the one who hit me are you?

MARI: You hit a truck. I was there watching it unfold in front of me like some awful flower. I watched you fly through the air.

STORM: How's the other person...the one who hit me.

MARI: She's in the hospital. I wanted to tell you—

STORM: She still knocked out?

MARI: She's unconscious, yes.

STORM: Serves her right.

MARI: You shouldn't say that.

STORM: It's the goddamned truth. She was looking dead at me wasn't she? She should have stopped.

MARI: It was no one's fault really.

STORM: I know what happened. That bitch shouldn't be out on the road.

MARI: Storm, she's your grand—

STORM: She sure took a mean hit. It was me against that truck...and I won. God I hate 4-wheeled vehicles.

MARI: Did you hear me? Your grandmother is in the hospital.

STORM: Granny? You didn't go and call home did you? You didn't go and tell her I got into an accident?

MARI: No—

STORM: That's good. Shit, you scared me. God, you don't want my

153

grandmother getting mixed up in any of this. She would just skin me alive. My Granny is not someone you want to fuck with. No. I'd rather be stuck in a bar with some horny mechanics than deal with Granny when she's mad. She always did things her own way. She had her own way of telling Little Red Riding Hood. Little Red wasn't a nambypamby, lavender and lace type, in her version, no, she saw the wolf for who he was right off. So when she asks the wolf, "My what big eyes you have, Granny," and the wolf answers back, "The better to see you with," Little Red doesn't miss a beat—she grabs the wolf by the throat, jabs her fingers in the wolf's eyes. Then she drags him out of bed and beats the living shit out of him. That's the way my grandmother told mother goose.

MARI: My father always said that Korean stories made more sense than American ones. They were more realistic he said.

STORM: I'm not Korean.

MARI: Okay.

STORM: No one ever told me who my parents were. I don't need to know. Look I've taken enough of your time.

She tries to get up, winces in pain,sits down again.

Shit! *(Pause.)* You know, in Little Red Riding Hood...the grandmother—she doesn't make it does she?

Scene 6

Garage. Morning. Jimmy and Mick are having breakfast. Jimmy eats his usual kimchee/beer/rice combo, Mick is eating a bowl of cereal. Suddenly Mick has a revelation.

MICK: Amino acids! I finally figured out how we can take the animals. We just take the essential amino acids along and then whenever we feel like it, we can regenerate the animals we can build them up from their DNA structure.

JIMMY: What do you know about amino acids?

MICK: I just read about them. Your sister is probably more knowledgeable in this area. Maybe we can ask her.

JIMMY: You ask her.

MICK: She's your sister.

JIMMY: She wouldn't listen to me.

MICK: No? Why is it that you don't seem to like each other?

JIMMY: I like my sister.

MICK: She doesn't like you.

JIMMY: She doesn't have to, she's my sister. Come on, let's get to work.

MICK: So no amino acids?

JIMMY: Where did you get this idea anyway?

MICK: I was in the supermarket checkout line. It was a long line, so I picked up this magazine on display there. This article was about how some scientist believed that life started from this primordial soup, this pool of broth that had DNA, amino acids, just the basic building blocks, and then life just kind of happened when electricity hit it. That's what they believe anyway. I couldn't finish the article because this stockboy was throwing vegetables at everyone and nearly caused a race riot.

JIMMY: I have a better idea. I've been thinking about how this engine should be powered. We need a special kind of fuel. Fusion, gas, none of it will work. This has been a mystery to me, because this mechanical element ties in with the spiritual element of the journey. And finally it hit me, the light bulb went off in my brain: emotional loss.

MICK: Emotional loss?

JIMMY: Yeah. It runs on emotional loss.

MICK: How?

JIMMY: I'm leaving that to you.

MICK: Does that mean we're going to be depressed on this whole trip?

JIMMY: It just means...look, it's all based on entropy. Harnessing the energy of emotional breakdown. It makes sense if you think about it.

MICK: How do you expect me to do any of this? Tell me that. Emotional loss. And why is everything so destructive with you? I think it's all that foul cabbage you eat. It warps your brain.

JIMMY: What do you think that primordial soup tasted like, Mick?

MICK: I don't know.

JIMMY: I bet it tasted good.

MICK: Yeah? Like minestrone?

JIMMY: Clam chowder.

MICK: Red or white?

JIMMY: Red.

MICK: You're making me hungry. I finally placed your face. You used to work at the supermarket. You were that crazy stockboy. What was that all about anyway?

JIMMY: You really want to know?

MICK: Please.

JIMMY: Bananas.

MICK: Bananas?

JIMMY: Yeah, bananas.

MICK: I see.

Scene 7

Porch. Mari has set up a makeshift hospital bed. She has just finished bandaging Storm's leg.

STORM: *(Grimacing.)* I need something.

MARI: You sure?

STORM: Yeah. It hurts...

MARI: Take these.

Storm swallows some pills, with water.

STORM: Thanks.

MARI: Just sit back and sleep for awhile.

STORM: You'll tell me if my bike happens along, won't you?

MARI: Of course.

STORM: Thanks.

Storm slowly falls asleep. Mari stares at her. She opens her medical book again.

MARI: *(Reading.)* "The medical student must learn to suppress the desire to ask too many questions. As a doctor there is a great danger in becoming too emotionally involved with one's patient. Empathy can only create a dangerous situation for the doctor. It will cloud the doctor's thought processes. It will in some cases lead to disaster."

Mari shuts the book. She takes a matchbook out and lights the medical book on fire. As the book catches fire, she kisses Storm very lightly on the forehead. She watches the book burn.

Mick enters.

MICK: Your book is on fire.

MARI: I know.

MICK: Don't you want to put it out?

MARI: Let it burn. It makes me feel good.

MICK: I see why you and Jimmy are related. He needs your help. He's beginning to crack.

MARI: Crack?

MICK: He's got some crazy idea for his engine now. *(Seeing Storm.)* Who's that?

MARI: A friend.

MICK: She looks like you.

MARI: How?

MICK: Well...it's just...I didn't mean it like...forget it.

MARI: Why do you think my brother is cracking?

MICK: He's making it run off of emotional loss.

MARI: Sounds like my brother.

MICK: Are all Koreans like you?

MARI: Are all mechanics like you?

MICK: No, I'm serious. I remember I used to watch that t.v. show, you know the one with Hawkeye and Klinger, that crazy crossdresser...

MARI: *M*A*S*H*?

MICK: That's it, and in that show, you people always seemed so, so—

MARI: So what?

MICK: Nice.

MARI: Nice?

MICK: Yeah, nice.

MARI: My parents were from Korea. I was born here. Just so you know.

MICK: Oh get off your high horse. My grandparents were from Germany. You don't see me having crazy dreams, burning my books, building boats out of Volkswagens.

MARI: Let's drop the subject.

MICK: It's dropped.

MARI: I hear you really like cars.

MICK: Sure I like them. I prefer trucks actually.

MARI: I hear you really like them.

MICK: I'm a mechanic, what do you expect? *(Moving to the fire.)* Do you mind if I put this out? *(He puts the fire out somewhat gingerly.)*

MARI: If you have so many doubts, why are you going on this trip?

MICK: I thought if I went along with him, I would learn something. I thought I could become...a better person.

MARI: And are you?

MICK: I don't know yet.

MARI: It's still not raining.

MICK: Oh, it's going to rain.

MARI: You're certain about this?

MICK: My leg's been hurting. It always knows when rain is coming.

MARI: Should I trust your leg?

MICK: My legs are very trustworthy. I have metal in mine.

MARI: You're a tin man. Are you looking for a heart?

MICK: Are you Dorothy?

MARI: I don't have any red shoes. And I don't live in Kansas.

They laugh.

I once thought the only thing that mattered was my music. I practised day in and day out. I thought I was above everyone else. I was a musician, an artist. Then I lost my gift suddenly. It was like a curtain fell from eyes. I suddenly saw that my brother didn't talk to my father and vice versa. I saw that I had never known my mother. I saw I saw I saw. I saw that my brother had a talent for hurting everybody around him, most of all, himself. And so I tried to do something different I tried to become a doctor. And the crazy thing is, my brother was responsible for all of that.

MICK: How do you mean?

MARI: He...just did things. An idea would come into his head and he wouldn't stop and think about it, he would just go ahead and act it out.

MICK: Internal combustion. The process by which a car burns fuel. The hydrogen bonds in the gasoline are destroyed, releasing energy. That's your brother alright.

MARI: And what about the rest of us?

MICK: I guess we're the fuel.

Scene 8

Focus switches back and forth between garage and porch. Later in the day. Jimmy is under the car. Mick is pacing around the car, clearly upset.

MICK: You told her. I can't believe you told her. That was a secret. That was like a code of honor, between men. And you broke that.

JIMMY: *(Sliding out from under car.)* What are you talking about?

MICK: Your sister. You told her.

JIMMY: About what?

MICK: Bessie.

JIMMY: Bessie?

MICK: My truck.

JIMMY: I did not.

MICK: Then why was she insinuating things? She was saying, "Mick, you like trucks don't you? You really like trucks." It was like she thought I was some kind of a pervert.

JIMMY: I didn't tell her anything.

MICK: Who else did then? The fucking mailman? You were the only one I told.

JIMMY: Okay, I may have made an offhand remark.

MICK: Like what?

JIMMY: Oh, I don't know, something like, like, uh...

MICK: I'm listening.

JIMMY: Like...uh...like—

MICK: LIKE WHAT?

JIMMY: Like "Mick fucks trucks."

MICK: "Like 'Mick fucks trucks'?" I can't believe—that's not even true! I told you I never did that! How could you tell her that?

JIMMY: I'm sorry.

MICK: Now your sister's going to tell her friends, their friends are going to tell their friends, and pretty soon the tv crews will be here, waving their cameras in my face.

JIMMY: It was just a figure of speech.

MICK: "Mick fucks trucks," is not a figure of speech! I trusted you too.

He picks up the jar of kimchee, threatens to heave it.

JIMMY: Put it down.

MICK: No! *(Mick opens the jar, but takes one eye-opening whiff...)* Oh my God...

Jimmy takes the jar away. He starts eating.

JIMMY: Look, I'll even set things straight with my sister. I'll do it right now.

He goes to the "door". Yells to Mari offstage.

Hey Mari! Mick does not fuck trucks! *(To Mick.)* There? Is that better?

Mick stands to the side, still angry.

You know what I think? You're afraid.

MICK: *(Show his fingernails, which are black.)* See that? That's built in grease. Doesn't wash out. Ever. I am a real mechanic. So don't give me any bullshit about me being scared. I could make your engine run off of fucking yogurt if I wanted to.

JIMMY: *(Beat.)* Really?

Lights crossfade to porch scene. Storm and Mari.

STORM: I had a very strange dream. As I was flying through the air over my bike, the windshield on that pickup truck, it became different, something soft, like skin and so when I hit it, it didn't hurt, and when I looked up I saw the face of the person driving the car...and it was you.

MARI: Me?

STORM: What does that mean?

MARI: You've gone through a very traumatic event. I have some bad news. I got a call from the hospital today. The other person in the accident...she passed away.

STORM: Oh.

MARI: I thought you would like to know.

STORM: I'm glad...you told me. Did this other person suffer?

MARI: I don't think so.

STORM: It's funny, isn't it. I was the one on the motorcycle. She was in a truck. I was the one who should have died.

MARI: No one should have died.

STORM: There's always a victim in an accident.

MARI: You're a victim too.

STORM: I always survive, Doc. How about you?

MARI: I survive too.

STORM: You have to. You're the doctor.

MARI: Please, call me Mari.

STORM: Okay, Mari, when can I walk?

MARI: Soon. Hopefully.

STORM: That smell this morning...that was kimchee, wasn't it?

MARI: Yes.

STORM: I like it.

> *Lights crossfade to garage scene. Mick has fashioned a large funnel on top of the engine. Jimmy looks at it.*

JIMMY: What the hell is that supposed to be?

MICK: You wanted an emotional loss engine, well, here it is.

JIMMY: How does it work?

MICK: You just stick things into this funnel, and then it runs.

JIMMY: You sure?

MICK: Let's put something into it and try it out.

> *They look around the garage. They look at each other.*

JIMMY: I don't really have anything. How about you?

MICK: It's your car, you should provide the fuel.

JIMMY: I don't have anything.

MICK: Nothing?

JIMMY: Just memories.

MICK: You have to have something.

JIMMY: Like what?

MICK: A photograph, a book, something.

JIMMY: I used to have some paintings. But I burned them.

MICK: What about your sister? Does she have something we could use?

JIMMY: She wouldn't give me anything like that.

MICK: How about this jar of kimchee?

JIMMY: No.

MICK: Just a piece?

JIMMY: No.

MICK: Why are you being so difficult?

JIMMY: Because...I'm a difficult person.

160

Scene 9

Light and sound suggests a dream, or an awful memory. We see Mari kneeling on the ground, Jimmy standing above her. They are younger, both in their teens.

JIMMY: I said, put your hands out on the floor.

MARI: But why?

JIMMY: Because I said so.

MARI: You're going to hurt me.

JIMMY: I am not.

MARI: Then why do I have to put my hands out?

JIMMY: You have to trust me.

MARI: Trust?

JIMMY: Yes.

She places her hands on the ground. With a swift movement, Jimmy steps on them. Mari yells out in pain.

JIMMY: Be quiet.

MARI: You said I should trust you.

JIMMY: One day, you'll understand.

MARI: I hate you.

JIMMY: I'm sorry.

MARI: You don't want me to play the piano, is that it?

JIMMY: I don't want you to leave me.

MARI: My hands hurt.

JIMMY: Let me hold them.

MARI: Don't touch me.

Scene 10

Night, on the porch. Storm is having a nightmare. Her words come out with very little control on her part.

STORM: *(Feverishly.)* Memory without a woman man life no meaning is is is without time meaning makes it with no lack loss the sky is so damn bright, where people, steep drop plunge down farewell goodbye only the woman no mother grandmother? Not dead, everyone dead yes, dead, yes, this shaking ground I walk every step a sinking please forgive don't forget old car driving now, flowers in the window little girl peeking over window broken glass everywhere so many faces. In the storm. Faceless. You got no face, no eyes. Burn my lips, break them. Grandma? *Halmuni?*

It begins to rain.

ACT TWO

Scene 1

Early morning. The garage is now the central part of the stage. In the dim morning light we see Jimmy and Mick asleep on the floor of the garage. The door bangs open noisily. Mari walks in, her clothes drenched and covered with mud. Her hands are covered in bright colors, like paints.

JIMMY: *(Barely awake.)* Mari?

MARI: Yeah?

JIMMY: It's raining.

MARI: Just a little.

JIMMY: No, a lot, it's raining a lot.

MARI: I was sitting out there. In the field. I wanted to listen to my thoughts. It was raining after all. Just like you said. And then I noticed that the dirt out there was oozing these—colors—this clay that had all these colors—I dropped my hands into it, this red and yellow and green—it's as if they were alive. But where did they come from?

JIMMY: Why are you looking at me?

MARI: I wanted to just find some ground I could attach myself to. And then this happened. I like these colors. Don't you?

JIMMY: I can't see them.

MARI: These colors—they remind me of those pictures that Mom did.

JIMMY: What pictures?

MARI: Those oil paintings. The cherries.

JIMMY: No—you must have dreamed that—I don't remember that. Your memory is too active—it makes things up.

MARI: I thought I saw him this morning. I thought I saw him shooting through this intersection, so I followed him, but he ran a red light and—

JIMMY: And what?

MARI: Then I saw Storm. I saw the accident. *(Beat.)* In that dream when you are up on the water...what happens then?

JIMMY: We...wait.

MARI: For what?

JIMMY: For things to change. For life to start fresh.

MARI: And how will that happen?

JIMMY: It will happen. On its own.

MARI: You still don't know where you're going?

JIMMY: The dream doesn't say.

MARI: I'm not asking the dream, I'm asking you. I think you know. You just don't want to tell your little sister.

162

JIMMY: You know that's not true.

Mick enters.

MICK: Have you ever taken a pee that gives you a whole new feeling about life?

Scene 2

Morning. Mari has fashioned a makeshift "table" around which she and Mick sit. A small kerosene lamp burns. They are drinking coffee. Jimmy is hammering away at the engine.

MARI: I thought you were a mechanic.

MICK: I already did the hard part. I built the engine.

MARI: It looks like a big wok.

MICK: He wanted an engine that runs off of loss. I tried to do what I could. But there's no fuel he said.

MARI: No fuel?

MICK: What does the word amino acid do for you?

MARI: It gives me hives. It makes me think of medical school and all those exams.

MICK: You've given it up?

MARI: For now.

MICK: That's a shame. We could benefit from your knowledge. I thought you could do some of the scientific work. You know, amino acids, DNA...

Storm comes in.

STORM: What does a person have to do around here to get a fucking cup of coffee?

MARI: Are you sure you should be up?

STORM: The rain was keeping me up anyway. *(Seeing Jimmy.)* You her brother?

Jimmy nods.

What's your name?

JIMMY: Jimmy R.

STORM: What does the R stand for?

JIMMY: Nothing.

MARI: It stands for Rodin.

STORM: That is so cool. Like Godzilla's arch enemy, right?

JIMMY: No.

STORM: Then who?

MARI: The sculptor.

STORM: Oh yeah? You an artist? *(Pause.)* I go by Storm.

MICK: As in the rain and thunder?

STORM: Yeah.

163

MICK: Hmm. The best kind.

STORM: Who's that?

JIMMY: That's Mick. He's a mechanic.

STORM: I can see that. What are you doing to that car?

MICK: We've modified the engine—we've made it run off of feelings. Because of the flood.

STORM: What are you talking about?

JIMMY: We're taking a trip.

STORM: Where to?

JIMMY: Don't know yet.

STORM: Sounds kind of dumb.

JIMMY: Haven't you ever just gone out on the road for a long ride?

STORM: Sure, but driving a car is like watching television.

JIMMY: I prefer horses personally.

MARI: Horses?

STORM: With horses there's too much shit. A bike's the best thing.

MICK: What kind of bike you ride?

STORM: It's black, like my eyes.

MICK: Big engine?

STORM: Feels like a F-16 when you ride it.

MICK: Well, is it a Honda? A Harley-Davidson?

STORM: It's a smooth ride, you understand? You forget the bike's even there.

JIMMY AND MICK: Must be a Honda.

STORM: I keep the chrome polished so that if I look down at the exhaust pipes when I'm on the road I can see the sky and trees, everything around me, reflected right there. My personal video unit.

JIMMY: You just said you hate television.

STORM: Not if it's my own show.

MICK: I own a pickup myself.

STORM: (Not listening.) And I've got these special mirrors on them so when I look back at the drivers I've just passed, I can see their faces.

MICK: It runs great. Pretty useful too.

STORM: I can tell if a couple's been fighting or even if they've just had a roll in the backseat.

MICK: If I roll the windows down I can get a great sense of speed actually.

STORM: Is it fast? Do you take it out and let 'er rip?

MICK: No...actually...speed scares me.

STORM: It's a damned Sony that you're driving. You imagine you're in some kind of sitcom while the cornfields race by at 17 miles per hour?

164

MICK: I thought you women like men who take their time.

STORM: For some things, yeah, but when it comes to driving, or leaving, it's best to just get the hell out! But where are you going?

JIMMY: We need to survive. That's what's important.

STORM: Survive what?

JIMMY: This flood.

STORM: Flood?

MARI: The flood.

JIMMY: There's a flood coming, haven't you noticed?

STORM: It's raining, sure, but there's no flood coming.

MICK: How do you know?

STORM: I just know. Anybody who's been on a farm for awhile knows how nature behaves. Don't you know anything Jiffy-Lube?

MICK: For me, a farm means shit. You wake up in the morning, you smell it, you go to bed at night, it's still there. And you got all your varieties: pig, horse, cow.

STORM: You scared of shit too?

MICK: I suppose you aren't scared of anything?

STORM: Actually, everything scares me. Except mechanics. They just make me laugh. (She laughs.)

MARI: You're feeling better.

STORM: I feel like I'm better. I don't have any bruises on my body or nothing. I feel like my body's good as new.

JIMMY: No one ever really gets healed. The wounds only get buried.

STORM: Your brother thinks he's one of those prophets in the Bible.

MICK: He is a prophet.

STORM: The question is, is he false or true?

JIMMY: I don't lie.

STORM: Have you seen my bike in any of your visions?

JIMMY: No.

STORM: Then what kind of prophet are you? How about you Goodwrench?

MICK: No, I haven't seen your bike.

STORM: You sure?

MICK: I am a mechanic.

JIMMY: This is a rain that will not be able to stop. It will just keep coming and coming. We will not be able to control the water. We will be overwhelmed and cleansed. I've been having these dreams for a year now. Dreams of rain, of Volkswagens floating. This flood that wipes this town, this house clean. I know it's going to happen. It has to happen. Doesn't it? You feel that don't you?

STORM: You know how I know this isn't going to be a real flood?

JIMMY: How?

STORM: There are no colors.

MICK: Colors?

STORM: When there's a real flood I see colors in the sky, or in the water, somewhere. I haven't seen any colors so far.

JIMMY: Who taught you all of this?

STORM: My grandmother.

JIMMY: Isn't she—

MARI: Jimmy!

STORM: Isn't she what?

JIMMY: Old?

STORM: She'd still kick the shit out of you.

MICK: You people are giving me the chills. All this dreaming and signs and floods. It's raining outside, we're making this Volkswagen float—what's the goddamn problem? Why can't you guys just let yourself be amazed?

STORM: It's not about being amazed. It's about seeing. That's all anyone can do with the weather. All those weathermen with their computers and satellites—it just comes down to seeing. Open your eyes.

JIMMY: That's funny. You talking about seeing. As far as I can tell, you don't see things either. You just see what you want to see.

STORM: Like what?

JIMMY: The way you behave.

STORM: How do I behave?

JIMMY: You pretend to be someone else.

STORM: Pretend to be who?

JIMMY: Someone else.

STORM: I know who I am.

JIMMY: I don't think you do.

STORM: And you know?

JIMMY: I think I know.

STORM: Tell me.

JIMMY: Look at yourself.

STORM: What about it?

JIMMY: You look like us.

STORM: I don't look like you.

JIMMY: You do.

STORM: Mick, do I look like him?

MICK: I don't know, he's a guy and you're a girl and—

STORM: Shut up! Mari, tell your brother he's out of line here.

MARI: Jimmy,

JIMMY: But I'm right.

MARI: That's not the point.

JIMMY: If that's not the point, then what is?

MARI: You shouldn't go around saying things like that. It's none of your business.

JIMMY: I can't believe you're falling for her game. It's all an act. The bike. The attitude. She's a fucking banana in a leather jacket!

MARI: Jimmy, what's your problem?

JIMMY: Who said there was a problem?

MARI: I say there's a problem when you're rude to my friends. Apologize to her.

JIMMY: What?

Mari picks up the exhaust pipe.

MARI: Apologize!

JIMMY: Storm, I'm sorry.

STORM: *(Seeing the exhaust pipe)* Wait a minute. This belonged to my bike. Oh, Jesus. Mari.

Storm picks up the pipe.

MARI: I can explain, this morning—

STORM: *(overlapping)* She's gone, isn't she? I hit her...and I was going fast...and...I didn't mean to hit her...you know? I didn't mean to.

God. Shit. God. Shit.

This belonged to my bike. What am I going to do?

MARI: Storm...I tried to tell you.

STORM: I know.

Mari holds her. Jimmy takes the exhaust pipe from Storm and puts it in the "engine". The engine turns over, then dies. They all stare at the car.

Scene 3

Mari is trying to wash her hands clean of the paint. Mick talks to her.

MICK: I really admire you.

MARI: What's to admire?

MICK: You're just so open...about everything. You aren't scared.

MARI: I am scared. I just don't let it bother me. Anyway, what are you so scared about? I've never met a mechanic like you. You're a bundle of nerves. Most mechanics I know are about as sensitive as a wrench.

MICK: I just have a lot of fears.

MARI: Like what?

MICK: Corn, mainly.

MARI: That's it?

MICK: It's a big one. You don't know what it's like to wake up every morning and see all that yellow and green staring you in the face. After we had a pile of it we would have to husk it all afternoon. Then we'd eat it for the next week. Every meal. I thought my skin would turn yellow. We gave the leftovers to the pigs and then that was another problem.

MARI: What problem?

MICK: All the corn, mixed with the pig's shit. One time I went out there into the fields with a friend of mine. And I got lost. No escape. My chest started to hurt. I couldn't breathe. My friend just left me there. All alone.

MARI: I was wondering if there was something else to your fear for corn. Whether it was the farm itself.

MICK: It's the corn, I tell you. Look around you, it's everywhere. If you close your eyes, you can still see it, you can still smell it. It's not a mystery—you don't need to have a vision to understand—there's just so much fucking yellow and green out here, it gets to you, you know, it just gets to you.

MARI: There's only one way to conquer your fears. You have to attack them. Stop running.

MICK: Yeah?

MARI: Just stop running.

Scene 4

Later that day. Mari and Storm sit in the car and talk.

STORM: I wanted to talk to her one last time. I thought I would just find my bike and go talk to her. Now I don't have her. I don't have anyone. Not even my bike.

MARI: Stop blaming yourself.

STORM: She drives too fast. I always told her that. And her eyesight was going on her.

MARI: It was an accident.

STORM: No, it wasn't, I must be doing something wrong in my life. I believe in fate. And punishment. I've done something wrong to deserve this. Maybe your brother's right. I'm escaping something. What's that on your hands?

MARI: It's paint.

STORM: Those colors.

MARI: I know.

STORM: Maybe there will be a flood.

MARI: I hope not.

STORM: A flood? Is that what I need? Something to cleanse me?

MARI: There's not going to be any flood.

STORM: But those colors.

MARI: This is just paint.

STORM: Where did it come from?

MARI: The ground.

STORM: You're kidding.

MARI: No.

STORM: That's even worse.

MARI: Why?

STORM: Color from the ground—that means the earth is upset—she's bleeding.

MARI: Upset about what?

STORM: Us. She's upset about us.

MARI: But I didn't even do anything. She should be upset at my father. Or my brother, or cars, or machines, or hospitals. Not me. I haven't done anything to anyone.

Scene 5

Mari is handing him tools as he works under the car.

JIMMY: Hex wrench.

Mari hands him a wrench.

No, the bigger one.

She hands him another one.

Does this mean you're coming?

MARI: I guess so.

JIMMY: You could be happier about it.

MARI: Now that would be lying wouldn't it? *(Beat.)* You think we'll find him?

JIMMY: For the millionth time, I've told you this isn't about him. We just need to get the hell out of here. We're following his example. Can you give me some more light?

MARI: When you stepped on my hands...did you know what you were doing?

JIMMY: Of course not.

MARI: Sometimes I could kill you for that.

JIMMY: I know.

MARI: I don't know why I don't.

JIMMY: I don't know either.

MARI: I burned my medical books.

JIMMY: That's stupid.

MARI: I don't want to be a doctor anymore.

JIMMY: What are you going to be?

MARI: A professional healer.

JIMMY: Like a faith healer?

MARI: No.

JIMMY: A therapist?

MARI: No. A healer. It's a new kind of job. Nothing destructive about it. No engines. No blood. No money. Just healing.

JIMMY: *(Wiping his hands.)* It's done. We can leave. I just have to wait.

MARI: For what?

JIMMY: The water. It has to come up to a certain level.

Scene 6

Jimmy stares out at the sky.

JIMMY: We have nothing. Our family was a ghost family. It looked and felt like a family. But it really wasn't there. It was this faded photograph. Black and white. Smudged. Grainy. If you looked too closely at the faces in it, you could see that everything was blurry. The shots were taken in Korea. The lens moved. A little. Or someone was in a hurry. Time, we never had any time. Everyone was working so hard. We were in such a rush to move on. To leave. To make it to the next day. That brighter next day. But we never looked hard at the day we had. And the photographs would get blurrier...and blurrier. Until finally all you had was dream pictures...faces that were ghosts.

Mari and Storm enter, drenched, clearly happy.

MARI: *(Singing.)* It's raining, it's pouring...

STORM: The old man is snoring.

MARI: Hey big brother, are you snoring?

JIMMY: What's gotten into you?

MARI: We're just happy. And we found something.

STORM: Someone.

JIMMY: Who?

STORM: Jack. Jack Daniels. *(She pulls out a bottle of whiskey.)* Want a sip?

JIMMY: No thanks.

STORM: Where's that lug-nut friend of yours?

JIMMY: He went out. Something about corn.

STORM: Oh God. Where'd you find him anyway?

JIMMY: Yellow pages.

STORM: What'd you look under, "Emotionally Disturbed Mechanics"?

MARI: You like him, don't you?

STORM: Too much of an oil-can.

MARI: He's a tin-man.

STORM: Looking for corn.

MARI: You hungry?

STORM: Starved.

MARI: Jimmy, what do we have?

JIMMY: Just the usual.

MARI: Okay. Storm, how do you feel about rice and kimchee?

STORM: Hey, I'll try anything. I need to prove to JR here that I'm open to Korean food I guess.

Mari sets the table with 3 bowls, serves food.

JIMMY: *(To Storm.)* So it's still raining isn't it?

STORM: Heavily.

MARI: I think it's letting up.

STORM: We washed Mari's hands.

JIMMY: How'd you do it?

MARI: The rain.

JIMMY: See, this is a magical rain.

MARI: Some people call it acid rain.

Jimmy starts to eat.

STORM: Don't you people say grace first?

JIMMY: *(Stopping.)* Uhh, sure.

STORM: Lord, bless this house, these people in it. Bless this rain that it may bring us food and happiness. Bless those who have left us, bless those of us left...who must deal with their pain. Amen.

MARI: That was beautiful.

STORM: This is spicy.

MARI: You like it?

STORM: I do.

MARI: *(To Jimmy.)* See, maybe she's Korean after all.

STORM: You guys are really hung up on being Korean aren't you? It's like bikers. We look down on the rest of the world. All the station-wagons, the trucks, the mini-vans. We know that deep down we're better than everyone else.

MARI: I don't think we're better than anyone else.

JIMMY: But there's a bond there. A secret code.

MARI: Storm says I should come along.

STORM: It's like one big fucking family.

171

MARI: Jimmy, my hands are clean. Don't they look nice? I just realized something when I looked at my hands in the rain. These hands of mine are strong. They endured a lot of things. They can still do things. Can still make things.

Mick comes in from the rain, covered with mud and brightly colored paint.

JIMMY: Mick. Where did you go?

MICK: *(Breathless.)* I was trying to get used to it. It's about time I faced up to all that corn, I told myself. Just like Mari said.

JIMMY: Mari?

MICK: So I waded into it as far as I could go. Pretty soon I felt lost. The same old feelings. Disoriented. Yellow and green on all sides of me, like I was held captive. Then I see the colors. Oozing out of the ground. So I start digging. These colors start flying with the dirt. They splatter all over the corn. Now it's not just yellow and green. It's red and blue and white and black. I can't stand it. It's too much. This is making me so happy— goddamn it—and then I find this.

Mick pulls a muddy oil painting from his jacket that had been folded up. It appears to be an old still life. He unfolds it and shows them.

STORM: It's a painting. One of your's Jimmy?

Mari takes the painting in her hands.

MARI: A year becomes a minute becomes a second becomes a lifetime.

JIMMY: You found all of this out there?

MARI: This was a painting that I would write long entries in my diary about. I would try to know my mother through this painting. And all along it was just laying out there under all that mud. All that corn. I thought I had only dreamed about it, but it's real. Why didn't you ever tell me?

JIMMY: Tell you what?

MARI: That you had this?

JIMMY: I don't know how it got there.

MARI: Yes you do.

JIMMY: I don't know.

MARI: I'm going out there. *(Beat.)* I want to see if it really is flooding.

Scene 7

Sometime later that night. Storm stands at doorway looking out. Mick testing the batteries of the car. Jimmy sits, stonefaced, staring at Mick.

MICK: Maybe someone should go look for her. Jimmy?

JIMMY: The water is going to come up soon.

STORM: It's true, it is raining a lot more than I had thought.

JIMMY: You never get everything to work out. Just some things.

172

STORM: You think she's coming back?

JIMMY: Yeah. She probably will. Is the water getting higher?

STORM: It's high.

Scene 8

Later, that same night. Storm, Mick and Jimmy are sleeping. Mari walks back in. Jimmy opens his eyes.

JIMMY: Hi!

MARI: I walked all through the fields, up and down the road. You know, walking is much better than driving. You can think about things. You really see things. The rain falling. The water beading to the stalks of corn. The feel of the drops as they run down your face walking through water.

JIMMY: *(Getting up.)* You should sit down.

MARI: No. You sit.

Jimmy sits.

Now talk.

JIMMY: Talk?

MARI: Yes.

JIMMY: You want me to start from the beginning?

MARI: That would help.

JIMMY: I don't know where to start.

MARI: Anywhere. Start anywhere.

JIMMY: Okay. This is my first memory. I see myself as a little kid running in from the back and knocking over her easel, spilling the paints everywhere. Instead of getting upset... Is this what you want?

MARI: Don't stop.

JIMMY: Instead of getting upset, she looks at the mess I made on the canvas and says, "Son, you're a born artist." I said, "Mom, why are you leaving us? Where are you going?" She couldn't explain she said. She tried, but she stopped. Her face is wet. She goes and kisses my baby sister. Mari. You. I didn't understand. "Mom, you're coming back, aren't you? You are aren't you?" The door shuts. I hear the car drive away. My father doesn't look at me. Only Mari looks at me. She doesn't know what's happened. And I think, isn't that the best thing? Why should she know any of this?

MARI: No, why should she? She's the baby sister after all. She should just be cute, the baby of the family. We're a family of leavers, aren't we? We leave Korea. Then we leave each other. And Dad?

JIMMY: He just took off. I think he was just sick of seeing me everyday. I was a walking monument to his failures.

MARI: Why didn't he come talk to me?

JIMMY: He was ashamed.

MARI: Ashamed?

JIMMY: He wanted to do things for you. But he thought maybe you and I were better off together. And he knew that he had to leave. For his own good.

MARI: Did you talk to him?

JIMMY: No. He did leave me something though. This note. *(He unfolds a piece of paper.)* "Remember to forget."

MARI: Remember to forget? That's all it says? I've been driving for miles and miles so that I can get a note that says "Remember to forget"?

JIMMY: I drove him away. He saw what happened.

MARI: Saw what happen?

JIMMY: The hunting accident.

MARI: That was years ago.

JIMMY: So what, it seems like it just happened yesterday. It wasn't an accident.

MARI: What was it then?

    Silence.

JIMMY: You think I really went out to hunt? I don't like hunting. I don't like killing things. He saw the whole thing. He knew all along that I was lying about it.

MARI: So he didn't forgive you for that?

JIMMY: No.

MARI: Jimmy, it's not your fault. It's just like you saw it in your head. The Volkswagen. The flood. Because that's the beauty of dreams. They're based on hope. They're based on maybe things changing from what they are today. From what they really are. You see yourself doing things you wouldn't do. You see a strange face. A car floating. Rain. *(Beat.)* Jimmy, they left because they could. Mom and Dad left because…they could.

    Water starts to seep across the floor of the garage.

    Mick and Storm wake up.

MAR: *(To Jimmy.)* You should be happy. All your dreams have come true. But I need to follow the family tradition. I have to leave too.

JIMMY: You can't do that.

MARI: Yes, Jimmy, I can. And I am. This family…it needs to be put to rest. It's an idea that's had it's day. Now we need to do something new.

STORM: Mari, you need company?

MARI: Love some.

STORM: What about you Mick?

MICK: I'm not going anywhere.

Mari gives him the painting.

MARI: Here, you can use this for your engine.

JIMMY: No, you keep it.

MARI: I don't want it. This has nothing to do with me anymore. Your dreams are not my dreams.

JIMMY: You're my sister. All we have is each other. We should hang on to that.

MARI: *Oppah.* Jimmy.

JIMMY: I'm sorry.

MARI: Yeah. *(To Storm.)* Storm?

STORM: I'm ready.

They exit. Long silence. Jimmy walks around the floor for awhile. He looks into the engine. He picks up the painting. He goes to the car and opens the oil-cloth in front of him. He stares at the painting. Mick opens the jar of kimchee. He starts eating a piece. He starts eating another piece. He sits down next to Jimmy.

Long silence.

Mick continues to chew and eat. Jimmy takes the painting and places it in the engine. It roars to life, glowing with a surreal and bright light. Jimmy and Mick look at each other. They smile. They get into the car.

The engine revs. Blackout.

EPILOGUE

As in the opening scene of the Prologue. Mari and Jimmy begin to speak, sometimes simultaneously, sometimes as echoes of each other.

MARI: The stories really matter don't they? I still have my memories.

And they live in me, like those wild flowers you see by the road. Those flowers survive even the most vicious storms.

You see them by the road, their colors get more bright in the rain. The water makes—

JIMMY: A brush. You start with a brush.

Paint. Rich and black.

See how it thickens near the brush? You have to control it.

the colors seem more vivid when the brush is wet—

MARI (cont'd): from the rain and the petals
      drip with what has newly fallen
      to the earth, small drops—

                              JIMMY (cont'd): of paint, which are to be
                                    avoided in the beginning
                                    if at all—

Possible. And you look out past   Possible. Watch the
road, the fields, you see   canvas carefully,
the infinite line of the land   imagine it as more than that,
against the clouds.   add depth to it,
Uhm-mah. Uhm-mah,   wrap the cloth around
play with me,   your eye, and paint
put your brush down   all the colors you see.
put your brush down.   From violet to red.

      They freeze. The lights fade.
      End of play.

HEIDI SCHRECK is a playwright and actor living in Brooklyn. Her other plays include *Creature, Backwards into China, The Boy Who Is a Bird,* and *Mr. Universe.* Her work has been produced by Printer's Devil Theatre, Soho Rep, On the Boards, The Uno Festival, and Consolidated Works. She has studied playwriting with Mac Wellman and Chuck Mee, Jr. and is a graduate of the 2005-2006 Soho Rep Writer/ Director Lab. As an actor, Heidi has originated roles in new plays by David Adjmi, Deron Bos, Sheila Callaghan, Erin Courtney, Bret Fetzer and Juliet Waller Pruzan, Kristen Kosmas, Kip Fagan, and Anne Washburn. She has also performed with Soho Rep, Target Margin, Playwrights Horizons, Two-Headed Calf, and Clubbed Thumb in NYC and in Seattle with the Empty Space, Sgt.Rigsby and his Amazing Silouhettes, New City Theatre, On The Boards and Printer's Devil Theatre, of which she is a founding member. She played the title role in Paul Willis's 2003 film version of *Hedda Gabler* and appears in Meredith Drum's film *The Pillow.* Heidi is currently a company member with both 2HC and Vinegar Tom Players in NYC.

Heidi Schreck

STRAY

SETTING:
A city. The present.

CHARACTERS:
Isa
May
Ellie
Girl
Frank

ACT ONE: THE NEW LIFE

1. Morning. *Isa is late for her new job. May follows her around like a dog.*

MAY: My tongue slides. Sometimes I can't understand anything I'm saying.

ISA: It doesn't mean you're pregnant.

MAY: Sometimes I can't talk at all. And sometimes I talk, but the things I say. I had this dream, Isa. I wish—.

ISA: What do you wish?

MAY: She was a girl and the dream—. We were holding each other. It was warm. And in the dream, I don't know.

ISA: You're not finishing your sentences. You need to do that. May, are you all right? Do you want breakfast?

MAY: No. I want my dream, to tell you what my dream.

ISA: It doesn't mean you're pregnant.

MAY: Isa—. In this dream. Every inch. In this dream all of our parts were touching. Even though she was so much smaller than I am. And we were smooth as two peeled stones. Or like otters. Yes. We were rolling otters in a warm. In a sea. I want to tell you about this dream because.

ISA: May.

MAY: She told me her name and no. I told her HER name, what I thought was her name and she said no. And she said, my name is—. And she told me her name. And I said, your name is—. And I said her name.

ISA: May you're not pregnant!

MAY: Pah. Shit. Tongue. My tongue.

Isa hands May something to vomit into. May Vomits. Isa holds her head.

ISA: You should eat something now.

MAY: My tongue slides when she's talking to me. I don't understand anything I'm saying.

ISA: It's because you don't finish your sentences.

Isa grabs her lunch and exits. Music comes from the floor. May looks around confused, and then slowly presses her ear to the floor. Lights change.

2. Later that night. *May sleeps with her ear still pressed to the floor. Isa speaks from the hallway.*

ISA: You can come back if you can't find anyone else to take you, you can come back. Where is your home? Don't you have a home? I would take you now but I'm allergic. You can come back though, don't worry, but please, first go and try to find your home. Try to find it. Try to find your home. *(to May)* I think I misled that cat. I led that cat on. I made that cat think this was its home. May?

The lights go out.

The lights went out.

The lights go back on.

The lights are now back on. May, are you awake?

MAY: Do you hear this noise coming from the floor?

ISA: I don't hear anything.

MAY: Someone is crying. It's coming from the floor.

Isa puts her ear to the floor.

ISA: It's music. It's music from that bar.

Isa walks slowly toward the door.

3. Enter Ellie. *An hour later. May sleeps on the daybed. Isa has brought home Ellie, a friend she met at the bar. Ellie's clothes are purposeful. She wears a hat. They stand uncomfortably for a moment until Ellie notices May.*

ELLIE: Do you live with someone?

ISA: No. Yes. Yes I do. I'm sorry I don't know why I said no.

ELLIE: Who is she?

ISA: What? Oh, she's my sister. Her name is May.

ELLIE: Oh. I thought you lived with someone—

ISA: What? Yes I do— .

ELLIE: She's your sister.

ISA: Yes, but she lives here.

Pause

ELLIE: It must be a big change living in the city.

ISA: What? I'm sorry you said that so quietly.

ELLIE: Do you like living in the city?

ISA: Do I look out of place?

ELLIE: You look like a foreigner.

ISA: I've thought about cutting my hair.

ELLIE: You shouldn't.

ISA: We'll see. *(Pause.)* Would you like water? Or juice?

ELLIE: Juice, I guess.

ISA: There's something unpleasant about someone starting a new life isn't there?

ELLIE: Yes. Maybe. Were you married? Is that why you left?

ISA: Where I come from, I'm past the age. I'm almost 29. Or 30. Are you married?

ELLIE: No. No. You don't know? 29 or 30?

ISA: It depends on who my mother wanted my father to be. Do you want ice?

ELLIE: In my juice?

ISA: Oh no, of course not. Well, sometimes I have ice in my juice—.

ELLIE: Do you look like your mother or your father?

ISA: What? Oh, I look like my mother. She's dead.

ELLIE: She was beautiful.

ISA: I'm not sure. Yes, she was. Thank you. I don't want you to misunderstand me. I walked into that bar and I saw you and you looked nice. You seemed like a warm person, a person I would like to talk to. And I don't like to talk to people often. Often I'm silent. I feel foolish now. Do you understand anything I'm saying?

ELLIE: I don't understand, but I don't mind.

ISA: I didn't know what kind of bar that was. I think I'll just sit down for a moment. I like you. You talk softly I like that. I'm sorry I'm just talking and talking.

ELLIE: How could have known what kind of bar it was?

ISA: I just needed some whiskey.

ELLIE: Sure.

ISA: When we were little, May and I sometimes pretended to be nuns, we took vows of silence. I was good at it. I could go for three full days without saying a word. When we were nuns, we ran around the yard in our mother's nightgowns with towels tied around our heads. I don't know why I'm talking now.

ELLIE: I like it when other people talk. I like it when you talk.

Silence.

ISA: It's almost light.

ELLIE: Mmmmmmm.

ISA: She's having a child. She's going to have a child.

ELLIE: Where's the father?

ISA: He's back there. I was supposed to move here alone.

ELLIE: Really? What happened?

ISA: The night before I left, I had a little party to say goodbye to all of my friends, and to May. She gave me a marble as a going away present, a green cat's eye she'd stolen from me when we were kids. I cried and told her how much I would miss her. And then when I arrived at the train station the next morning, there she was, waiting for me. She didn't even have a suitcase.

ELLIE: You didn't tell her to go back home?

ISA: No.

ELLIE: Could I have a little more juice? I'm so thirsty.

ISA: Of course.

ELLIE: I don't look spongy do I?

ISA: No, I don't think so.

ELLIE: I'm kind of hungover.

Isa brings the juice.

Why did she leave him?

ISA: I don't know. Before she left, she cut off pieces of her hair, though, and left it on the doorsteps of the people she loved. Even people she was only fond of, or thought she might someday have become fond of. She scattered her clothes in the street and all of the comic books she'd collected since childhood.

ELLIE: She didn't really want to leave.

ISA: She wanted to leave traces.

Silence. Isa lights a cigarette. She looks intently at Ellie.

ELLIE: What are you thinking? You aren't going to write some kind of poem about me are you?

ISA: I was thinking that there's something unconvincing about you.

ELLIE: Really?

ISA: I think it's your clothes.

ELLIE: What is?

ISA: I think those aren't your clothes, I don't buy it.

ELLIE: No, they're my clothes.

ISA: They're unconvincing. For one thing, they're way too big. And why the hat?

ELLIE: These are my clothes, this is how I dress! That hat was a gift.

ISA: Is it true you sing in that bar? I saw your picture on the wall. Is it true that you sing?

ELLIE: Yes, I do. Why are you laughing? Why are you laughing?

ISA: I don't know.

Ellie takes a drag of Isa's cigarette and hands it back to her.

ELLIE: Do you still want to kiss me?

ISA: Did you think I wanted to before?

ELLIE: Are you worried about how my mouth will taste now, because of the cigarette?

ISA: It was my cigarette.

ELLIE: My mouth is usually sweet. I often use a refreshing spray after I smoke.

ISA: Oh.

ELLIE: We probably shouldn't be smoking, anyway.

ISA: What? *(looking at May)* Oh. Oh God. No. No we shouldn't.

Isa puts out her cigarette.

ELLIE: Could I touch your face?

ISA: I don't know. Yes.

Ellie walks over to Isa and gently touches her face.

ELLIE: You can close your eyes.

Isa does not close her eyes.

ISA: This is awkward.

Ellie touches Isa's face tenderly.

4. Two weeks later. *Darkness. A song.*

ELLIE: Do not take yourself by the hand...
Do not lead yourself across the river...
Do not point a finger at yourself...

Morning. light reveals Ellie, Isa and May sitting together at the table. May watches Ellie carefully.

ELLIE: *(still singing)* Or tell fairy tales about yourself...
Go on, go on – and stumble.
It's a lullaby.

ISA: I have to go to work. *(Pause.)* Well, goodbye. I'll be home for lunch.

Ellie kisses Isa. Isa exits. May looks at Ellie.

ELLIE: You have good eyes.

MAY: I have a boyfriend.

Ellie laughs.

ELLIE: You do? Does he live here?

MAY: No.

ELLIE: Oh. Do you miss him?

183

MAY: Yes, I do. He has his own house. I lived there with him before we moved here. I lived with him in his house.

ELLIE: I miss someone too. Do you know what I do when I miss this person too much?

MAY: No.

ELLIE: You think I know a secret, but I don't. I go crazy when I miss this person. I want God to take everything out of me and give me a new heart.

MAY: Well he won't. It's not going to happen.

ELLIE: No, it won't happen.

MAY: Anyway, now you like my sister.

ELLIE: Yes, I like your sister.

MAY: That's good. A lot of people don't like her.

ELLIE: Oh?

MAY: But I'm happy that you like her.

ELLIE: What's your boyfriend's name?

MAY: Frank. I left him though, so he's not really my boyfriend.

ELLIE: But you still miss him?

MAY: I miss his house.

ELLIE: Oh.

MAY: Sometimes I think about it just sitting there after we're dead and it's like we never lived there at all. We might as well never have lived there.

ELLIE: Does he still live there?

MAY: I'm not sure. Sometimes I think I see him here, on the street, but of course it's never him. It never is. Sometimes I imagine it's him though. I imagine him on the streets of the city and it makes me laugh.

ELLIE: Why?

MAY: His funny walk in this city. His walk it would stick out. He would walk like this—carefully.

May walks like Frank.

He would be looking at everything with a funny look in his eye. He wouldn't know what to say to anybody. And if he went into a store he would just stand still in one of the aisles and stare at the shelves. And if I saw him in the store, at first I wouldn't recognize him. He would be walking down the aisle toward me and I would look at him but I wouldn't see, because he would be in the wrong place. I would never expect to see him there, and so I wouldn't. Until he got very close, and then I would see.

ELLIE: What would you see?

MAY: He would be wrong somehow. I would see that his teeth were rotten and how his shoulders slumped. I never saw that before.

ELLIE: Could you forgive him for it?

MAY: I couldn't say for sure until I saw him.

ELLIE: Oh, then you couldn't for sure. You've got to plan ahead for things like that. What are the rules of this house?

MAY: What do you mean?

ELLIE: I would like to take off my coat and lie in this patch of sun here. May I do you think?

MAY: Isa makes the rules. What are the rules at your house?

ELLIE: At my house I was not allowed to lie on the floor.

MAY: Was your father a minister?

ELLIE: No.

MAY: What about your house now?

ELLIE: I don't have a house.

MAY: I mean apartment.

ELLIE: I don't have one.

MAY: Could I wear your hat?

ELLIE: Sure you don't even have to ask.

MAY: Look, you're half in shade already.

ELLIE: That's time passing.

MAY: It's going to come to me soon. I'd better keep your hat on. Light hurts my eyes.

ELLIE: I feel easy here.

MAY: Sure if you don't have any place else to go.

ELLIE: I don't need another place to go.

MAY: You can't live here. There isn't enough room here.

ELLIE: Isa says you're going on assistance.

MAY: It fell through.

ELLIE: Well, in any case, you can't keep living off of her.

MAY: Who says that I live off her?

ELLIE: You don't work do you?

MAY: I'm having a baby. I'm pregnant. I'm having a baby.

ELLIE: Well, whose problem is that?

MAY: You can't live here.

ELLIE: Isa loves me. She tries to love you but you are hard to love. You're like a black hole sucking up everything she gives and never giving anything back. You never remember her birthday. She tries to help you, but you ignore her. Lie to her. You're cruel to her when she doesn't deserve it. You make her feel like she's the one incapable of loving when really it's you. It's you. People like you are good at pretending to love. You have a light around you, a luminescence that people mistake for love. But it's not real. It's a dead light.

185

MAY: You don't know about me.

ELLIE: You make her feel like she doesn't care. Like she doesn't know how to love. You make her feel like that because that's what you need.

MAY: Get out of our apartment.

ELLIE: Do you want me to ask Isa? Do you want me to see what she says?

MAY: No.

ELLIE: I need my hat now.

5. May looks for a job. *Night. May, Isa, and Ellie. May is reading the newspaper.*

MAY: We are looking for a sharp journalist to lead our local news efforts in Alaska. That sounds like a good job for you, Isa. Anchorage offers world class entertainment, yet the adventurous spirit will find the wilderness in his backyard. And here are some cars for sale. When Frank comes we can buy a car.

ISA: Have you been writing to Frank?

MAY: Yes, but I don't send the letters.

ISA: I see.

ELLIE: Why don't you work in a restaurant?

MAY: My mother worked in a restaurant I don't want to work in a restaurant

ISA: May, we have enough money. I don't think you should work for a while.

ELLIE: I could ask about a job in the bar.

MAY: I don't want to work in a bar.

ELLIE: I love working in the bar.

> *(Singing)* In my room lives a beautiful
> Slow black snake
> She is like me
> She is like me
> Just as lazy
> Just as cold

MAY: Don't sing. Why is she singing that? What does that song mean why is she singing that?

ISA: Ellie, please don't sing. May—

MAY: Does that song mean I'm lazy? I'm not lazy.

ISA: May, we'll find you something. Here give me the paper. I'll look for something.

ELLIE: Usually it cheers people up when I sing.

MAY: Pass me the front page, Isa. I'm going to read the newspaper.

ELLIE: I'm going to read my book then if no one is going to talk.

ISA: I'm circling the jobs I think you might like, May. I'm circling them.

MAY: Don't bother. I'm going out to find a job.

ISA: It's night. Where will you look for a job at night. May? May?

May exits.

ELLIE: I'm going to open the window. I'm going to let the night come in.

Ellie opens the window.

ISA: I'm going to work. I haven't worked in days. It's a strange smell. The smell of the night.

ELLIE: I like it.

ISA: How can it smell so strong? Like a person or an animal. Are you cold?

ELLIE: Let me hold you. Like this. I can feel the night on my face, thick like fur. It's filling up the room. I can taste it. It tastes like dirt. When I was in the first grade I played a child in the school play, a child who dies and is buried in the dirt. I lay still with my arms like this, and around me all the other children cried. As I lay there, I pretended that I wasn't really dead, that I had been buried alive. I like the feel of dirt on my face. I like its smell.

ISA: What a terrible play for children.

ELLIE: We were not like children. We were like old men and women. I am not like other people, I'm not.

ISA: I know.

ELLIE: Isa, are you okay?

ISA: I think I'm allergic to something in the air.

ELLIE: I'll shut the window.

Ellie shuts the window.

There. You're allergic to the night, Isa. Don't you think that's funny?

ISA: I should work.

ELLIE: Don't work, don't work.

ISA: I have to.

ELLIE: Don't work. Don't work. Don't work. Don't work.

6. Isa sleepwalks. *A week later. Grey and glimmery. Isa crawls into May's arms like a child. May wakes and looks at her.*

MAY: Are you sleeping?

ISA: No.

MAY: You are sleeping.

ISA: No.

MAY: Is your name Isa?

ISA: No.

MAY: Yes you are, you're sleeping. And I know what you see: Field of corn, early morning farmhouse—.

ISA: I'm not sleeping.

187

Isa wakes.

Where am I now?

MAY: You're sleeping.

ISA: No. I'm awake. Where am I now?

MAY: You must have been walking in your sleep. You crawled in bed with me. Into this black hole with me.

ISA: Stop that. I feel sick.

MAY: You were walking while you were sleeping.

ISA: Oh good god. *(ISA gags.)*

MAY: Gosh, Isa, do you think you're pregnant?

ISA: I hate the thought of sleepwalking it makes me sick thinking about running around unconscious. Running around like a monster or a chicken. Remember that chicken? That chicken's name was Helen.

MAY: Isa are you even awake?

ISA: Will you hold my head? Just hold it you don't have to be tender about it. Where is Ellie? It's almost morning she hasn't come back. Where is Ellie?

MAY: Maybe she's dead.

ISA: Don't joke about that.

MAY: I'm just saying maybe she got killed. By a killer.

ISA: It's not funny.

Isa listens at the floor.

MAY: What are you doing?

ISA: Do you hear anything? Do you hear any music?

MAY: I don't hear anything.

ISA: I think I hear something. I think I hear music.

Isa relaxes onto the floor.

MAY: Isa get up. Get up, Isa.

Isa stands.

ISA: I'm sorry, May. That was silly

188 **7. Ellie remembers Marya.** *Minutes later. May sleeps. Isa kisses Ellie. Ellie is drunk.*

ISA: I don't want you staying out all night anymore. It's dangerous.

ELLIE: It's not anymore dangerous than it was before.

ISA: I didn't love you then.

ELLIE: I was just a person you didn't know before. You didn't care what happened to me?

ISA: I know that seems wrong doesn't it. I don't understand it either.

ELLIE: I find it hard to believe that you love me when you were so careless about my welfare before.

ISA: I didn't know I loved you then.

They kiss. Ellie suddenly moves away.

ELLIE: You should have known. You should have loved me just as another person. You should have loved me even though you didn't know me. I don't think you really love me now. I think you can't love me now if you didn't love me then.

ISA: That's not true.

ELLIE: It's all right though because there's another woman who really loved me. She truly did. And I still love her.

ISA: What?

ELLIE: I've been in love with her for a year. Her name is Marya. You don't know her.

ISA: I see.

ELLIE: Marya loved me from the first moment she saw me. She grabbed me by my hair and kissed and kissed and kissed me. She couldn't let me go after that. She never wanted me out of her sight. All from just looking at me.

ISA: You should go to her then. Ellie you should go to her.

ELLIE: She loves someone else now. She fell in love with a girl. She can't help it, I forgive her. Her heart is on fire. She loves one way then the other, but she really loves each time. Not like you. She really loves.

ISA: I don't know what to say.

ELLIE: You could try to convince me that you really love me.

ISA: I tried. I told you I wanted you to stop staying out all night. What do you want me to do?

ELLIE: I don't know. I don't want anything from you. I want to be with her.

ISA: I can't help you with that.

ELLIE: If you were Marya you would grab me now and kiss me and kiss me.

ISA: I don't think I could possibly do that right now.

ELLIE: That's your biggest problem, Isa.

ISA: And what's your biggest problem Ellie?

ELLIE: That she doesn't want me. That's my only problem.

ISA: I see.

ELLIE: Do you want me to leave?

ISA: Yes.

ELLIE: I don't have anywhere else to stay.

ISA: I know. You can stay.

ELLIE: She would have kicked me out. And then later she would have taken me back.

ISA: I know and she would have pressed her body against yours until the heat emanating from her fiercely burning heart branded the shape of a heart into your skin, here, where your own heart should be. And then you could have gone down to the tattoo shop and had her name engraved there.

ELLIE: You're making fun of me.

ISA: Because you have stupid ideas about love.

ELLIE: I'm not going to stay here.

ISA: Yes you will. You don't have anywhere else to go.

    Silence.

ELLIE: I'm going.

ISA: Ellie you can stay. You know you can stay.

ELLIE: I want to find this girl she loves. I want to meet her. I want her to meet me and I want her to feel sorry for me. I want her to feel sorry for how ugly I am.

ISA: That's not right, Ellie. You're not ugly.

ELLIE: Every day she becomes stronger and I become weaker. She's a monster. I have to meet her.

ISA: Why would you want to meet a monster?

ELLIE: I mean who is she? What is she like? Is she taller than me? I'm so short. She's tender isn't she? I'm not tender enough. She's sexy. I want to know her. I want to see her. I have to see her.

ISA: Ellie. Ellie. She'll be less than you think.

ELLIE: She won't. She's a miracle. I can feel it.

    Ellie shakes.

I have to see her! I have to see her! Don't try to stop me, Isa.

ISA: I'm not. Where are you going?

ELLIE: I'm going to find this girl. I'm going. I'm going.

    Ellie exits. Isa follows her.

8. Marya's girl. *The next day. Marya's Girl is alone in the apartment. She peeks at Isa's papers.*

MAY: Who are you? Who the fuck are you, I said.

GIRL: ELLIE.

MAY: You're not Ellie.

GIRL: I know. I meant to say I'm a friend of Ellie's. Actually I'm a friend of Ellie's ex-girlfriend, Marya.

MAY: That's weird.

GIRL: I got scared.

MAY: I'm not scary. I'm going to be a mother. How can I be a mother if I'm scary? I'm nice. I'm caring. I'm going to be a good mother.

GIRL: I believe you.

HEIDI SCHRECK

MAY: You do?

GIRL: Yes I do.

MAY: What's your name?

GIRL: Ellie said I could stay here.

MAY: You can't stay here. There's already too many people living here. There's too many people ever since Ellie got here so don't think you're going to sneak in here on her recommendation.

GIRL: I don't have anywhere else to go.

MAY: Well me either but I'm pregnant and it's my sister's apartment so I guess fuck you. Sorry.

GIRL: Okay.

MAY: Okay? Are you giving up then?

GIRL: Is it all right if I wait for Ellie to come back?

MAY: Yeah sure.

GIRL: Can I wait inside?

MAY: If you think someone else is mean, you should ask yourself why do I think that person is mean? And probably you will come up with the answer, because I am mean. I am mean for not believing in that other person. For not believing they are a good person.

GIRL: You came from a mean place.

MAY: Is this what your friend Ellie told you? Did she tell you where I came from?

GIRL: Yes.

MAY: You're friend Ellie is stupid. She's stupid and mean.

GIRL: You should lie down. It's extremely tiring to be pregnant.

MAY: You're right, it is tiring. And I have to work, too. I have to be pregnant and I have to have a job.

GIRL: What kind of job?

MAY: I don't want to talk about it.

GIRL: You should work from home. That way you can set your own hours and it's all up to you. Do you know if your baby is going to be a boy or a girl?

MAY: Yes.

GIRL: I think it's going to be a girl.

MAY: You're right. Have you had a baby before?

GIRL: I'm not as old as I look. Babies are miracles.

MAY: Where did you hear that? Did you read that somewhere?

GIRL: I think it's true.

MAY: Well not everyone agrees with you.

GIRL: What about you? Do you think babies are miracles?

191

MAY: I would never say it in such a stupid way.

GIRL: What is her name?

MAY: She doesn't want the name I gave her.

GIRL: Oh. What does she want to be called?

MAY: I don't want to tell you.

GIRL: Okay.

MAY: Sometimes I want her out of me even though I know I'll be lonely for her then. The way my mother used to be lonely for me. If my mother took me back now I would eat her up from the inside out, I wouldn't be able to help it. I'm so hungry all the time.

GIRL: My mother was not smart but she was beautiful. She was the most beautiful mother. Once I wanted to prove to the other students at school how beautiful she was so I cut her picture out of her passport and I brought it to school as proof. But no one believed that she was really my mother. They thought I had stolen the picture.

MAY: Don't you look like her?

GIRL: Not at all. I look so different from her that I could be any other mother's child in the world before hers.

MAY: Are you sure she's your mother then?

GIRL: She's not alive anymore. She died in the town that we came from. She always wanted to move somewhere else, but after I cut her picture out of her passport, she couldn't. She had to live the whole rest of her life where she was born. She couldn't go anywhere without her passport.

MAY: Was she a criminal?

GIRL: Maybe. I don't know. But she always hated me for cutting out that picture. She died in that town and she never forgave me.

> Pause.

MAY: Did you make that up?

GIRL: I don't think so.

MAY: Maybe you dreamed it.

GIRL: Maybe.

MAY: It's all right if you made it up.

GIRL: Yes.

MAY: It's a good story.

GIRL: Yes.

9. Later that night. *Ellie stands before Isa with her hat in her hands. She is a little bit drunk.*

ISA: I don't want to love with a burning heart. I distrust people who say they are in love. I look into their eyes and I see what the need. They desire only one thing, to be near the thing they love. They will do anything to be near the person they love, and you cannot trust someone who will do anything. A person who will do anything is an untrustworthy person. I wanted to learn to love moderately and you're making it very hard for me Ellie. I don't want that girl to stay here, but you know I won't say no.

ELLIE: It wasn't what I expected Isa. She answered the door and she was just a skinny girl. She looked like she had been crying. I said, "I'm Ellie, are you sorry for me?" And she said, "Yes I am. I am sorry for you, Ellie."

ISA: Where is her girlfriend? Where is Marya?

ELLIE: I don't know. She's gone. She doesn't love either of us now.

> *The sound of crying.*

ISA: What is that?

MAY: *[os]* It's that girl. What should I do?

ISA: Why don't you go to her?

MAY: I don't know what to do.

ISA: You could hold her.

MAY: I don't know.

ISA: You're going to be a mother it will be good practice.

MAY: I don't think I can.

> *Isa opens her curtain.*

ISA: Just walk over and put your arms around her.

> *Pause.*

MAY: I don't want to Isa you do it.

> *Isa walks over and puts her arms around the Girl.*

MAY: Isa, is she all right?

ISA: Why don't you ask her?

MAY: ARE YOU ALL RIGHT? ARE YOU SICK? Is she all right? She won't answer. ARE YOU ALL RIGHT? Shhhhhhh. Oh no. Oh no. She's not all right.

ISA: Shhhhhhh.

MAY: Why doesn't Ellie help her? *(to Ellie)* HEY! Why don't you help her for God's sake.

ISA: May, be quiet. You're upsetting her more.

MAY: Shhhh. Shhhh. Maybe I'll hold her now. Oh fuck. I can't. I can't. *(To Ellie)* Why don't you help her you stupid drunk?

ISA: Stop it May.

MAY: Who are you to tell me that I can't do anything that I'm mean that I don't care about anything. *(The Girl cries more loudly.)* Oh no. I'm sorry. Please don't cry.

ELLIE: I need some sleep.

193

10. Ellie finds ease; Isa is graceful for a moment. May's baby kicks. *Three months later. Morning. The Girl is typing on Isa's typewriter.*

ISA: What are you doing?

GIRL: Writing.

ISA: Don't do that.

The Girl moves away from the typewriter. Isa sits down.

GIRL: What are you writing?

ISA: It's just a poem.

The Girl watches Isa.

GIRL: Is it a love poem?

ISA: I'm not sure.

GIRL: Can I read it?

ISA: Do you read much?

GIRL: I've read about a hundred books.

ISA: When I'm finished you can read it.

Isa continues writing.

GIRL: I started writing a love poem for my girlfriend, but she stopped loving me before I could finish it.

ISA: Marya?

GIRL: Yes. Do you know her?

ISA: No.

GIRL: Would you like to hear the beginning of my poem?

ISA: Not right now.

GIRL: Okay. I'm also working on a story.

ISA: About Marya?

GIRL: No. It's about you and May. About how you came here. It's just from my imagination. It's not really a story, it's going to be more like a play. And guess what? I'm going to play the part of you.

ISA: Why?

GIRL: Because I like your face. Sometimes when people are sad their faces twist up like they've just eaten a lemon. But you look beautiful when you're sad.

ISA: Thank you.

GIRL: Isa? Isa?

ISA: What?

GIRL: Is it true that May cut off her hair before she moved here? ·

ISA: Yes.

GIRL: Maybe I'll play the part of May.

ISA: Why?

194

GIRL: Because if I play May then I get to be bald.

ISA: And pregnant.

GIRL: Yes. If I play May I get to be bald and pregnant.

> *Ellie enters. Her face is red and her hair a mess.*

ELLIE: She was putting some cans of peaches on a shelf and the thing I
noticed was her stockings. They were silver with violet seams. I knew they
were real stockings, silk probably, and I wanted to touch them. I wanted
to trace that seam with my fingers – well she turned as I was thinking this
and looked at me—. Isa, do you want me to stop?

ISA: No, it's all right.

GIRL: I need to go to the store.

ELLIE: I don't have anyone else to tell these things.

ISA: I know. I want you to tell me.

GIRL: May needs some oranges.

ELLIE: She turned while I was thinking this and I didn't know what to do so I
said, "I'd like to buy a can of peaches. My name is Ellie."

> *Isa laughs.*

Isa? Isa?

> *Girl exits.*

ISA: You can tell me anything Ellie. Anything at all. I feel wonderful for some
reason suddenly easy. Empty.

ELLIE: Maybe we should talk about something else.

ISA: No, Ellie, you should tell me now while it lasts.

ELLIE: Well, I said, "I'd like to buy a can of peaches. I'm Ellie."

ISA: Was she charmed? She must have been charmed.

ELLIE: She was, she laughed like you are laughing now. And she looked at
me and I could tell she liked me. She'd seen me before. We had—. We had
noticed each other before. And I said I don't know how I could have been so
bold I said, "I've never seen stocking like those stockings. May I touch them?"

ISA: What did she do?

ELLIE: Slowly without turning she lifted her skirt above her knees and then
my hand moved along that vein. We were both shaking and then my
hand, I don't know how, was between her legs. And she was so warm, Isa,
she was warm. I pulled her down to her knees and leaned against her back
and for the first time I felt that I was resting.

ISA: I think that's wonderful.

ELLIE: Do you mean it Isa?

ISA: For this moment I think it's wonderful, Ellie. I'm happy for you.

ELLIE: Thanks, Isa.

> *Pause.*

195

ISA: Ellie?

ELLIE: Yes.

ISA: Will you leave me?

ELLIE: You wanted me to tell you. You asked me to tell you—

ISA: I'm so empty, Ellie. It's amazing, right now, I can imagine anything. I am expanding at a terrifying rate.

ELLIE: Isa—.

ISA: I am empty and full of love, look at me.

ELLIE: I want to tell you something Isa I don't know what it is.

ISA: You found a moment of ease.

ELLIE: Yes, maybe. I was graceful. You seem so calm, I've never seen you so calm.

ISA: I don't know how long it's going to last it could end at any moment. Are you going to leave me Ellie?

ELLIE: Is it what you want?

ISA: I think you should leave me. I am graceful now too. Look at me. I'm going to stand up now, to say goodbye to you.

She stands slowly, looks at Ellie, and falls down.

ELLIE: Isa are you all right? You fell.

ISA: I hit my head. Can you sit me up?

ELLIE: I'm sorry I upset you Isa.

ISA: Ellie? Will you just tell me that you don't want me, that you don't want to be with me.

ELLIE: Is it what you're waiting for? Have you been waiting for it all this time?

ISA: Yes. I don't know.

ELLIE: Will you tell me when you know?

ISA: I—

When I know—.

Yes.

May enters. She wears a movie usher's costume from the 1930s.

MAY: I don't think I was made for anything, Isa.

ISA: Did they fire you already?

ELLIE: Were you late? Did you talk too much?

MAY: No. I didn't get fired. I just think I wasn't made to be a movie usher. I felt like a phony, I was sure all of the movie patrons could see I was only pretending to be a movie usher.

ISA: You love the movies, May. Especially old movies. You are not a phony.

MAY: I do love movies but I was all wrong. When I spoke my voice got stuck, it stuck. I tried to say, "There is a single seat in this row, sir," but it sounded hollow and fake. THERE IS A SINGLE SEAT IN THIS ROW SIR. After a while I stopped speaking, I kept my head down at my knees. I was afraid to let people see my eyes because I knew they would look right in and see only the bad in me. Then right before the curtain went up, an old lady walked by and I thought I heard her say, right as she passed me, she said, "You're not fooling anybody."

ISA: She didn't say that.

MAY: Maybe she didn't. I couldn't be sure though, Isa.

ELLIE: If you love movies so much maybe you would rather be in the movies.

MAY: Maybe.

ELLIE: I'm sure the audience could sense your genuine affection for movies, though. It's rare to meet someone with a true passion for their work—.

MAY: I don't have a passion for work, though. I have a passion for movies. Isa has a passion for work not me.

ISA: I don't know if it's really a passion. I'm not a good example.

MAY: You mean because you're special.

ISA: No, it's not exactly what I mean.

ELLIE: I think May is right, that is what you mean. Admit it, Isa, you think you are more special than the rest of us.

MAY: It's true you should be honest with us. Please confess now, Isa, confess that you know you were made for something and that we were not made for anything. Then we will all be able to relax. We can stop pretending.

ELLIE: I was not made for nothing. I was made for everything.

ISA: I think that's true Ellie.

ELLIE: I have been so many things already. I could be anything.

MAY: Have you been a movie usher?

ELLIE: No.

MAY: Am I the only one who was made to be a movie usher?

ELLIE: If you were then it's a gift. At least you have one thing, you know what it is, you can devote your life to it. The problem with being made for everything is that you are never devoted to one thing and therefore never happy. I'm not sure I've ever been happy.

MAY: Have you ever been happy Isa?

197

ISA: Yes.

MAY: When?

ELLIE: Don't tell us!

ISA: I'll tell you some other time.

ELLIE: I've even worked in foreign countries. How many people can say that? I've been a dancing instructor, a jewelry-maker, a baker—. More things than I can remember. And I was good at all of them.

MAY: I've never been good at anything.

ISA: That isn't true, May.

MAY: What have I ever been good at?

ELLIE: A friend said to me once, "I think you would be good at anything you tried. That's a gift." But she was wrong. It means a life without devotion. A life that has not been blessed.

ISA: Once May, when you were little our mother got so angry. I can't even remember why, now. She said she didn't want to live with us anymore, she wanted to move somewhere where the people were gentle. Your father was already gone by then, May, and she was alone with us. I never understood before how lonely she was. She was crying, she ran into her bedroom and I thought I should go in there, I should do something now. Now I'm going to do something. But then I heard her voice from the bedroom, it was so small. "You don't love me," she said. "My own daughters are afraid of me." I was afraid of her. I couldn't pretend it wasn't true, so instead I pretended not to hear. But you, May, you ran straight into her room and started yelling "YOU'RE CRAZY IF YOU THINK I'M AFRAID OF YOU" and then you climbed into the bed and put your arms around her and fell asleep. The two of you slept the whole day and when she woke up in the evening, our mother was fine again. She was fine.

MAY: I don't remember any of that, Isa.

ISA: Well I remember.

MAY: I don't know what it means, though, Isa. What was I good at?

ELLIE: You were good at not being afraid of your mother.

MAY: I don't remember it though.

> *May climbs the stairs to Isa's room.*

Look at my knuckles. Why are they so big? *(To her stomach)* She's a beast.

ISA: Good night, May.

> *Ellie and Isa sit looking at one another.*

Ellie?

ELLIE: Yes?

> *Isa stands, turns her back to Ellie, lifts the hem of her skirt, slowly. Ellie watches her.*

ISA: I don't want to have to ask you.

> *Ellie kneels down behind Isa.*

ELLIE: Don't cry Isa.

> *Ellie on her knees wraps her arm around Isa's waist and leans into Isa's back. The Girl enters carrying a huge sack of oranges, which she sets down immediately. She finds a towel and hands it to Isa who wipes her eyes.*

ISA: You are never surprised by anything.

GIRL: No.

ISA: Will you tell me something? What is she like? The woman Ellie loves what is she like?

ELLIE: Isa—.

GIRL: She has a loud laugh. Her voice is lazy when she answers the telephone. She says, "Hello." She owned a hat shop and whenever a customer was unsure about buying a hat, she would just try the hat on herself and immediately the customer would see what a perfect hat it was, and buy it.

ISA: Do you miss her?

GIRL: Not if I don't think about her. Do you want to see her picture?

ISA: No. I'd like to keep the picture I have of her in my imagination.

GIRL: She's more than you can imagine. Most people are less than you can imagine, but not her.

ISA: I'm tired.

May enters in her pajamas.

ISA: Aren't you sleeping?

MAY: My oranges!

The Girl opens the sack of oranges and dumps the fruit at May's feet.

MAY: Isa, would you peel this for me?

GIRL: I'll do it. I can do it all in one peel.

Whenever May finishes an orange, the Girl peels her a new one.

The thing to be careful about is not to get any diseases while you're pregnant. That's one thing. You know it's scary if you get the chicken pocks when you're an adult, it's deadly, just like if you get the chicken pocks when you're a baby. So adults are just like babies. A lot of people don't realize that. Children are strong and healthy, but adults and babies are weak.

ELLIE: I think that's true.

MAY: My baby is not weak. My baby is ferocious.

ISA: *(to Girl)* I changed my mind. I would like to see that picture.

The Girl hands Isa the picture.

GIRL: Even a ferocious baby can be weak. I knew a baby once who was the most ferocious baby. Every time someone came near this baby, she would scream, and if they got too close, she would attack. Most babies retreat, but this one would attack. And she couldn't walk either, so she rolled. She would just roll toward the person very quickly and this would usually scare the person off. This baby learned to walk, but she never learned to crawl because she rolled instead of crawling. She just rolled everywhere until she wore all of her hair off and she was bald.

ELLIE: She doesn't sound very weak.

GIRL: Her hair never grew back. And so she grew up very shy. She looked like a refugee all her life or a cancer patient. So the other kids never wanted to talk to her. And she wanted them to talk to her. She needed them to talk to her. And this need made her weak.

ISA: Do you know that when Ellie leaves me I will be fine? I'll buy a car. I'll drive down the coast until I find a beach where the ocean is warm. There will be a little hotel, pink sandstone, cracked shells on the porch. A window. When I walk outside, things will look different, the boardwalks will glimmer, people's faces will seem larger than usual. Big gentle cow faces with limpid eyes. The feeling of this day will be one of unmistakable benevolence. The sand, the buildings, the sky, even objects in store windows will seem like kind old grandmothers and grandfathers looking out for all of us.

GIRL: Will you have forgotten about Ellie?

ISA: Ellie will be everywhere, but I won't miss her. And eventually she'll stop being everywhere. She won't be forgotten. She will have become part of another life. A life that will seem, looking back, as if it were lived by a different person than me.

Silence. Isa looks at Marya's photograph.

GIRL: What are you thinking?

ISA: I like her hat. I like it very much. The shape is exactly right.

May cries out in pain and leaps up from the floor.

MAY: FUCK! Holy FUCKING Fuck! YOU TINY FUCKING BITCH!

GIRL: What happened?

MAY: SHE KICKED. SHE KICKED ME!

GIRL: She kicked!

MAY: NO SHE KICKED ME! SHE FUCKING KICKED ME.

ISA: Here, May. Lie down. Help me lie her down.

MAY: *(to the baby)* I could kill you. Do you hear me? I'm shaking. I'm shaking,

ISA: Shhhh. May—.

The baby kicks again.

MAY: YOU FUCKING ALIEN BITCH!

ISA: MAY—.

MAY: I CAN'T DO IT ISA. I WON'T DO IT.

ISA: MAY, LIE DOWN!

MAY: NO!

GIRL: What is it? Tell us how it feels.

MAY: FUCK YOU!

GIRL: What does it feel like?

MAY: I'M IN FUCKING PAIN. I CAN'T SAY IT ANY BETTER THAN THAT. I'M LIKE A DUMB FUCKING ANIMAL I'M IN PAIN AND ALL I CAN DO

IS moooooo. Mooooooooooooooooooooo. Moooooooooooooooooo.

ISA: Ellie please help me—.

MAY: SHE KICKED ME AGAIN.

GIRL: She kicked! She kicked!

MAY: *(to baby)* I'll kill you. I'll kill you. I won't eat oranges I'll eat shit I'll eat rocks I'll eat scissors I'll eat rocks.

> *May pulls buttons off her uniform and begins to shove them in her mouth. The Girl who turns out to be very strong restrains her and fishes them out. The Girl cradles May like a child. May wails. The Girl slowly releases her. May crawls to the floor.*

MAY: Puh puh puh puh puh puh puh puh puh puh puh

GIRL: Are you going to throw up?

MAY: Isa.

ISA: Yes?

MAY: I'm remembering all the times I tried to do things but I couldn't. They weigh me down. Such a heavy body. *(pause)* Ow.

GIRL: Did she kick again? May I touch?

> *May nods. The Girl rolls May over and places her hand on May's stomach.*

MAY: Isa?

ISA: Yes.

MAY: Can you say something to comfort me?

ISA: I'll try.

> *She begins to hum. Embarrassed, she stops, then begins again with more determination.*

MAY: That's a nice song. *(To baby)* I'll tell you all of my furious secrets. I'll tell you every one.

ACT TWO: PARTURITION

I. The play. *Three months later. Darkness. Isa enters. She wears a black 1940s dress. May, Ellie and the Girl perform the Girl's play. May lights her candle and begins to speak.*

201

MAY: I am the mountain we crossed.
   Four days and three nights
   We walked the pass
   And I am the mountain we crossed.

GIRL: I am May. I wore hardly any clothes.
   I had given them all away.

ELLIE: I am Isa. I carried everything that day.

> *Their shadows appear on the wall behind May.*

GIRL: Our mother followed us
Until we reached the forest.

ELLIE: I would like to come with you
She said. But I have no passport.

GIRL: She turned around and walked back alone.
Goodbye. I'm tired, Isa. I can't walk any farther.

ELLIE: I know, May, but here is the mountain.

GIRL: The mountain! Which road do we take?

ELLIE: The road to safety.

GIRL: But the mountain heard us, and it spoke.

MAY: YOU NEED A PASSPORT FOR THAT.

GIRL: We have passports. Isa show the mountain our passports.

ELLIE: Here they are.

MAY: THERE ARE NO PICTURES IN THESE PASSPORTS.

GIRL: No pictures!

ELLIE: No pictures. Our mother has taken revenge.

GIRL: Quick, look back, see if she's still there.

ELLIE: She's faded.

GIRL: Where do we go now, Isa?

There is a knocking at the door. May, Isa, Ellie and the Girl look toward the door.

ELLIE: *(to Girl)* You think it's her. You think she's come back for you. Why
don't you answer it, then? Haven't you been waiting for her?

ISA: It's late. Nobody should answer it.

MAY: Should I go on?

More knocking.

GIRL: I'm sorry, Isa. I have to answer it.

The Girl runs to the door. she opens it.

It's the army.

Frank enters. He is carrying a box.

FRANK: These are all my things. There were others with me, but they're gone.

ISA: You should sit down, Frank.

FRANK: We didn't sleep and then on the third day, I turned around and they
others gone. I didn't know then whether to keep walking. I don't think I
ever decided. Hello, May.

GIRL: I'll bring you some water.

FRANK: Will you come here?

MAY: I don't know.

FRANK: I'm too tired to walk anymore.

MAY: I'm tired, too. I'm pregnant.

FRANK: Will you look at me?

MAY: I'm the mountain. I don't move.

ISA: These are all of your things?

FRANK: They aren't mine, they're May's. I collected some of the things she gave away, I brought them back. Just her comics, mostly. I thought she probably wishes she hadn't given those away. All of my things are gone.

GIRL: Can I look at your things, May?

May nods. The Girl takes May's things out of the box and sets them in little piles.

MAY: What happened to the house?

FRANK: I stopped paying the lease. Some men came, they cleaned me out, left a sign on the door. When I opened the door and saw the house was empty, I just cried like a little baby. Then I went out to the garage and there were your things. For some reason, your things were all still there, as if you'd never left. I just picked up as much as I could carry and started walking.

GIRL: *(to May)* I bet these were your favorite shoes.

The Girl puts on May's shoes. The lights go out.

ELLIE: They're out again.

GIRL: We're going to eat soon, Frank, don't worry. It's Isa's birthday.

ISA: I'm 30.

2. A Purple Mystery. *The Girl reads from Andrei Bely's novel* St. Petersburg. *Isa and Ellie dance to soft music coming through the floor from the bar.*

GIRL: 1. It was a holy night. The last little cloud melted away in the enamel sky.
2. The enamel sky burned with golden stars; the streets were empty, clean and white.
3. If you went out onto the balcony of a three-storied house, you could see two lines of golden lamp lights along the sleeping streets.
4. In the distance the lights merged into one, single golden thread.
Now he starts over.
1. The horizon did not die down at all that night, but shone. As if a sacred candle were flaming beyond the horizon.
2. As if, beyond the horizon, St. John the Divine had prayed all night, enacting a purple mystery.

Loud noises from Isa's room.

ISA: MAY. MAY!

May appears.

MAY: I was dreaming that I was hitting. I dreamed that I hit him. I was dreaming. I was sleeping.

Frank appears.

FRANK: She hit me.

MAY: I hit him in my sleep. In my sleep!

FRANK: I don't care. I don't care if she hits me.

MAY: You can't sleep with me anymore because I hit you in my sleep.

FRANK: I don't care. I don't care if you hit me in your sleep.

MAY: I'm sorry. I'm sorry we disturbed you. It won't happen again.

May returns to Isa's room. Silence. Isa and Ellie sit down by the Girl who continues to read.

GIRL: 3. Grieving, the fairy-tale sat on a high window ledge. She was looking at the amber cloud.

4. Her red hair had fallen about her shoulders, and the golden stars shone into her face.

5. Tomorrow she would leave the city and say farewell to her dreams.

6. …As if a sacred candle were flaming beyond the horizon. As if, beyond the horizon, St. John the Divine had prayed all night, enacting a purple mystery.

Ellie has fallen asleep. Isa starts to clear the mess from the party. The Girl closes her book. When Isa finishes her task, she returns to the Girl, who has fallen asleep.

ISA: Someday I'll tell you where May and I came from. I'll describe the sky we lived under and then it will seem to you that once you lived under that sky, too. But I am afraid now to tell you what I know. I am afraid that no one is watching over us now.

3. Frank comes down. *The Girl sits on May's bed playing a clarinet while May works at the table. A letter flies down from Isa's room. The Girl picks it up.*

GIRL: Here's a letter for you. It's from Frank.

MAY: I don't want it.

GIRL: Can I have it?

MAY: Sure. I was only 16 when I met him and now I'm supposed to be his for life? I liked his eyes. He seemed creepy and I liked that.

GIRL: Don't you love him?

MAY: It was always so hot next to him in the bed. You know what, though? When I left, I hoped he would follow me here. I hoped he would and so he did. I made him do it with my mind. I wrote him letters and I didn't even have to send them.

204 GIRL: I think he's kind. He's aimless and tender. May?

MAY: What?

GIRL: I think he's listening to us.

MAY: Is he singing?

GIRL: Yes, I think he's singing.

FRANK: I wish you were here, dear,
I wish you were here.
I wish you sat on the sofa
And I sat near.

The handkerchief could be yours,
The tear could be mine
Though it could be, of course,
The other way around.
I wish you were here, dear,
I wish you were here.
I wish I knew no astronomy
When stars appear,
When the moon skims the water
That sighs in its slumber
I wish it were still a quarter
To dial your number.
I wish you were here, dear,
I wish you were—

MAY: Stop it, Frank. No more singing.

FRANK: I was having a dream, but I woke up. It was a good dream. You and I were in my old Buick and I was driving without a license and we got pulled over. But instead of giving me a ticket, the cop got in and said he'd drive us wherever we wanted to go.

GIRL: You slept all day, Frank.

FRANK: Can I come down?

GIRL: Sure. Why do you wear your dog tags if you're not even in the army anymore?

FRANK: I like how they feel. And I like the way they make my body important.

GIRL: I think they make your body unimportant.

FRANK: Well, that's how you see it. Anyway, if I die they could send them back to my uncle, he'd like that. What are you doing, May?

MAY: Working. I work now.

FRANK: What kind of work?

MAY: I make things at home. It's a good job. I set my own hours, and it's all up to me. It's a good job. I like it.

FRANK: May?

MAY: What?

FRANK: Could I touch you?

> *Pause.*

GIRL: Well, I have to meet some of my friends. There's a parade today. See you.

> *Girl exits.*

MAY: Where do you want to touch me?

FRANK: Anywhere. I don't know.

MAY: You can hold my arm. It's sore. My legs are sore, my arms are sore. My muscles are angry.

Frank holds May's arm.

MAY: You're supporting my arm. That feels good. You can put your other hand on the back of my neck, here.

FRANK: Can I touch your hair?

MAY: Okay. What are you doing?

FRANK: Hovering.

MAY: Stop it.

FRANK: You could put your head here. You could rest.

MAY: I can't rest.

She tries to rest against him.

I can't rest.

He holds her awkwardly.

FRANK: When I first started walking, all I could think about was our house and the things inside it. I just started naming out loud all the things that were gone. Bed. Blue lamp. My favorite hat. The only letter you ever wrote me. I tried to stop but then I'd whisper: Table. Grandfather's watch. The way the orchard looked from the window. Your quilt. When I named your quilt, the one we kept on the old couch I thought this is too much, I can't stand this. And then suddenly I felt nothing. The quilt disappeared just like you disappeared. And then for a long time I thought of nothing.

MAY: What I think about now is my old house, the one I grew up in. I think about my mom.

FRANK: I met your mom, once.

MAY: I know.

FRANK: She was wearing an orange dress. She told me I looked like an orphan.

MAY: You do look like an orphan. I look just like my dad. I look just like a man I never met who wasn't even nice. I was born with so much already. I have violence in my bones. In my eyelashes.

FRANK: I have my dad's chest. Look at it. (*Frank takes off his shirt.*) I'm nothing like my dad, except for this, here. When I was a little boy, my mom left us for a while and when she was gone, I had to take care of my dad. I'd wake him up in the morning, I'd say "Dad, it's time for me to go to school and you to go to work." I'd pour us both a bowl of cereal. He wasn't good for much, but here he is, look at him.

May looks at Frank.

FRANK: That's my dad's chest making you breathe like that.

Isa enters carrying grocery bags.

MAY: I'm going to lie down by myself.

May exits to Isa's room.

FRANK: Can't you talk to her, Isa?

ISA: No, I can't. (Pause) I'm sorry about your house, Frank.

FRANK: I just stopped paying the mortgage. I stopped doing anything. Why did she leave me?

ISA: I don't know. You'll be alright without her. You will.

FRANK: That's not true, Isa. I love her.

ISA: I know you do.

FRANK: And she doesn't have any skills. What will happen to her? How can she get along without me?

ISA: We all have poor skills, Frank. We all get along.

FRANK: But she's different. She's having a baby. She needs a father for that baby.

ISA: She's never had a father before, what does she need a father now for?

FRANK: I don't know. It's better with a father.

ISA: That's not always true.

FRANK: But I would be a good father.

ISA: I think that's probably true.

FRANK: I mean what is she looking for? Am I holding her back somehow? Am I stopping her from doing something? I'm not stopping her from doing anything. She makes me feel like I'm in the way. Am I in the way?

ISA: Maybe.

FRANK: Don't say that, Isa.

ISA: Sometimes I feel I'm in the way here. Last night I had a dream that the souls of dead people were getting stuck in my room on their way up to heaven.

FRANK: Don't you think about going back?

ISA: No, I never do. (pause) I understand you, Frank.

FRANK: You do?

ISA: Hm. You know the woman you met last night. Ellie?

FRANK: Yes.

ISA: I love her.

FRANK: You love that woman?

ISA: Yes, I do.

FRANK: Oh.

ISA: You're surprised.

FRANK: Yes. Sorry. I am. I am surprised. And she doesn't love you back?

ISA: Not in the way I would like her to, no.

FRANK: What are you going to do?

ISA: Should I do something?

FRANK: Well, sure.

ISA: No, I'm not going to do anything. Well actually, I'm going to make

207

dinner for myself. Would you like some dinner?

FRANK: No, thank you. Isa?

ISA: What?

FRANK: If May changes her mind—.

ISA: Yes?

FRANK: Well.

ISA: Oh. I see.

FRANK: I don't have anywhere else to go.

ISA: Yes. I see.

FRANK: I'm sorry.

ISA: No. No. Of course. Don't be sorry.

> *Ellie enters carrying a large bag. She wears a sundress. The Girl follows her carrying another bag.*

ELLIE: It's like a seaside resort out there! It's like a holiday! You have no idea, Isa. You have no idea. At the market this woman gave me tomatoes just for smiling at her. Just for smiling, I can't believe it! People are out. They're barbecuing and laughing. *(To Frank)* Hello.

FRANK: Hello, Ellie.

ELLIE: I've brought so many things.

ISA: It's not like a seaside resort out there, Ellie.

GIRL: Doesn't she look beautiful? You look like a girl in photograph, Ellie.

ELLIE: And here is your ice cream, Miss Isa. And I brought May something.

GIRL: May! MAY!

FRANK: MAY!

MAY: What is it?

GIRL: Strawberries.

MAY: Strawberries!

> *May enters.*

ELLIE: And I brought wine.

ISA: It wasn't like a seaside resort though, Ellie. Was it?

ELLIE: I'm telling you Isa, it was like a seaside resort. My arms were bare and I was just walking along like this, and there was the smell of lilacs and I was swinging my arms. This is how the man with the tomatoes noticed me. Because of my bare arms. I'm telling you Isa, what you see out of this window is not what it was like out there today.

MAY: These strawberries are delicious, Ellie.

ELLIE: And I bought this for you, Isa. I bought this for you at the seaside resort.

ISA: You just smiled at this man and he gave you tomatoes?

ELLIE: It's an orchid, Isa. It's rare.

ISA: I know that it's rare. How did you find it? Did your friend with the tomatoes help you find this orchid?

ELLIE: I'm telling you, what you can see from this window is not what it was like out there today.

GIRL: It's a perfect orchid.

ELLIE: I thought we could have another birthday dinner. I brought asparagus and oranges and fresh bread.

ISA: That's lovely, Ellie, but tell me, why would I want to have dinner with someone who lies about how she got tomatoes?

MAY: Isa—.

GIRL: We could have another party. We could act like we lived at a seaside resort.

ISA: Looking at these tomatoes makes me sick, looking at these tomatoes makes my hands shake and my tongue taste like iron. I don't want these tomatoes in my house, I don't know why you thought I would want to even look at these tomatoes much less eat them. I shouldn't have to look at these fucking tomatoes.

GIRL: Please don't throw them out. I'll make a salad.

ISA: You whore. you liar. You cunt. You liar.

MAY: Isa.

ISA: Do you think I'm stupid, Ellie? Do you think I'm weak? Do you think I'm nothing? Do you?

ELLIE: I brought you the orchid.

ISA: I can smell you, Ellie. I can smell you right now. And I remember what you taste like. You should have to be standing close to a person to smell them. That's only fair. But I can smell you from here. And that makes me want to kiss you. And it also makes me want to hit you very hard with my fist.

ELLIE: Well?

ISA: I want those tomatoes out of my apartment.

Isa exits to the kitchen.

MAY: We should set the table.

GIRL: You really do look like a beautiful girl in a photograph.

ELLIE: I'm hungover. I don't look spongy?

FRANK: No, you don't. You look tired.

GIRL: You should lie down. May and I will set the table.

Isa returns from the kitchen. Ellie exits. Isa follows her out the door.

4. The new new life. *Later that night. May and Frank asleep in Isa's room. The Girl sits alone on May's bed. Isa enters through front door and stands in doorway.*

GIRL: What's wrong with you? Isa? What's wrong with you?

ISA: I found something inside of me I didn't know I had. Now I'm afraid to make a move. I know that for now, no kind of movement is required. And I should not move until I have to.

GIRL: What did you do, Isa?

ISA: I ran after her. I wanted to tell her that I love her but instead I said, "Where are you going?" She didn't understand. She thought I was following her. I said, "I want to know where you're going because I love you." She said, "No, you want to know where I'm going because you want to make sure I'm not fucking anyone else." I tried to explain that isn't what I wanted, I wanted to know where she was going because I love her. I ran after her. I took my ring off of my finger and I tried to give it to her. I just wanted anything of mine to be near her. I chased her down the street. She wouldn't take it, she won't take anything of mine. I ran after her like an idiot. I wanted to tell her I love her. I wanted to tell her gently, but instead I was screaming. I was a monster and all the time I wanted to be gentle. Oh, I have to sit. Why don't you tell me something. Please talk to me, tell me something.

GIRL: I could tell you about my friends. Do you want me to tell you about my friends?

ISA: Yes, tell me about your friends.

GIRL: There's my friend John. He's mystifying. He writes down how much he spends every day in a little notebook. And my friend Eric, everyone knows him, even the bums. Everyone loves it when he comes around. He can flip a cigarette from the pack to his mouth in one move. He's skinny but with muscles. He looks like a tree. And my friend Radial, she's crazy, everyone knows it but the never say anything. Why do you think we never say anything?

ISA: It's hard to talk about that kind of thing.

GIRL: Yes. Some of them I just don't know what to do with. Sometimes I wish I had new friends.

ISA: What would they be like, these new friends?

GIRL: They would be more considerate, I guess. Isa?

ISA: I don't know if I can keep living in this city without her.

GIRL: What will you do?

ISA: I'll leave. I'll start a new new life.

GIRL: I love you. You are a like a family and I am part of it. I know it's hard to be a family. It's not always going to be easy. It's all I ever wish for though. I don't have anyone who has to love me no matter what. Only people with families have that but I don't have a family. That's why I have you, now. You are my family and I belong to you. There is always someone who has to come visit me if I'm sick. If I'm dying you will have to come or you won't be able to live with yourself. That's what it means to have a family, you have to keep loving them just in order to live with yourself. And there is no one bad in this family. Sometimes in a family there is someone who doesn't understand what a family is and that person can ruin everything. But even if you live in a family where no one really takes care of you, when that family is gone you still feel unprotected. You can't leave, you are my family.

ISA: I'm not your family, though. I can love you without being your family and that's better, trust me.

GIRL: No, it's not Isa. You know that it's not.

ISA: You have your friends. You should love them. You could teach them things. Teach them to be considerate.

Pause.

GIRL: All right.

ISA: *(gently)* I'm not your family.

GIRL: Is this May and Frank's house, now?

ISA: I don't know. I suppose it is.

GIRL: I have people I can stay with. Don't worry.

ISA: That's good. It's good that you have friends.

The Girls gets up as if to leave. She doesn't know whether she can stay a while longer. She goes to the door. Isa watches her but still cannot make a move.

GIRL: Isa, can I tell you something?

ISA: What is it?

GIRL: I lie. Sometimes I lie. And I've stolen things before. I've wanted to tell you for a long time. Because I love you.

ISA: It's good that you told me. Why do you lie?

GIRL: Sometimes I lie because it's easy, that's the worst thing, how easy it is for me to lie. If you are a person who lies, even just sometimes, then you know there is no reason for anyone to ever trust you, or love you, and then it's hard to go on living after that. If I had a family they would have to love me even if I lied.

5. Minutes later. *The Girl has left. Isa remains sitting. May looks down on her from Isa's room.*

MAY: I've been watching you for so long.

ISA: Yes?

MAY: When we were little, you only paid attention to me when you needed me for your games, but I noticed everything about you. I knew all of your favorite books: *The Hidden Staircase, The Midnight Clock.* I knew that sometimes you couldn't sleep at night and that you cried when you had to cut your hair short. Then you went to junior high and I didn't know anything about you anymore. You were like a foreigner just visiting us from another land. You always came home thinking about so many things. What were you thinking about?

6. Waiting for the baby. *Frank and Isa are taking care of May in Isa's room. May is wrapped in a sheet.*

FRANK: We're at the lake. Lune Lake. It's hot and dry and you've got your blue suit on.

ISA: Uncle George is there and he tells you not to put your feet in the water or the fish will eat your toes. He puts his feet in the water and we say, "What are you doing?" and he says, "Letting the fish eat my toes."

FRANK: The lake smells like gasoline. And we're walking along the road to Pat and Mike's.

ISA: We're going to get ice cream. Our hair is full of lake water and our skin is burning from the inside but the wind is cool. It pets our skin. We're going swimming in just a little while, don't worry.

FRANK: When we get to Pat and Mike's, Mike says, "What's your favorite ice cream?"

MAY: Orange sherbet.

FRANK: That's not ice cream, there's no cream in that!

MAY: I know Mike, but it's still my favorite. *(Pause.)* I hate waiting!

ISA: We stand around in front of Pat and Mike's with our cones. Our feet are burning. We watch the cars pull in at the gas pumps and we wave at the people we know.

MAY: Which people?

FRANK: Harry Olson.

MAY: Harry Olson!

ISA: Harry Olson never came to the lake.

FRANK: Well now we're letting him come to the lake.

MAY: What will Harry Olson do there?

FRANK: Harry Olson, he's going fishing. He's going to wear big hip-waders and walk into the water.

MAY: I think you only use those for the river.

FRANK: Harry Olson uses pieces of old corn for bait. And when you fish with him, he's always hooking you in the butt on his first cast.

212

May groans.

FRANK: *(To Isa)* Should we take her now?

MAY: Not yet.

ISA: We wait as long as we can. There's still time to wait. Do you want some whiskey?

FRANK: Mary Holly's old dog is there.

ISA: Oh, I liked that dog.

MAY: He must be dead for sure.

FRANK: Here May, let me hold your head.

The Girl opens the door and looks around. She crawls to May's bed and climbs in.

MAY: You know just a few months ago, I was eating chicken wings at the bar, and I almost choked on a bone. I almost died. And here I am having a baby.

FRANK: The water is cool but not cold. When you slide into the lake, there's no temperature. There's no difference between the water and your body.

The Girl begins to cry softly.

MAY: What's that noise?

ISA: Shhhhhhhhhhhhhhhhh. There's no noise. Let me hold you.

End of play.

AMY WHEELER is a Seattle-based playwright whose nationally produced plays include: *Wizzer Pizzer* at 7 Stages in Atlanta (2005), *Weeping Woman* (2003) and *Kiss It!* (2004) at Stark Raving Theatre in Portland, and *Two Birds & A Stone* at Seattle's Capitol Hill Arts Center (2004). *Two Birds* was developed in Portland Center Stage's JAW/West Festival. Her new two-part epic *Atomic Agape* is being developed by Stark Raving for a 2007 premiere. Amy's work has also been produced in New York at the Greenwich Street Theatre and the Guggenheim Museum, and through the New York Drama League's New Directors/New Works project. Awards include a New York Foundation for the Arts sponsorship, two fellowships from Artist's Trust in Seattle, and a Yaddo residency. Amy is Executive Director of the Hedgebrook women writer's retreat, and teaches playwriting in Seattle at Cornish College of the Arts, Freehold Theatre Lab, and in ACT Theatre's Young Playwrights Program. She holds an MFA from University of Iowa's Playwrights Workshop.

Amy Wheeler

Two Birds & A Stone

This play is dedicated to the mothers and children of war.

*"We who were born from the war know what it is.
The war is in us, but it is also in everyone."*
— Thich Nhat Hanh

"Every heart to love will come but as a refugee."
— Anthem, Leonard Cohen

CHARACTERS

BOY—who talks to the Sun & Moon, an orphan

WOMAN—who is 8 months pregnant, a refugee

INTERROGATOR—who has stopped dreaming

GIRL—who is searching for her mother, an orphan

ENSEMBLE—(KING CARP, MOON, SUN, COOK, DEAD SOLDIER, BIRD, SOLDIERS 1, 2 & 3) Doubled as follows: Dead Soldier & Soldier 1, King Carp & Soldier 2, Sun & Soldier 3, Moon & Cook, Girl & Bird

[Total cast size: 8]

TIME: Winter.

PLACE: A war torn country, in and around a bombed out village, following a tenuous ceasefire.

NOTES: Time is fractured in places, as in dreams and memory. In other places, it flows, overlaps, converges and circles back. Each character experiences time differently: for the Girl, it is a moment of watching a flock of birds take flight and wondering what happened to her mother; for the Woman, it is the night she gives birth; for the Boy and Interrogator, it is the last day of their life. Theatrically, there are synchronized moments when time bends, past and future converge, and we experience several events simultaneously - flying, birth and death. These are stylized moments, using movement and sound, and should have a very different feel from the harsh realities of the Interrogation

Room and abandoned Barn, and the vivid world of the Boy's imagination. It is recommended that the theatrical spaces be delineated simply, with light, sound and minimal set elements - creating a fluidity to the movement of bodies and objects that echoes the poetic language of the piece, and shifting!

The invented language spoken by the Soldiers and Interrogator is followed by its translation in English.

ACT I

In the darkness, sound of a flock of birds taking flight.

Lights reveal Girl at a window perched high above, searching. She cranes her neck to follow their path across the sky.

We hear Woman singing a lullaby. Her voice is hushed and desperate.

WOMAN: *(singing)* One bright morning in the springtime
    in the budding trees
  A dark hunter shot an arrow
    through a young bird's wing.
  She lay broken on the ground
    bleeding out her plea
  I found her laying silently
    as if she were asleep.

Interrogation Room: The song continues as light discovers Woman slumped in a chair, hands tied behind her. She wears a pretty dress, ripped and dirty, and red high heels caked with mud.

WOMAN: I let her rest beside my window
    bound her wing in silk
  Fed her blossoms from the meadow
    and butterflies milk
  As the brilliant summer passed
    she relearned her song
  She sang it as the trees grew gold
    and the shadows long

Barn: Boy sits cross-legged on the floor, holding a baby wrapped in a bundled shirt. It is night. A few strands of light filter through the window and across his face. He gently hushes her soft cries.

BOY: Shhhhh…don't cry…it's okay…I'm here…I'll take care of you…

A flashlight beam scans the room through the window, catching the Boy's face. Soldiers 1 & 3 yell from outside. Note: [ ] indicates English translation of line. (for actors only, not spoken)

SOLDIER 1: Baçik orusila! *(Pause)* Istupi! [Throw down your weapon! Step forward!]

SOLDIER 3: Kazi ko si! [Identify yourself!]

SOLDIER 1: Kazi ko si—o zjhaste! [Identify yourself—or we'll shoot you!]

> *Boy stands, protecting the bundled baby. Lines overlap.*

BOY: I don't understand…

SOLDIER 1: Baçik orusila! Kazi ko si! [Throw down your weapon! Identify yourself!]

BOY: Please! I can't understand you!

SOLDIER 3: Kazi ko si—o zjhaste! [Identify yourself—or we'll shoot you!]

> *A gunshot. Woman'S singing stops abruptly. Lights out on Woman.*

BOY: NO!

> *A 2nd gunshot. The Boy is hit. He falls, the baby underneath him. Lights out on Boy. Lights out on Girl.*
>
> *Silence.*
>
> *Darkness.*
>
> *Interrogation Room: Lights bump up bright. Woman snaps to life, her body tense, her eyes wild. Soldier 2 enters, roughly spreads Woman's legs and lashes her ankles to the chair. Interrogator enters briskly from behind them, carrying a bunch of limp flowers.*

INTERROGATOR: Dobar dan…good evening. Are you comfortable? Too warm? *(to Soldier)* Da ste oma svuce? [Should we have her undress?] *(Soldier laughs)*

> *Interrogator moves in front of Woman and sees she is pregnant.*

Ah ha—Sala un promo botzance. [This one is full of surprises]. You are with child. How nice. Now I shall have two of you to question. *(to Soldier 2)* Sala da façi. [This should be easy.] *(to Woman's belly)* Vat cuve du y Mama dontant, eh? [What were you and Mommy doing today, huh?] Is your Mommy a spy?

> *Pause. He circles her, then thrusts the flowers under her nose.*

You were carrying these at the time of your arrest. What is their meaning? *(Pause)* Everything has a meaning. Everything tells a story.

> *Plucking petals off flowers.*

Zasto? [Why?] This is the question I have to answer. Why was she on the wrong side of town…in a cemetery…after curfew? Why would she risk her life? Why tonight? Would you like something to drink? *(to Soldier)* Donsi casu vode! [Bring a glass of water!]

> *Soldier 2 exits. Interrogator looks out the window.*

A full moon…she betrayed you…no shadows to hide in.

> *Soldier 2 reenters with a glass. Interrogator gives her a sip, spilling water down her dress, then sticks flowers in the glass.*

Pretty flowers. We don't want them to die of thirst.

217

Barn: Soldiers 1 & 3 enter and discover the Boy's lifeless body.

Soldier 1, agitated and pumped up with adrenalin, rushes in. Soldier 3 moves with caution.

SOLDIER 3: Pazi! [Be careful!]

SOLDIER 1: Vat ficken?! Esje dar kindish. [What the fuck?! It's that kid!]

Soldier 3 checks the Boy's pulse.

SOLDIER 3: Uszbekt om. [You killed him.]

SOLDIER 1: Om ajza bet. Te grosse es egate. [He's just bait. The big one got away.]

Soldier 3 kneels by Boy and prays in silence.

Soldier 1 discovers Boy's notebook.

(He reads, in English) "Sometimes the only thing that keeps me from crying is knowing that we see the same moon."

Soldier 1 drops the notebook, laughing.

Sound of a flock of birds taking flight.

SOLDIER 3: Uskut! Asawey! [Shhh! Listen!]

A baby's muffled cry.

Soldier 1 aims his gun at Boy's body.

SOLDIER 1: Ne je sta! [Don't touch it!]

Soldier 3 gently shifts Boy and discovers the baby underneath him.

SOLDIER 3: Oma uvek bres. [She's still breathing.]

Soldier 1 points his gun at the baby.

Soldier 3 reaches for her.

SOLDIER 1: Ne je sta! Bis du lut?! [Don't touch it! Are you crazy?!]

Soldier 3 carefully lifts baby and she begins to cry.

Soldier 1 holds his gun on both of them.

Sputi je! Sputi je! [Put it down! Put it down!]

Soldier 3 sings lullaby on "la la la".

Vat ficken u cuve!? [What the fuck are you doing?!]

SOLDIER 3: Sabrisj, kindish. [Patience, boy.]

SOLDIER 1: Vat u kukir ma? Vat u kukir ma?! [What did you call me? What did you call me?!]

SOLDIER 3: U flaub uszbekten mak te om. [You think killing makes you a man.]

A whistle from outside.

SOLDIER 1: Hey! Tachte oma! Uiga! Uiga! [Hey! He's got her! Let's go! Let's go!]

Soldier 1 runs out.

Soldier 3 holds the baby, making a decision.

Blackout.

Interrogation Room: Some time has passed, interrogation is in progress.

INTERROGATOR: You're really very lucky. You have no idea. Do you know what happens to the women brought here? You hear them crying out from the other rooms? *(Pause)* We all die. It's a matter of how we die.

Interrogator sits facing Woman, settling in. He cleans his fingernails as he speaks.

You're just a body to them. They keep you alive long enough to have fun. You've heard of this? Electrodes attached to various body parts, a blow torch, or simple objects, like pliers to yank out your fingernails. They play music to drown out your screams and create the right mood. Springsteen or Mahler, depending on your torturer's taste. You are a spectator sport. Officers crowd around on cardboard boxes, drinking beer and cheering. Placing bets on how long you last. The longer, the better. Female victims receive special treatment. *(Pause)* I prefer talking. A dialogue, you understand? *(Pause)* Shall I begin?

Woman stares him down.

Very well.

He signals Soldier 2, who swings Woman around to face him, towering over her.

Why did you go out? Why alone? So far from home.

Interrogator nods at Soldier 2, who slaps her. Her head snaps back in defiance.

My dead sleep in that cemetery! My people! Not yours!

Interrogator nods, Soldier 2 slaps her.

There are no markers, no headstones, no names, just holes in the ground, piles of dirt, how would you know which grave to place the flowers on?

Interrogator nods, Soldier 2 slaps her.

You were meeting someone? A secret rendezvous? That would explain why you're dressed like a whore. Who are you protecting?

Soldier 2 raises his hand. Interrogator shoves him out of the way and faces Woman.

Your silence is deafening. *(Pause)* All it takes is a word from you. A few answers…simple.

He waits, expectantly. She spits on him. He controls his rage, laughs, wipes his face.

(to Soldier) Ucini vat u sta jete oma. [Do what you like with her.]

Interrogator exits, but stays just outside the door.

An awkward moment, Soldier 2 unsure what to do. He holds her face and tries to kiss her hard on the mouth.

WOMAN: (singing, a yell) One bright morning in the springtime
in the budding trees!!

Interrogator hears song and is shocked. He briskly reenters.

(to Soldier) Ostavite nas. [Leave us!]

Pause. A stare down, then Soldier 2 exits, confused.

219

How do you know this song? How do you know it?!

Simultaneously:

Barn: The room is becoming lighter—a shift in time. Boy moves in his sleep, waking from a dream.

BOY: Mama?!

Boy wakes, disoriented. He sees his shirt bundled under his arm and unfolds it, confused. Sound of wind. A window on loose hinges bangs open and closed. He notices these things as if he's still dreaming.

INTERROGATOR: (*sings*) [One bright morning in the springtime in the budding trees…]
Dah dah dah dah dah dah dah dah…
What is it? What comes next? I can't remember…

Boy pulls his jacket on, trying to get warm. He stomps around the barn.

BOY: Mama…can you hear me?

INTERROGATOR: I'm curious…who taught you this song? Where did you learn it?

BOY: Why did you have to go? Why, Mama, I don't understand.

INTERROGATOR: My mother used to sing this song to me.

BOY: Do you think about me?

INTERROGATOR: You shouldn't know it. It's not your song.

BOY: Do you wonder if I'm thinking about you?

Interrogator moves close to Woman.

INTERROGATOR: What is your story? I want to know it. I do.

Boy finds his notebook and begins to write.

BOY: "Sometimes the only thing that keeps me from crying is knowing that we see the same moon."

INTERROGATOR: Shall I tell you a story?

Interrogator removes his belt. Boy goes outside.

Once upon a time there was a boy.

BOY: Hello stars. Thank you for keeping watch.

INTERROGATOR: And this boy hid in a basement everyday and sang a song…
(*sings*) "She fluttered at the window pane trapped in a cocoon, I kissed her once, unwrapped her wing, released her to the moon…" Do you know why? Do you know why he sang this beautiful song? He sang it because he was scared. You see, each night a man would come home smelling of whiskey and drag him outside and beat him senseless. The world was unfair to this man, this father, and he needed someone to take his rage.

BOY: Where is the Moon tonight? It's so dark.

Boy begins wandering in the dark, searching for food.

As Interrogator speaks, he begins whipping himself with the belt:

INTERROGATOR: …with every lash of the belt the boy felt the father pushing him to something. Egging him on. The father planted the seed of hate in the boy. Nurtured it. Watched it grow. And it thrived, like ragweed cropping up its ugly head in a garden of lilies. It grew roots and spread. Lurking beneath the flowers. Until one day—quite unexpectedly—it sprouted a stem that surged out of the boy's fingers and wrapped itself around the father's throat. Like this… *(he demonstrates)* …I watched the life drain out of him. His eyes rolled back in his head, and his fingers began to twitch and…I laughed. He looked so ridiculous. *(He imitates)* You see?

Interrogator flails on the floor, laughing. A knock at the door.

SOLDIER 2: Zapovednice?! Zapovednice, vreme je. [Commander?! Commander, it's time!]

Interrogator is on the hysterical edge between laughing and crying. Louder knocking. He hears it and starts, confused by where he is.

INTERROGATOR: What…what is it…?

Soldier 2 enters, catching Interrogator on the floor.

SOLDIER 2: Zapovednice?! [Commander?!]

Interrogator composes himself, embarrassed.

INTERROGATOR: Da, da, dolazim! [Yes, yes, I'm coming!] *(to her)* We do look so absurd in death. Truly. It's a weakness.

Interrogator exits. Outside door:

SOLDIER 2: Cov oma spake? [Did she speak?]

INTERROGATOR: The bitch is sealed up tight.

Barn: A cloud passes over, blocking the Moon's light.

BOY: Sister Moon? Where are you?

Moon appears.

MOON: Hush, Boy. You shouldn't be prowling around in the dark.

BOY: I'm hungry.

MOON: Wait until it's light.

BOY: How long will that be?

MOON: When the birds start to sing, of course.

BOY: I have to wait for the birds?

MOON: It's their job to get a rise out of the Sun. Now, go back to sleep.

BOY: I can't. My stomach hurts. *(Pause)* BIRDS! WAKE UP! Get to work!

MOON: *(overlapping)* Now, be careful. You know how grumpy he is when you wake him up early.

LITTLE BIRD begins whistling from her perch as lights rise on her.

See there? You woke the little one up. She doesn't know any better.

221

BOY: Come on, little bird. You can do it. Sing louder! Come on.

MOON: Oh, he's not going to be happy with you.

> BIRD'S whistles grow louder. Boy joins her, running and whooping. They are joined by a Chorus OF BIRDS, calling to the Sun, who wakes:

SUN: What's all that noise?!

BOY: Wake up, Brother Sun. It's a new day!

SUN: Says who?

BOY: Me and the birds!

> Sun looks at Moon, who shrugs her shoulders and disappears.

SUN: (to the Moon) Where are you going? Hey! Come back here!

BOY: It's her turn to sleep.

SUN: I determine when it's dawn, Boy! It's been that way since the beginning of time.

BOY: Then how come you need the birds to remind you?

SUN: I don't *need* the birds, for heaven's sake. They're just part of the ritual. Now you've got the dumb things all confused. Listen to them!

BOY: But if they didn't sing, would you still wake up?

SUN: Well, that's the big question, isn't it? The mystery.

BOY: I don't like mystery. I like to know.

SUN: Ah, but you see, every morning is an experiment in faith. (To the chirping birds) QUIET! That's better. You see, there are those who believe that I will always come up, and they don't give it a second thought. There are those who are convinced that I won't show my face tomorrow, and they grumble when their predictions are wrong. And there are those who watch with wonder, expectation and hope, willing me awake by the sheer force of their imagination. (Pause) And then there are impatient little Boys who wake me *early* on a whim.

BOY: I haven't eaten in two days and I can't find any food because of all the snow, especially when it's so dark, and...

SUN: (overlapping) Yes, yes, fine...please. Not before my morning ablutions. I'll tell you what. There's a big, juicy Carp in that pond over there just waiting to be somebody's breakfast. Go wake him up. Tell him I sent you.

> He tosses Boy his scepter to use as a fishing pole and Boy sets off.

> *Interrogation Room:* Interrogator enters quietly. Woman's head droops. He watches her quietly as she sleeps.

INTERROGATOR: Do you dream? (she snaps awake) I close my eyes and see a white door imprinted on my eyelids. Then I wake. Nothing in between. (Pause) I just watched a man die. They forced a tube down his throat. I held him while they turned on the water. He thrashed, his body tense, his head jerking around, as if he was trying to swim away. I made eye contact.

222

They tell you not to, but his eyes locked on mine and I couldn't look away...strange...

Boy approaches King Carp's icy domain:

BOY: Yo ho, King Carp!
You have a visitor.

INTERROGATOR: ...it feels like catching a fish with your bare hands. It writhes, fighting its way back to water. You could toss it back...like that. *(he gestures)*

A blue light illuminates King Carp in all his regalia, sleeping beneath the surface of the ice. Boy begins chipping a hole in the ice.

BOY: Wake up, King!
From your long winter's nap.

INTERROGATOR: You could save it. So simple just... *(gestures again)*

KING CARP: What's that? Who's there?

Interrogator cautiously curls up in a fetal position at Woman's feet— less a gesture of devotion than an experiment. As he falls asleep, tension seeps out of his body.

BOY: The Sun sent me.

KING CARP: The Sun, eh? And what does his royal solarity wish to convey at this hour?

BOY: I'm hungry.

KING CARP: And?

BOY: He said you'd be my breakfast.

KING CARP: Oh, he did, did he? And you believed him? You know, for being such a big star, he's really not very bright.

Boy drops his hook in the water and dangles it carelessly.

My dear boy. Who taught you how to fish?

BOY: I taught myself.

KING CARP: Oh, my. No technique. And even less finesse.

BOY: Come on, Carp! My mouth is watering.

KING CARP: But there's no bait on your hook! How do you expect to entice me?

BOY: You mean I have to feed you first?

KING CARP: That's generally the way it works.

BOY: But I don't know what you eat.

KING CARP: Go away, child.

BOY: Wait! Listen to my stomach growl! *(King Carp swims away, disgusted)* King Carp? Are you there?

Boy sits dejectedly. Eventually he goes on a walk, investigating rubble and pretending to fly—an action coinciding with Interrogator's dream.

Interrogation Room: Interrogator stirs in his sleep, dreaming awake. He moves through the dream slowly, as if underwater.

INTERROGATOR: dark room. leaky faucet. cup my hands. so thirsty. blood drips on my palms.

He wipes his hands on his shirt—can't get them clean.

reach in again. tiny silver fish slip through my fingers. I grab one. it thrashes. grows heavy. I fall backwards. it lands on my chest, and becomes…

He sees the Boy pretending to fly and watches, fascinated.

…a Boy. he looks at me. a drop runs down his cheek. sweat. a tear. maybe blood. I lick it off. he flaps his arms. wind rushes. fish flop in puddles of blood. turn into birds…

Amplified sound of wings and screeching. He covers his head, crawls for cover.

…beating down…they fly…across the room and out the window.

Interrogator cowers in a corner of the room.

Boy hears a rustling and thrusts his fishing pole in front of him.

BOY: Halt! Who goes there?!

Interrogator suddenly snaps out of dream and sees Woman.

INTERROGATOR: What does this mean…please tell me…everything has a meaning.

BOY: Present yourself!

Boy crawls toward the sound.

Interrogator crawls to Woman.

INTERROGATOR: You are so different from the other women they bring here, begging for their lives, talking incessantly. It wears me down. But you listen to me…you listen…

Boy spies a little bird that has fallen out of its nest.

BOY: Hello there, little bird. Where's your mother? Did she forget about you?

INTERROGATOR:	BOY:
I want you to resuscitate me.	
	You should be flying South with your friends.
I'll bring you food and water.	
	Are you hungry?
	Me too.
I'll let you walk around the room. It will be our secret. No one will know.	
	Oh look, your little wing is hurt.
I won't hurt you.	
	Shhh…it's okay…don't worry.

224

INTERROGATOR:	BOY:

INTERROGATOR:

Did the people who let you get caught and dragged here care for you?

I think they did not.
Not like I will.

BOY:

I'll take care of you.

Interrogator moves behind Woman, humming the lullaby. He encircles her and rubs her belly.

Boy sits cross-legged on the ground, holding the little bird carefully.

BOY: I found a puppy once. I brought him home, but Mama said we didn't have enough food for three. So, I gave him to John. He lived in a big house with a garden. His papa was a policeman. I used to pretend like he was my papa and John was my brother. I was jealous that he had one. One day, some soldiers came to their house and dragged John's papa out into the street. They beat him with their clubs. Me and John could see from the window. They kept kicking him. Even after he died. I never told John, but I was happy then that I never had a papa.

Boy places bird carefully in her nest. From his perch, he spies several Dead Soldiers lying nearby. He goes to them.

INTERROGATOR: Is he dead, this father? You were visiting his grave? *(Pause)* You don't know who he is. It was dark. He entered your room so quietly. A breath of air. Shoved a pillow over your face. Never spoke. He could be anyone. A Soldier. One of my men. He could be me.

Boy searches a soldier's pockets and takes a medallion from around his neck. He inspects all three soldier's boots for wear.

Let me hear your voice…just one word…I just want to hear your voice. *(Pause)* You don't trust me. You think I'm trying to trick you?

Interrogator strips down to his underwear and mismatched socks.

I understand. You don't see a man. You see a soldier. But I am a man. Look…please…look at me…

Interrogator traces a line with his fingertip down the Woman's face, around her mouth, trailing down her chin to her throat. She jerks her head away. He continues down to her chest, circling her breast in concentric circles that get smaller until he is circling her nipple.

225

Boy pulls one of Dead Soldier's boots off, and he snaps to life:

DEAD SOLDIER:

He points a gun at your head.
Your senses snap to life.
Feel your heart pounding out of your chest.
Taste acid washing up from your empty belly.
Hear water drip drip dripping in the sink.

DEAD SOLDIER:

   It's been dripping all along.
   You were just too dull to notice.

   Green. The color of his eyes.
   You can see the whites all the way around.
   He's scared, too.

   He's going to have to take your life.

   A drop of sweat runs down your spine
   and settles at the base of your back.
   In the small indentation. That soft place you
   used to lick on your lover's back.

   You focus on the drop of sweat.
   Become it.
   Crawl into that safe place to hide.

   He clears his throat. Cocks the gun.

   The sound echoes in your head.
   Sends chills through your body.
   "This is it."

   You breathe.
   Your bowels loosen.
   Piss runs down your leg.

   Green eyes says:

   But you don't give an inch of his pity back.
   He's looking death in the eyes in your face
   and you want him to wake up in a cold sweat
   every night for the rest of his life.

   Hear the click.
   Feel the bullet whistle toward you.
   Become the bullet.
   Wind whips past as you careen toward your
   point of destination.

INTERROGATOR:

Softly…softly…

Don't be scared.

I won't hurt you.

You're safe here.

Could you sing for me?

The song my Mother
sang.

Please, little bird?

Shh. Don't be scared.

I'm sorry.

There are ways to get
what youwant without
talking.

226

AMY WHEELER

DEAD SOLDIER:	INTERROGATOR:

DEAD SOLDIER:

Your whole life is lived in the hair of a moment
that falls between action

and reaction.

INTERROGATOR:

Sing, little bird.

Sing.

(Woman sings the lullaby.)

The solitary instant as the bullet flies.
It finds its mark.

Yes…oh, yes…

Your heart bursts all over your chest
Pours out all the love you've ever felt.
All over your body.
You're filled with it.
When you and the bullet
become one.

Interrogator tucks his head under her blouse and suckles her breast as he touches himself. Woman is rigid, tears streaming down her face. Lights shift on them until only her face is lit. [Note: This is a sexual experience for him, a violation of intimacy, but it is not rape. It should be staged as a stylized moment, juxtaposed with the Dead Soldier's visceral description of his death.]

Dead Soldier strikes a match on his boot, its light flickers on his face. He speaks directly to Boy:

DEAD SOLDIER: A dead man's boots carry the moment when he left this world in them. The dry sweat is his fear. You pull them on and you see things for what they are. *(Pause)* Hardest thing to live is a moment. But it's the only thing that counts.

Dead Soldier hands his other boot to Boy and lays back down.

As Boy pulls the boot on, a flock of birds flies over. He follows them across the sky, then raises his arms. The wind draws him up, he becomes one of them. The 3 dead soldiers rise up around him, their arms raised, a circling flock.

Boy speaks an incantation. Soldier's words begin on a whisper, light as air. Gradually, the sound picks up and their words become the wind that lifts and carries him:

BOY:

Wind…here I am
Catch me, lift me
Breeze, come down from the branches
Flutter my feathers
Blow through my hair
Yes…yes…I feel you

SOLDIERS:

Air…air…air…air…
Push…push…push…push…
Flutter…flutter…flutter…

BOY:
    Whispering whispering
    Take me wind
    Take me take me take me
    Now lift me!
    Lift me up!
    Now! I'm ready!
    Away from earth
    Away from earth
    Away from earth

        (he catches current & whoops)

    Yes! Yes!
    Carry me away from here!
    Carry me away!

        (current shifts and he slips)

    Oh no no slipping
    Falling slipping
    Spiraling
    Spiraling
    Spiraling

    Yes! Up to the sky!
    To the sun!
    Past the moon!
    Up up up!

SOLDIERS:
    Caress…caress…caress…
    Shhhhhhhhhhhhhhhhhh…

    Lift up Lift up!
    Take me take me!
    Away.
    Away.
    Away.
    Up Up Up UP.

    Push push push
    Air air air air

        (flock splits and retreats)
    uP uP uP uP
    Shhhhhhhhhhhh
    Shhhhhhhhhhhh
    Shhhhhhhhhhhh

        (flock swoops him back up)
    Up up up!
    Push lift up!
    Climbing climbing climbing
    Floating…gliding…
    Hushhhhhh.

Woman hears a flock fly over. She cranes her neck to see them through the window, willing her spirit to leave her body. Lines overlap & converge—a 'suspended dialogue' across space & time.

BOY:
    Look! I see you!
    You want to fly?

    On my back.

    Lift your wings.

    Don't wait.
    Now!
    Fly now!

WOMAN:

    Carry me.

    Spread my wings.

    Wait for the wind to ease
    itself under me.

    Strange current
    whips & spins

228

BOY:

Catch the wind.

Now!

Yes!

Yes!

WOMAN:
    wings beating down.

    Up up up

    I'm flying…

    I'm flying…

INTERROGATOR:
    Down. Push down. Hard.

WOMAN:
    No. Slipping.
    Falling.

No!
Don't go back.
Don't go.
Slipping
  back
    down.

    Slipping.
    Blood on my wings.
    Your hungry mouth.
    sucking the life out of me
      sucking me dry
        Sucking me back
        to earth

    (Pause)

    (Pause)

INTERROGATOR:
    Why so sad, little bird?

You'll fly to me.
On my Mama's breath.
Beat your wings.

    Others would beat you.

Map a path across the sky.

    I make love.

I'm on the other end.
Come find me.

Boy closes his eyes and floats back to the ground. Soldiers lay back down.
Woman sits, limp, her head hanging. Interrogator lies on his back on the
floor—breathless, overwhelmed with emotion.

INTERROGATOR: BOY:
    It feels like flying—
    like
    falling and flying—I
    forgot…

                 Did you see me, little
                 bird? Did you see me fly?

    We could fly away
    together.

INTERROGATOR:	BOY:	
	These are magic boots. They're going to take me places.	
Would you like that, little bird?		
	Do you want to go, too?	
Would you like to fly away with me?		
		BIRD:
		I want to go with you! I want to go!
…leave this madness…		
	Can you fly?	
		Fly, yes, fly! I want to fly!
	Maybe we'll fly together.	
		Yes! Yes! I'll fly! Watch me fly!
	When you get a little bigger.	
I can't…I can't feel… all these things it's too much I want…I want you to…touch me…I ache for your touch. Please? Just once…	*(Boy climbs up to nest.)*	*(BIRD open her eyes and sees Woman.)*
	What do you see from up here?	
		I see her! I see her!
…once with your hands free.		
	What? What is it?	
		Yes! Yes!
	It's okay, little bird. I'll find your mama. I'll bring her back home.	

Boy goes tramping off in search of the Bird's mother.

Interrogator unties ropes that bind Woman. Slowly, carefully, she rises and moves to him, gently touching his face.

INTERROGATOR: Yes…oh yes…

Blackout.

A coffeeshop. The same day. Cook sits alone in a darkened café, surrounded by rubble, taking slugs from a bottle. She's singing and mumbling to herself. Boy sneaks in quietly, making his way around the room to the kitchen.

COOK: (*singing, making it up as she goes*) One black morning…in the winter
When the moon was…red
Soot was forming on the window
And the bird is dead…
(*mumbling, laughing*)…that bird is dead… that goddamn bird…

She mimes shooting a bird. Boy drops something that clatters.

Who's there? We're closed for business…closed for pleasure! Who's there, I said?!

BOY: (*singing sweetly*) One black morning in the winter…la la la la la…

Cook's face changes, she thinks he is her son. She staggers towards the voice.

COOK: Tomas…?

Boy steps out of the shadows cautiously.

BOY: Ma'am…could you spare a scrap of bread…?

COOK: You again! I thought I told you to get lost!

BOY: What?

COOK: Beat it—before I beat you!

BOY: Do you treat all your customers this way?

COOK: Not the ones who pay! You was here last week with your buddies. Stole a loaf of bread from in front of my store—

BOY: I don't have any buddies!

COOK: (*leering*) I kicked you in the seat of your pants! Bet the tread of my boot is still there—

A chase ensues in the dark, big commotion. He ducks under a table.

Ha!—where'd you go you little thief? Little Boy…poor starving Boy…so lost and cold…As if I care! As if I've got time to care about you. We all got troubles, little Boy, take me, for instance, a woman running a café with no food rusty water moldy bread and yesterday's crusty stew…the rats eat better than we do. This place used to be the hot spot in town…always crowded, people singing, toasting, carrying on, and me…the belle of the ball. Only soldiers come here now, take what they want and blow up the rest. No help…no husband to pay the bills…no son…no son…no son… (*she weeps*)…how's anyone supposed to be a mother in a war?…

Boy comes out from hiding and kneels near her. He takes the medallion from his neck and dangles it in front of her. It glints in the light.

What's this?

BOY: St Anthony. The Saint of Lost Things.

COOK: What good's a Saint do me?

BOY: You've lost something.

Cook takes it from him and examines it.

COOK: Where'd you get this then?

BOY: Found it.

COOK: Stole it, more like.

BOY: It's silver.

COOK: Who's got money for silver?

BOY: Maybe someday you will.

Boy puts medallion around Cook's neck. A smile creeps over her face.

COOK: Clever Boy…face like an angel…you could get away with murder.

Cook takes a swig of whiskey and offers him one. He takes a gulp and gags.

Your parents know where you are? *(Boy shrugs.)* Let's see what we can rustle up.

Cook heads to the kitchen.

BOY: Thank you, Ma'am! Bless you!

Boy hears Soldiers coming down the street, boisterous, joking around, looking for a good time. He starts to run out, realizes they'll see him. Scurries to hide. They spill into the room noisily.

SOLDIER 1: Hey! Susla avasay?! [Hey! Where is everybody?!]

SOLDIER 3: Service! Vim ste service! [Service! We want service!]

SOLDIER 2: Don cu ste gut service a gonde? [How do we get service around here?]

Cook reenters, gesturing. She doesn't want trouble.

COOK: We're closed! We're closed!

SOLDIER 3: Ah! Ste glista! [Ah! We're thirsty!]

Soldier 3 grabs whiskey bottle and gestures with it.

COOK: I don't have anything! Natejz! [Nothing!]

SOLDIER 1: Bring us a drink. Whiskey!

COOK: *(relieved)* Ah! Yes yes, okay, whiskey.

Cook bustles to kitchen.

SOLDIER 3: Istavake! Eh?! [Now we're talking!]

Soldier 3 slaps Soldier 1 on the back. Boy sneezes. Instant shift: Soldier 3 draws his flashlight, Soldier 2 draws a gun, Soldier 1 draws a knife.

SOLDIER 1: Uskut! [Shhhh…]

Soldiers 1 & 2 cautiously advance toward sound. Soldier 3's flashlight catches Boy in his hiding place.

Ah…vat ste kol gonde… [Well…what have here…]

Boy suddenly bolts. Soldier 2 catches him and hauls him up. Soldier 1 approaches with his knife. Cook reenters with whiskey and 3 glasses. She sees what's happening and moves with caution.

SOLDIER 2: Susla cu flaub u gute, eh? [Where do you think you're going, eh?]

SOLDIER 1: Who were you hiding from?

SOLDIER 3: Bak om ga. Ajza kindish. [Let him go. It's just a kid. *(to Cook, gesturing)* Donsi ma casu. [Bring me a glass.]

SOLDIER 1: Om koli orusila! [He could have a gun!]

Soldier 2 pats him down.

COOK: I gave you 3 glasses.

BOY: I didn't do anything.

SOLDIER 2: Uskut! [Shut up!]

SOLDIER 1: It's past your bedtime, little Boy.

SOLDIER 2: *(leering)* …little Boy…

SOLDIER 1: You know what we do to little Boys who break curfew? We make filets out of them. You like that, huh? …tasty little fish filet?

BOY: No thanks. I'm planning on living until Christmas.

SOLDIER 2: Oh ho ho—Nicolas donsi toys, little Boy?

BOY: I'm hoping for a coat actually, and maybe some socks.

SOLDIER 3: Ha! Rusti sol dar betja! [Ha! Cocky son of a bitch!]

SOLDIER 1: Listen you little piece of shit, I could sharpen my knife on your throat, you hear me?

Boy nods, his eyes wild. Soldier 1 pushes Boy to his knees. Soldier 2 laughs, egging him on.

SOLDIER 3: Bak om ga. [Let him go.]

SOLDIER 1: Om zavri ma! [He insulted me!]

SOLDIER 2: Ovo cu je. [Let's do it.]

Soldier 2 grabs Boy's hair and pulls his head back, exposing his throat.

SOLDIER 3: E DIT BAK OM GA! [I SAID LET HIM GO!]

Woman enters, in a rush. All eyes turn toward her.

COOK: Help you?

WOMAN: Could I use your ladies room?

COOK: No room for ladies in here!

Soldier 1 laughs and Cook joins him, pleased. Soldiers 1 & 2 lose interest in Boy and drop him. He scurries away, his eyes on Woman.

233

WOMAN: Please.

COOK: Only customers get to use the facilities. Paying ones!

WOMAN: I'd like a cup of coffee.

COOK: Cream and sugar?

WOMAN: Yes.

COOK: We're out of sugar.

WOMAN: Fine.

COOK: Got some molasses.

WOMAN: Good.

COOK: But it'll have to be milk. Cream's gone sour.

WOMAN: Please...

COOK: Around the corner to the left.

> *Woman rushes out of the room.*

And don't be messin on my floor! (*to Soldiers*) Always the same thing. Day in, day out. People taking advantage of my hospitality.

SOLDIER 3: (*laughing*) Un casu—donsi ma un casu! [Another glass—bring me another glass!]

SOLDIER 1: He wants you to bring a glass.

COOK: Yessir, right away. (*to Boy*) You—don't cause any trouble.

> *Cook motions for him to sit and goes to kitchen. Boy sits by the door. He suddenly seems old and tired. Soldier 1 stares him down. Woman reenters and sits near Boy.*

SOLDIER 2: Susla es oma faan? [Where is she from?]

SOLDIER 1: My friend wants to know where you're from pretty lady.

SOLDIER 2: E kino oma. [I know her.]

SOLDIER 1: Hello? Are you deaf? You can trust us. It's peace time, did you hear? (*he waves his weapon*) We're peacekeepers.

SOLDIER 2: Peacekeepers, ya!

> *Sound of a helicopter flying over. Everyone stops and looks toward a window.*

SOLDIER 3: Hey—ga vise vat es guten. [Hey—go see what's happening.]

> *Soldier 1 heads outside. Soldier 2 follows, keeping his eyes on Woman.*

BOY: (*without looking up*) Better to sit by the door. Faster to get out.

WOMAN: I don't plan on leaving fast.

BOY: You will.

> *Cook reenters and gives whiskey to Soldier 3 and coffee to Woman.*

COOK: Out of molasses and milk.

WOMAN: As long as it's hot.

234
> *She roughly hands Boy a bowl of stew.*

COOK: Eat fast, then you're gone.

BOY: Saint Anthony will bless you for this!

COOK: The devil take you and your Anthony!

> *Soldier 3 gestures for Cook to join table, extends 4th glass of whiskey.*

COOK: Who me?

SOLDIER 3: (*to Boy*) Hey kindish...dom gonde...dom dom... [Hey kid...come here...come come...]

Boy cautiously goes to Soldier 3.

Cu ma prima...din su oma espojza. [Do me a favor...ask if she's married.]

BOY: I'm sorry, I don't understand what—

SOLDIER 3: Espojza...espojza...don dis u...uh...*Mister*? [Married...married... how do you say, uh...*Mister*?]

BOY: Oh, he wants to know where your husband is.

COOK: Dead.

BOY: He's...uh...

Boy makes a confusing gesture that Soldier 3 misinterprets.

SOLDIER 3: Ah! *(He raises a toast)* A te belista omanya. [To the beautiful lady!]

Awkward pause. He senses his mistake.

Yasa...ne cu solya katavake...a dir gravis oman y...a dir belista lunir. [Sorry...I don't mean disrespect...to your brave husband and...to your beautiful smile.]

BOY: He drinks to your café.

Cook, puzzled, downs her whiskey. Soldier 3 happily refills her glass and she joins his table. They drink and flirt quietly. Boy returns to his chair and dives into the stew. Woman stares at him. After a moment, he feels her eyes and looks up. She looks away quickly.

BOY: Have you seen the moon today?

WOMAN: The moon? No.

BOY: She came out by mistake. I think she's embarrassed.

Woman turns her back to him.

Of course, the sun isn't helping by being so angry that she's taking up his time. And with the clouds making fun of him for having to share the sky, I guess he's having a pretty bad day.

Boy wipes his spoon on his pants, crosses to her, and places the bowl in front of her. Soldier 3 watches them.

SOLDIER 3: *(quietly gesturing)* Ah...vise dar kindish. [Ah...watch that boy.]

COOK: He's a wiley angel, that one.

WOMAN: *(whispering)* Leave me alone.

BOY: You're hungry.

WOMAN: They're looking. Sit down.

BOY: She gave me too much. I'm full.

She pushes the bowl, less aggressively, toward him.

WOMAN: I don't have any money.

BOY: This would be my third meal today.

WOMAN: You shouldn't lie.

BOY: You need your strength.

235

WOMAN: How do you know what I need?

BOY: Eating for two.

> *She glances about nervously. Sound of Soldiers outside, laughing and talking. She tastes stew and makes a face.*

Sometimes I pretend it's something else. Makes it taste better.

WOMAN: Like what?

BOY: The broth is an ocean and the carrots are sharks chasing the little celery-fish around. I eat the sharks first, to save the celeries. And the chunks of meat are big ships carrying gold and silver and sometimes kings.

WOMAN: Don't watch.

> *He looks away and she quickly licks her plate.*

I did notice the moon, actually. She didn't look so embarrassed.

BOY: Well, she is. She told me.

WOMAN: The moon talks to you?

BOY: So does the Sun.

WOMAN: I see.

BOY: They talk to everybody. I listen.

> *Soldiers 1 & 2 enter again. Cook jumps up.*

COOK: Alright, beat it, kid! *(to Woman)* Pay up!

WOMAN: Um. Oh. I was hoping that I could help you with some dishes...

COOK: WHAT?!

WOMAN: ...in exchange for the coffee and your hospitality.

COOK: You ordered coffee and you don't have money?

WOMAN: Well, actually, I thought I had some change but there is a hole, see? In the bottom of my pocket...

COOK: *(overlapping)* GET OUT OF HERE! BOTH OF YOU!

> *Cook runs them into the street, snowing and bitterly cold. Boy wraps his blanket around his shoulders. Woman catches her breath, visibly shaken.*

BOY: She's an ass, anyway. And a drunk. I go in there everyday, and she never recognizes me. *(Pause)* Do you have somewhere to stay?

WOMAN: Yes.

BOY: You shouldn't lie.

WOMAN: Thank you for the stew.

BOY: You're welcome.

> *Boy hangs back. Woman huddles against the wall, frightened. Lights up on Interrogator, writhing on the floor. Woman covers her ears and sinks to the ground. Boy approaches her cautiously.*

I'm staying in a barn. It's not very far. Some cows were there until the soldiers took them away. There's fresh hay to sleep on.

He reaches for her hand. She hesitates, then takes it. He helps her up and they walk together.

Blackout.

ACT 2

Barn. Boy walks ahead Woman, proudly displaying the room. She hesitates at the entrance.

WOMAN: This is it?

BOY: Yes!

WOMAN: It smells like cow.

BOY: I know. I wish they were still here. I miss having milk for breakfast.

WOMAN: Are there rats?

BOY: I haven't seen any.

WOMAN: Mice?

BOY: Just some little brown furry ones.

WOMAN: What about lice?

BOY: The cows had some.

WOMAN: Do you?

BOY: I don't think so. They would have bitten me by now.

She enters the room, cautiously.

WOMAN: *(Pause)* Has anyone seen you go in or out?

BOY: I don't think so.

WOMAN: What about the soldiers?

BOY: I hid in the woods behind the barn.

WOMAN: Have long have you stayed here?

BOY: About two weeks. Two Sundays, anyway.

WOMAN: Why Sundays?

BOY: That's when I go to church. I usually go to the Catholic service first and take the Blessed Sacrament.

WOMAN: I haven't taken the Sacrament since I was your age.

BOY: You could go with me.

WOMAN: Oh, no. I gave that up a long time ago.

BOY: I like the wine. It warms me up. But they serve thin little wafers that aren't very filling, so I go to the Protestant service next. They serve big chunks of bread with their communion. I usually go up to the altar twice.

WOMAN: Doesn't the pastor notice?

BOY: I cry the second time, so he'll think I really need it. My mother always

237

said, "The Lord helps those who help themselves."

She suddenly doubles over with a sharp contraction.

What's wrong?

A second one brings her to her knees. She is nauseous. He reaches for her and she pushes him away. She crawls out of the Barn and dry heaves.

Interrogator watches from the shadows. A blood stain over his heart soaks his shirt. She hears him, but does not look up:

INTERROGATOR: They're doing scientific experiments in the next room. Trying to find the secret place. Hidden deep inside. Where love sleeps. Fascinating, isn't it? These men in white lab coats donning rubber gloves. Slicing the human heart lengthwise. In halves. Then quarters. I'm their guinea pig. They cut me open. Fully awake. Staring straight up into the blazing lights as they probe my heart for the chamber that houses my love for you.

Woman suddenly rushes back into the Barn.

Interrogator moves back into shadows.

BOY: It's dry over here.

She makes her way to the corner and lies down. He covers her with his coat.

WOMAN: How do you know so much? I know men three times your age who don't know half as much.

BOY: Your husband?

WOMAN: *(Pause)* I'm not married.

BOY: Oh. Neither was my mother. *(Pause)* What is your name?

WOMAN: No. We can't use names.

BOY: Where are you from?

WOMAN: The less we know about each other the better.

BOY: When I meet someone I like, I let them name me. I will be a different person with them than with anybody else I've ever known. It's an honor to name someone.

WOMAN: I'll call you Truong then. After my brother.

BOY: It has to be my name. Not a used one.

WOMAN: He was a brave man.

BOY: But when you say his name, you'll think of him. I want my own name.

WOMAN: How about...Sevko?

BOY: Sevko? Okay. And you will be...Arta.

WOMAN: Arta. That's a pretty name.

BOY: I've never called a grown-up by their first name before.

WOMAN: I need to rest. You keep watch.

BOY: Okay.

Woman curls up and falls asleep. Lights shift.

Boy moves to his "watch post" and watches her closely.

BOY: Why do I lie to you?

He crawls to her and speaks to her stomach.

Little Sister, can you hear me? I'm going to give you some good advice. You'll thank me for it later. Stay inside as long as you can. It's better than being out here, I can tell you that. Out here nobody sees you. I go for days sometimes with nobody to talk to. Then somebody kicks me or calls me a name, and I want to thank them.

He touches her stomach. The baby kicks, Woman stirs.

Don't worry. I'll take care of you.

Boy approaches King Carp's icy domain.

BOY: King Carp. Yo ho. It's me again.

KING CARP: Hello, Boy. Did you bring me something tasty this time?

BOY: Oh, yes. Something you can't refuse.

KING CARP: Try me.

BOY: You have lived a long life, King Carp. Preparing for this day. You're a wise old hunter.

KING CARP: Thank you.

BOY: Fat and fine.

KING CARP: Flattery will get you everywhere.

BOY: So I don't expect to outsmart you.

KING CARP: Not a chance.

BOY: But I ask you to consider this.

KING CARP: I wait with bated breath.

BOY: Someday you will die.

KING CARP: True.

BOY: And so will I.

KING CARP: Your point?

BOY: Today...today you have the chance to give your life for a cause.

KING CARP: I beg your pardon?

BOY: Few men have that opportunity, let alone a fish.

KING CARP: A cause? You are stirring me for a *cause*?

BOY: You could feed a woman who carries a baby inside her. What more excellent tribute to a great, cunning King than to sacrifice your old life for a new one.

KING CARP: Sacrifice?!

BOY: Yes!

KING CARP: I have not lived this long life to sacrifice it now! That would make me a traitor to the survival I have tirelessly pursued! A laughing stock to the death I have dodged!

239

BOY: Please, listen...

KING CARP: Life is a gift! Given mysteriously and taken away!

BOY: I need your help!

KING CARP: What do you take me for, Boy? I have lived a long and happy life. I've devoted entire days to dodging the shiny tip of a hook. I used to be frightened by them as a boy, their sharp points dangling in the water. Glinting...beckoning...enticing me to taste the delicacies that only humans can provide. Minnows, mmmm. Peanut butter, MMMmmm. Plump, juicy, fat earthworms, MMMMMM. I've been seduced by the best of them. All the pleasures of the world a desperate fisherman will offer at the end of a long and nibbleless day.

But I...I have always been...the one who got away. Yes! The big, beautiful, shining one that tasted the bait—just enough to wake them up—tickled the tip of the hook, made love to the worm, darting back and forth, a breathtaking dance. Oh, I've fallen in love with many a dancing worm in my time.

Then, my crowning glory. Just as they give up...after they've pulled the line out of the water, broken down the pole and called it a day...that's when I plummet deep to the bottom of the lake, muster every bit of strength in my slippery, sinewy body—and BULLET to the top, cresting the surface of the water, turning a triple somersault in mid-air, and smashing back into the dark abyss with a purposeful, shocking splunk. As the force of my dive drives me back to the bottom, I see in my mind's eye the look of disbelief on their faces. The son-of-a-gun expression. "Did you see that?" they exclaim to each other, or to no one in particular.

And I haunt them. Late into the night. As they recount the tale to hungry ears in the dark paneled safety of their murky taverns. Telling and retelling their woeful yarn 'til their eyes are bleary. Making me bigger each time, and faster and more beautiful, until I reach mythic proportions.

Through the wake of their sweaty dreams I glide… beckoning... teasing... the one who got away.

BOY: That is a beautiful story.

KING CARP: Thank you.

BOY: And I do admire your pride.

KING CARP: But?

BOY: ...if Arta doesn't eat soon, she'll lose the little bit of strength she has, and little sister will die!

KING CARP: Not my problem.

BOY: How can you be so cruel?

KING CARP: I don't have to see you to know that you are just a boy. A man would never ask another to give up his life. The indecency in that request.

BOY: What would a man do?

KING CARP: Take my life from me, of course.

BOY: I don't want to kill you!

KING CARP: Then you don't deserve my life. Have some respect here.

BOY: I'm sorry.

KING CARP: You should be.

BOY: I didn't know you are so selfish.

KING CARP: My father was caught by a boy. A kid. Caught him for sport. Hauled him up out of the water by his fins. Paraded him around until his eyes bulged out, then tossed him back in the water. I watched him as he bloated up and floated to shore. I smelled his death for weeks.

BOY: I'm sorry. I didn't know.

KING CARP: Come back to me when you're a man. I'll teach you to dance.

Boy starts slowly back to the Barn. Woman is still sleeping.

Barn: Woman's Dream: Interrogator enters and circles Woman, holding baby. She reaches for him, groping, as if she's blindfolded.

INTERROGATOR: Oh...look...she has my eyes.

Boy enters. Woman looks at Boy, disoriented. Interrogator disappears.

BOY: Are you okay?

She looks back to where Interrogator was. Pause.

I brought you these.

He hands her some berries.

WOMAN: Where did you go?

BOY: To look for food.

WOMAN: I thought you left me.

BOY: Where would I go?

He watches her eat.

WOMAN: You want some?

BOY: They're for you. Were you having a nightmare? *(Woman nods)* I have those sometimes.

WOMAN: We should take turns sleeping.

BOY: Okay.

WOMAN: You go ahead.

BOY: I'm not sleepy.

WOMAN: You need to rest so you can hunt again when it's light.

He moves away from her and curls up, his back to her.

Woman moves around, stretches. A contraction starts, and she tries to keep silent. Boy watches. When she turns again, he pretends to sleep. She picks up his notebook and flips through it, then begins to read.

241

BOY: Nobody's ever read it before.

She puts it down.

WOMAN: I'm sorry.

BOY: Mama gave it to me. It was hers when she was a girl.

WOMAN: It's a beautiful book.

BOY: She told me to write in it whenever I feel lonely.

WOMAN: I would fill the pages of a book like that in one night.

BOY: I haven't written anything since you came.

WOMAN: What happened to her?

BOY: It only has 40 pages, and I'm going to live a long life. On the ocean. There's room for me there. I'll sail my own ship out onto the wide, blue water. I'll trim the sails and scrub the deck and steer the ship myself. And I will be so happy that I'll toss this book in the water and let the sharks swallow my sadness. *(Pause)* I've forgotten how her voice sounds.

WOMAN: That happens after awhile.

BOY: Have you watched someone die?

WOMAN: *(Pause)* No.

BOY: She held my hand, like this...when she felt herself slipping she squeezed. Hard. Until it went numb. Like somebody else's hand on the end of my arm. I liked that feeling. I gave her the life from my hand. *(Pause)* I kept myself awake. For three days. I knew if I stopped watching she would leave me, but...

Pause. He moves away from her.

WOMAN: What happened?

BOY: I fell asleep. Just for a second. I closed my eyes and...her hand dropped. The life fell out of her body. Out of the room. There was a big space in the air where her breath had been.

WOMAN: She didn't want to leave you.

She touches his back. He flinches and jerks away from her.

BOY: No! I let go! I let her go!

He runs outside. Woman gradually falls asleep again.

Outside Barn: It is dark, Boy is desperate.

BOY: Sister Moon, come out! Stop hiding behind the clouds!

Moon appears, irritated.

MOON: The sun has sent them to block me. He's angry about this afternoon.

BOY: Be bold! Assert yourself! I need your light!

MOON: But my light is his light! I glow in his reflection. I'm afraid you'll have to talk to him if you want to see my face tonight.

BOY: SUN! Yo ho! Brother Sun, I'm talking to you!

SUN: Pipe down, kid. You're giving me a headache.

BOY: Why are you blocking Sister Moon from me?

SUN: The lady had her time today. It's not my problem she came out early.

BOY: But I need her light.

SUN: Listen to me, boy. Her crazy night light is just going to get you into trouble. Understand? She's cunning and deceptive, as females usually are. She only lights what you want to see. I, on the other hand, light the truth. Harsh? Sometimes. But real, little brother. And true.

MOON: I beg to differ.

SUN: Of course you do, she always *differs*.

MOON: I reveal a different reality. Hidden beneath the surface. I cast shadows and throw the truth into relief.

SUN: Your shadows create illusions! That's exactly what the kid wants!

BOY: I do not!

SUN: You want to see this Woman as young and beautiful.

BOY: She is!

SUN: And yourself as man—strong and brave.

BOY: What about it?!

SUN: Ha! Tell him, Moon. Warn him of the dangers that lurk in your shadows!

MOON: I can illuminate this night for you, any way you like.

SUN: Watch out!

MOON: But only for one night. When day comes around again, and HE'S in charge, you are on your own.

SUN: Don't do it, kid.

MOON: It's up to you. It is your night.

SUN: I'm warning you...don't be seduced.

BOY: Please...let me see her.

SUN: Big mistake, Boy. You'll be mad at me tomorrow, when you see the light.

MOON: Your desire will guide my light. But first, I have to coax the clouds away.

> *Moon gestures with a flourish and Sun grudgingly stirs up wind, as Boy enters Barn.*

That's better. Now let me see. Oh, she looks so tired and sad.

BOY: Little Sister is coming soon. I think she's scared.

MOON: I'll erase those hard lines around her mouth and eyes. There.

BOY: That's better.

MOON: And highlight her face with a warm glow.

BOY: Oh, yes. Thank you.

MOON: My pleasure.

> *Boy crouches near Woman.*

BOY: Look. Even the moon loves you. See how she touches your face.

Interrogator appears at the edge of the Barn.

WOMAN: *(in her sleep)* ...getting...closer...

Interrogator moves behind Boy.

BOY: You don't look anything like my mother. I used to watch her sleep, too. You don't look anything like her. Your face is a book. When you sleep, all the pages fall away and leave the story. Just the story. Not the one you want me to hear...not the one you tell me. But the other one, the true one, written on the surface of your face.

Interrogator reaches for Boy's neck. Woman wakes, sees him and yells out, startling Boy. Interrogator backs into the shadows.

WOMAN: Why are you looking at me?!

BOY: I wasn't.

WOMAN: Stop! Stop looking at me! Go away! Every time I wake up, I see you crouching like a hungry animal.

BOY: I'm keeping watch.

WOMAN: You're watching me!

BOY: I'm keeping you safe!

WOMAN: I don't need you!

She has a sharp labor pain, and cries out.

BOY: What?

WOMAN: God! *(She beats her stomach.)* Dead dead dead dead dead!

He grabs her by the wrists and they struggle.

BOY: Don't! She's alive!

WOMAN: What do you know about it?!

BOY: I wish I had her in me.

WOMAN: Oh is that right?!

BOY: I would be so happy.

WOMAN: What do you think is in here? A baby? Oh no—my dreams tell me what sleeps in here! Clawing it's way out of me, sharp little fangs tearing at my flesh—

BOY: No—stop it!—

WOMAN: They took turns! They took turns while my mother watched. All night. In the morning when she couldn't cry anymore they slit her throat with a steak knife. Laughing. I wanted them to kill me, but I reminded one of them of his sister. He sang me a lullaby over and over. I held onto his voice. He squeezed my hand and smoothed my hair. He never hurt me. When they left, he whispered, "We planted our seed. Kill it before it kills you." It's my body. *It's my body and I can do what I want with it!* No one will want her anyway. She shouldn't suffer. *(Pause)* Listen. Now you've got me calling it a "she".

244

BOY: (quietly) Maybe she'll look like me.

WOMAN: Get away from me!

> Woman shoves him away, and has another contraction.

Get me some water.

> He doesn't move.

Please.

> He drags the bucket to her and walks away. She struggles to drink, spilling it.

I need your help.

> Boy grudgingly scoops water in his hands. She holds them and drinks.

WOMAN: How old are you?

BOY: Old enough.

WOMAN: When will this be over?

> She buries her face in his hands and cries. He stays, awkward and uncertain.

So soft. Your skin is a surprise. Like a girls.

> He pulls away.

WOMAN: Don't become a man.

BOY: I am a man.

WOMAN: Don't.

BOY: I love her.

WOMAN: Who?

BOY: I want her to be mine. I want to say she's mine.

WOMAN: She's no one's—she's nothing—forget her—forget both of us!

> Woman exits.

BOY: Where are you going?

> Outside, Woman is overcome with emotion. As she speaks, Moon appears.

WOMAN: …oh god…Mama…why…why aren't you here…I don't want to do this…I can't…I can't do this without you…what do I do?…

MOON: (overlapping) Shhhh…I'm here…you are not alone…you're never alone…shhh…I'm here, I'm here…

> Moon makes a gesture of comfort. The Woman feels it, turns her face upward and is bathed in moonlight.

> Barn: Time has passed, the shadows are longer. Woman enters and paces the room, tottering on her high heels.

BOY: Why are you wearing those shoes?

WOMAN: Why do you ask so many questions?

BOY: I want to know you.

WOMAN: What for. We're just going to die.

BOY: At least I'll know someone who is good and beautiful…I haven't known

245

anybody like you before…

WOMAN: Shut up. Please. Stop.

BOY: Okay. *(Pause)* If we can't talk, what do we do?

WOMAN: We rest.

BOY: Okay.

> *He doesn't move. Woman lays down, facing away from him.*

BOY: *(Pause)* What were you like before?

WOMAN: Before what.

BOY: You probably liked to dress up and go to parties and dance with strangers. You probably had lots of friends.

WOMAN: Listen you just… you can't know me. This is what's left. The leftovers. *(pause)* You can't know that I used to ride my bicycle very fast downhill with my hands in the air, or that my sister could make me laugh until my sides hurt, or that boys whistled at my ass when I walked by, or that I stole cigarettes and smoked them on my parent's roof. You can't know these things.

BOY: Did you ever crash your bike?

WOMAN: Too many times to count.

BOY: Do you have scars?

> *She rolls up her sleeve and shows a scar on her elbow.*

Oh, that's a good one.

WOMAN: You probably don't have any.

> *Boy rolls up his pants leg and shows her a red line up his calf.*

BOY: I fell out of a tree. I thought I was a bird.

> *Woman laughs. Boy points to another scar on her head.*

BOY: What's this one?

WOMAN: We were playing football with empty mortar shells, me and Truong. We tried to hide it from my mother, but the blood gave us away.

> *Boy shows her another scar on his back.*

BOY: This is where a soldier hit me with his gun.

WOMAN: Oh…that hurt.

> *She gently traces the scar with her finger.*

BOY: I didn't cry.

WOMAN: *(Pause)* When they made me leave my home, I decided to wear my best shoes. They gave me 5 minutes. If I could take nothing, at least I was going to wear my best shoes.

BOY: Why did they make you leave?

WOMAN: We should rest.

> *She tries to get comfortable. He lays near her, and rests her head on his lap.*

246

BOY: Here...I'll keep you warm.

He wraps his arms around her. She gradually relaxes.

(*to baby*) What's it like, floating in her ocean? Dark and safe and warm. I wish I could crawl in there with you.

Boy falls asleep. Girl, Sun and Moon appear, and he dreams:

GIRL: BOY: MOON:

I want to fly with you
to the ocean.

                              ocean

Sail out together   White sand beaches
on a big ship   sparkling in the sun
                          ship   underneath

The blue, blue sky

                          sky

                                    That is kissed and
                                    caressed by the ocean.

Seagulls diving and soaring
and swooping overhead.   diving . soaring

                                 SUN:
                                    Be careful, Boy.
                               MOON:
                                    The water is a tease.

Sound of the water flapping   flap flap flap
against the side of the boat
                                    It licks and leaps at
                                    the shore
                                    and slow pulses under
                                    the heat of the sky.

Sails snapping in the wind
                          Shadows

                                 SUN:
                                    Stay out of her
                                    shadows.

                               MOON:
                                  You swim very deep.

Underneath playful waves   **247**
                                    Lose your whole self
                                    in the pulsing
Fly with me
                                    safe
                        safe
                                    rhythm
To our home
                        home
On the island.   Of the ocean.

The Carp swims into Boy's dream. They are speaking in a dream state:

KING CARP: Through the wake of their sweaty dreams I glide...

BOY: You won't refuse my request this time, Carp.

CARP:

    I didn't refuse, Boy.
    I merely danced.

WOMAN:

    I feel your heat.
    Drawing me in.
    Like a moth to
    a flickering candle.

The life and death tango.

    If I dance too close
You can't ask your partner   I'll be burned to death.
to give in.
How boring that would be.

    Before I have time
    to think.
You have to communicate
your intentions   Think.
with a subtle tilt of
of the head,   I have to keep my
    head on.
a flick of the wrist,
shifting of the eyes...   Too much longing in
    your hungry eyes.
So that the other senses...

    Stay away, Boy.
FEELS your request.

And resists...
or yields.

    Keep your heart
    in your chest
Resists...   and your chest
or yields   BOY: in your body
    Resists or yields   and your body

248 Resists...   across the room
or yields   from me.

    Resists or yields

Carp swims off in a flourish. As lights shift to indicate deeper levels of dreaming, Boy & Woman move in various stages of sleep. The Woman wakes briefly and glances at Boy:

WOMAN: Why does love always come to me in disguise?

She curls up next to him and falls back asleep, spooning. Carp swims back on and circles him. Lighting and movement indicate a surreal dream state as the

Boy & Woman's dreams intermingle:

KING CARP: ...glistening...beckoning...the one who got away.

Boy rises and goes to the Carp.

BOY: I've come back, King Carp.

KING CARP: Is that you, Boy?

BOY: It's time, old fish. Teach me to dance.

Boy lowers himself into the water. Carp swims around him.

*Woman rises and moves to the **Interrogation Room**, where Interrogator slumps in the chair. The four characters move in a stylized dance around each other—the life and death tango.*

KING CARP: And what is it about the dance that you don't know?

BOY: How to finish.

KING CARP: The ending. Of course. The eagerness of youth. Jumping right to the climactic moment. Skipping the seduction.

BOY: What do I do?

WOMAN: If I had a knife, I would slit your throat.

KING CARP: First, you have to entice me.

WOMAN: Watch you gagging. Your eyes wild with panic.

BOY: How?

WOMAN: I kill you a thousand times a day in my head.

BOY: Tell me how!

WOMAN: So many different ways.

KING CARP: Patience...patience...

INTERROGATOR: *(waking)* Did you say something?

KING CARP: Catch my eye from across the water.

INTERROGATOR: Were you talking to me?

KING CARP: Imitate the actions of a worm.

WOMAN: Untie me.

KING CARP: Slipping and sliding on the hook.

BOY: Like this?

WOMAN: Untie my hands.

KING CARP: ...yes, not bad...

WOMAN: So I can touch you.

KING CARP: ...wriggling with life...

WOMAN: Would you like that?

INTERROGATOR: Yes.

KING CARP: Oh, yes...good...good.

INTERROGATOR: They'll take you away from me.

KING CARP: You see, it is life that attracts me...

WOMAN: You don't want me to touch you?

INTERROGATOR: I ache for your touch.

KING CARP: ...that illusive ingredient. Breath...

WOMAN: Release me.

KING CARP: ...heartbeat...

INTERROGATOR: If we get caught?

KING CARP: The salty taste of fear.

INTERROGATOR: They will put us to death.

BOY: I'm not afraid.

WOMAN: Would you die for me?

KING CARP: Of course not. You're young. You'll live forever!

WOMAN: Can your love be complete if I can't respond?

INTERROGATOR: So, you love me now?

WOMAN: I can't know until you let my hands free.

> Boy stops dancing with Carp and sees Woman.

KING CARP: Watch out, Boy. Don't look away!

INTERROGATOR: You birthed me into this world. Like a baby. I see things that I never noticed before.

KING CARP: We're approaching the ending, Boy. Are you ready?

INTERROGATOR: You opened a chasm and sucked me under. Then, just as my lungs filled with water...you taught me to swim. Kiss me...once...with your hands free.

KING CARP: That's it...good, good.

INTERROGATOR: One kiss and you can have my life.

> Woman moves to Interrogator. Carp draws Boy back into dance.

KING CARP: Now, when you've found your rhythm, when you have me in your sites, thrust forward for the kill.

> Interrogator and Woman kiss.

KING CARP: Now! Kill me!

250 BOY: NO!

KING CARP: What are you waiting for?

BOY: I can't.

KING CARP: But I'm ready!

> **Simultaneous gesture:** Woman chokes Interrogator as Carp lunges at Boy. A tremendous struggle for life is punctuated by sounds of breathing and a racing heartbeat. The four characters move in slow, exaggerated movements. Boy overpowers Carp. Interrogator and Carp rise to the surface of the dream and gasp for one last breath before going limp. As they sink, sounds continue to

build under the Woman's cries. She is in labor.

BOY: I'm sorry.

GIRL: Wake up!

CHORUS: Wake up wake up wake up…

> *The Birth: Stylized movement in which Sun, Moon, Girl, Dead Soldier and Carp become a Chorus, moving Woman through the stages of labor: "preparing", "riding the wave" and "revelation". A soundscape under their movement echoes the earlier sounds of flight—"air, push, lift me up, push down, feathers flutter", etc.—heightened by amplified breathing and heartbeat that builds to a cacophony. The following lines are interspersed with soundscape.*

WOMAN: Wake up!

BOY: What? What is it?

WOMAN: Wake up. It's coming!

BOY: What do I do?

WOMAN: SEVKO!

BOY: I'm here.

> *Girl appears at the edge of the shadows.*

BOY: I see her. I see her! Oh—here she is!

> *Boy holds bundled baby. He rushes to clean blood off of her.*

WOMAN: What does she look like?

BOY: She's so little.

WOMAN: What does she *look* like?!

BOY: There's a lot of blood.

WOMAN: Is she breathing?

BOY: Yes, she's got tiny hands and feet and dark hair—

> *Sound of a baby crying.*

WOMAN: Shhh. Make it stop…make it stop crying! They'll hear it!

> *Boy quickly bundles the baby in his shirt and tries to shush her.*

BOY: It's not working. What do I do?

> *Boy walks with the baby. Cries continue.*

WOMAN: I don't know!

> *He holds her close to his chest and breathes deeply—she grows quiet.*

BOY: There, she stopped crying. I got her to stop. *(Pause)* Oh…she's looking at me. Hello.

WOMAN: Give her to me.

> *Boy hands her to Woman, who takes her clumsily. Baby whimpers.*

BOY: Be careful.

> *Woman places baby on the floor.*

251

BOY: What are you doing? She'll get cold.

WOMAN: Leave me alone. Go outside. I need to be alone.

BOY: *(quietly)* You're not alone.

WOMAN: Go!

> *Boy quietly leaves the Barn.*

WOMAN: I'm not alone…I'm never alone…

> *Woman slowly uncovers the baby, and she begins to cry. Woman covers her and quickly moves away, pacing, making a decision.*

Shhh…shush…shut up! They'll hear you!

> *Woman crouches across the room, watching the baby as if it were an animal.*

Why did you come here?

BOY: *(from outside)* Arta…I think I hear someone coming.

WOMAN: Quiet! Go hide!

BOY: But what about you and the baby—

WOMAN: Go hide in the woods! I'm coming!

> *Woman crawls to baby.*

You can't stay, you know. You can't stay. This is no place for a life.

> *Woman holds her hand over the baby's face, preparing to smother her. Girl appears at the edge of the darkness.*

GIRL: Mama…?

> *Woman hesitates.*

WOMAN:	GIRL:
You should have been a boy.	
	Mama…
Your life will be so hard. People will hurt you because you are a girl.	
	…where are you?
Stay hidden. Watch. Listen.	
	I'm a stranger here. Nobody sees me.
Learn the language of secret thoughts	
	I look at their faces, listen to their voices.
The meaning underneath the words.	
	Something to tell me where I'm from.
Woman hears Soldiers approaching. Never love anything so much it will hurt to let it go.	
	Do you think about me?

WOMAN:	GIRL:
Especially a daughter.	
	Do you wonder if I'm thinking about you?
Never have a daughter.	
	Why didn't you want me?

Woman kisses baby's palms and Girl sees her own hands.

GIRL: My mother's hands are a map of her life. The traces and lines of her journey. My fingerprints are mine. My hands are my mothers.

Woman carefully lays the baby on the floor, and runs out of the barn, yelling. Girl disappears.

Barn: Boy creeps back in. It is too quiet.

BOY: Arta? Where are you?

He discovers the baby on the floor, grabs her up and sits cross-legged on the floor, rocking her. A few strands of light filter through the window and across his face. He gently hushes her soft cries.

Shhhhh...don't cry...it's okay...I'm here...I'll take care of you...

Sound of Woman singing the lullaby as in beginning of play (may be live or recorded).

WOMAN: *(singing)* One bright morning in the springtime
　　in the budding trees
A dark hunter shot an arrow
　　through a young bird's wing.
She lay broken on the ground
　　bleeding out her plea
I found her laying silently
　　as if she were asleep.

I let her rest beside my window
　　bound her wing in silk
Fed her blossoms from the meadow
　　and butterflies milk
As the brilliant summer passed
　　she relearned her song
She sang it as the trees grew gold
　　and the shadows long

One autumn evening as she sang
　　the stars into the sky
The hunter like a crimson storm cloud
　　came to claim his prize.
She fluttered at the window pane
　　trapped in a cocoon,
I kissed her once, unwrapped her wing,

253

released her to the moon.

As the song continues: A flashlight beam scans the room through the window, catching the Boy's face. Soldiers 1 & 3 yell from outside.

SOLDIER 1: Baçik orusila! *(Pause)* Istupi! [Throw down your weapon! Step forward!]

SOLDIER 3: Kazi ko si! [Identify yourself!]

SOLDIER 1: Kazi ko si—o zjhaste! [Identify yourself—or we'll shoot you!]

Boy stands, protecting the bundled baby. Lines overlap.

BOY: I don't understand…

SOLDIER 1: Baçik orusila! Kazi ko si! [Throw down your weapon! Identify yourself!]

BOY: Please! I can't understand you!

SOLDIER 3: Kazi ko si—o zjhaste! [Identify yourself—or we'll shoot you!]

A gunshot. Woman's singing stops.

BOY: NO!

A 2ⁿᵈ gunshot. The Boy is hit. He falls in slow motion, the baby underneath him. Girl's voice picks up with the lullaby where Woman left off.

Barn: Soldiers 1 & 3 enter the Barn and see the Boy's lifeless body.

THE Soldiers REPEAT SCENE 3—GOING THROUGH THE MOTIONS EXACTLY AS IN THE BEGINNING—BUT MOUTHING THE WORDS IN SILENCE, AS IF THE VOLUME IS TURNED DOWN.

[* indicates new stage directions]

SOLDIER 3: Pazi! [Be careful!]

SOLDIER 1: Vat ficken?! Esje dar kindish. [What the fuck?! It's that kid!]

Soldier 3 checks the Boy's pulse.

SOLDIER 3: Uszbekt om. [You killed him.]

SOLDIER 1: Om ajza bet. Te grosse es egate. [He's just bait. The big one got away.]

Soldier 3 kneels by Boy and prays in silence.

Soldier 1 discovers Boy's notebook.

(he reads, in English) "Sometimes the only thing that keeps me from crying is knowing that we see the same moon."

Soldier 1 drops the notebook, laughing.

Sound of a flock of birds taking flight.

SOLDIER 3: Uskut! Asawey! [Shhh! Listen!]

A baby's muffled cry.

* *Girl appears at a window.*

Soldier 1 aims his gun at Boy's body.

SOLDIER 1: Ne je sta! [Don't touch it!]

Soldier 3 gently shifts Boy and discovers baby underneath him.

* Boy slowly rises, as if he is underwater. Soldiers continue scene, uninterrupted—they do not see him. Boy stands slowly, his body limp, his eyes closed.

SOLDIER 3: Oma uvek bres. [She's still breathing.]

Soldier 1 points his gun at the baby.

Soldier 3 reaches for her.

SOLDIER 1: Ne je sta! Bis du lut?! [Don't touch it! Are you crazy?!]

Soldier 3 carefully lifts baby and she begins to cry.

Soldier 1 holds his gun on both of them.

SOLDIER 1: Sputi je! Sputi je! [Put it down! Put it down!]

Soldier 3 sings lullaby on "la la la".

Vat ficken u cuve!? [What the fuck are you doing?!]

SOLDIER 3: Sabrisj, kindish. [Patience, boy.]

SOLDIER 1: Vat u kukir ma? Vat u kukir ma?! [What did you call me? What did you call me?!]

SOLDIER 3: U flaub uszbekten mak te om. [You think killing makes you a man.]

A whistle from outside.

SOLDIER 1: Hey! Tachte oma! Uiga! Uiga! [Hey! He's got her! Let's go! Let's go!]

Soldier 1 runs out.

* Soldier 3 holds the baby. A moment of decision—he takes her with him, exiting the barn in the opposite direction of Soldier 1.

Boy slowly raises his arms, like outstretched wings. Pause.

A suspended moment.

GIRL: (sings) Winter's cold has faded now
    like her melody
that promised she would fly back home
    with the blooms of spring
I sing each night to weave a path
    to my window sill
I strain each dawn to hear her voice,
    and fear I never will.

Girl's singing continues as:

Boy opens his eyes. In a swift motion of flight, he lowers his arms and extends his body upwards.

A rush of air.

Boy disappears into the darkness.

Sound of a flock of birds taking flight.

Girl watches from her window as the flock flies over.

Darkness.

APPENDIX: PRODUCTION INFORMATION

RCP#160 **GREAT MEN OF SCIENCE** premiered in Los Angeles at the Lost Studio Theater, March 19 to April 26, 1998, produced by The Circle X Theater, directed by Jillian Armenante.

> Chatelet — Alice Dodd
> Vaucanson — Matthew Allen Bretz
> Spallanzani — Jim Anzide
> Condorcet — David Wichert
> Le Cat — Paul Morgan Stetler
> Housekeeper — Melanie van Betten

BACK OF THE THROAT was co-produced by Thick Description and Golden Thread Productions, San Francisco, April 18, 2005. Tony Kelly was Artistic Directors for Thick Description) and Torange Yeghiazarian for Golden Thread Productions. Tony Kelly directed the production with set design by James Faerron, lighting design by Rick Martin, and costumes by Isabella Ortega.

> Khaled — James Asher
> Bartlett — James Reese
> Carl — Paul Santiago
> Shelly/Beth/Jean — Chloe Bronzan
> Asfoor — Brian Rivera

RCP#17 **TORNADO & AVALANCHE** were produced by Poisonous Toy Theater under the joint title *Stormy Weather* at On the Boards, Seattle, WA, Jan 10-20, 2002, directed by Bret Fetzer and Juliet Waller Pruzan, stage managed by Jennifer Moon, with technical assisance by Alan Pruzan. Set design for *Tornado* was by John DeShazo; set design for *Avalanche* was by Curtis Taylor.

> Windy — Corey Quigley
> Flora Bell — Heidi Schreck
> Buster — Matt Ford
> Teacher/other voices — Audrey Freudenberg
> Henrik — Mark Boeker
> Carla — Heidi Schreck
> Dagmar — Audrey Freudenberg
> Albert — Matt Ford
> Border Guard/townspeople — Corey Quigley
> Townspeople — Bret Fetzer, Juliet Waller Pruzan

RCP#82 **CLEVELAND RAINING** was developed at Pan Asian Rep, the Brown University New Plays Festival, Seattle Group Theater, Grinnell College, and the Mark Taper Forum New Works Festival. It received its world premiere at East West Players in Los Angeles in March 1995. Tim Dang was Artistic Director, and Shishir Kurup directed the play with the following cast:

> Jimmy — Nelson Yamashita
> Mari — Peggy Ahn

Mick — Mark Bringelson
Storm — Kei Rowan-Young

Michael Daeho Chung and Kerri Higuchi were understudies; Edward E. Haynes, Jr. designed sets; David E. Hadsell designed lights; Naomi Yoshida Rodriguez designed costumes; Joe Romano designed sound and composed music; Kent Hirohama and Anne Williams were Production Stage Managers.

Special Thanks to Paula Vogel, Stephen Weeks, Honour Molloy, Tisa Chang, Ernest Abuba, Daniel Dae Kim, Nanci Griffiths, Chiori Miyagawa, Brian Peebles, Tim Dang, Chay Yew, Shishir Kurup, Tony Kelly, Karen Amano, Octavio Solis, Mom & Dad, and Helen, for their help in bringing this play, my very first, into this world.

STRAY was produced by Printer's Devil Theatre in Seattle, Washington in June 2001. Heidi Schreck directed, with production design by Jessica Dodge, lighting design by Lindsay Smith, music by Chris Caniglia. Meaghan Maloney stage managed, and Jessica Pregnolato was dramaturg and assistant director.

#161

ISA — Trica Rodley
MAY — Alissa Ford
ELLIE — Tina Kunz
GIRL — Kristen Palmer
FRANK — John Paulsen

Special thanks to Deron Bos, Jennifer Creegan, Bret Fetzer, Stephen Hando, Kip Fagan, Matt Ford, Hilary Ketchum, Clayton McCarl, Larry, Sherry, and Carl Schreck, Aaron Thomas, Carolyn "Blade" Thompson, and Paul Willis

TWO BIRDS AND A STONE received its world premiere at Capitol Hill Arts Center in Seattle in February 2004, Artistic Director Matthew Kwatinetz. The production was directed by Christine Young, with set design by Matthew Kwatinetz, sound design by Nathan Anderson and lighting design by Patti West. Production team included stage manager Audrey Murray, assistant director Joe Rettenmaier and line producer Deron Sedy, with the following cast:

#194

Boy — Kalan Sherrard
Woman — Marie Broderick
Interrogator — Nathan Breskin-Auer
King Carp & Soldier 2 — Jose Gonzales
Sun & Soldier 3 — John Farrage
Dead Soldier & Soldier 1 — Connor Toms
Moon & Cook — Susan McIntyre
Girl — Rachel Abramson

Special thanks to Nilo Cruz, Portland Center Stage's JAW West Festival, Seattle's FringeACT Festival and translators Dragana Milutinovic, David Nash and Ravenna McQuill.

ERIK EHN is married to patricia chanteloube. he is a playwright. he is dean of the school of theater at the california institute of the arts. peace is the plot of creation.

A manifesto is a communication made to the whole world, whose only pretension is to the discovery of an instant cure for political, astronomical, artistic, parliamentary, agronomical and literary syphilis. It may be pleasant, and good-natured, it's always right, it's strong, vigorous and logical.

— Tristan Tzara, *Feeble Love & Bitter Love, II*

I n dramaturgical terms, we're looking for narratives whose several parts are available simultaneously —we can shift back and *forth* at (private) will across a range of possible interpretations. In terms of distribution, we need the Black Rock Rangers —environments, sites, districts— ON A GLOBAL SCALE; the transglobal freak, World Social Forum, *motion-motion-motion* so you can find s t i l l n e s s at any point in your process on the globe. Theater converts the world to the flesh computer – one large, integrated, SIMULTANEOUS drive. Per the Brit sitcom: unanimous with itself.

11001010010101011101101100110100
01010001000101101011101101101001
11001010011001101001001101011011
10110010101001011001010011010111 0
10100100110010100110101101101100
01011101101100011010010110010100 1
11010011011011011000110100100 00
11010010110100111011011000110 10
11111000010010010111001011101010 11
11001001001100111010101101101100 1101
01010010101000110101110110110011
00101001101011101101000011101001
11001010010101011101101100110100 1
01010001000101101011101101101001
11001010011001101001001101011011
10110010101001011001010011010111 0
10100100110010100110101101101100
01011101101100011010010110010100 1
01010011010110110110000110100100 00 1
11001010011010011101101101100011010
11111000010010010111001011101010 11
11001001010011010101101101101100 1101
01010010101000110101110110111001 1
00101001101011101101000011101001
11001010011010101010110100101011 0
10001001101011010110110011000010
11001001001010101110110110011010 01
01010001000101101011101101101001 1
11001010011001101001001101011011
10110010101001011001010011010111 0
10100100110010100110101101101100 1
11010011010110110110000110100100 00 1
11001010011010011101101101100011010
010100101010001101011101101101100110
Plays are files—means of bundling and distributing affinities of information. PLAYWRIGHTS GRIND CODE.
11001010011001101001101101110011010
01010001000101101011101101101001

OWNERSHIP

MANIFESTO: like other o-terminus words—

PRESTO CHANGE-O , BOO HELL'O ... ● A WAY OF

ANNOUNCING APPEARANCE. THEATER, THE MAYFLY, IS ALWAYS AND ONLY *HERE*. THIS PRINTED ISSUE COLLECTS SIX PLAYS, MORTAL CODES FOR VITAL INTENSITIES. They're good: involving, surprising, subversive. They also shake out driving trends in narrative and eschatology.

Narrative

The plays are narrative without being descriptive. Narratives are

actions; the plays and the people in them use acts of telling to

create motion in landscape and character, not through recounting

events by demonstrating structures of memory and imagination.

That one chooses (or is forced) to build a certain kind of story at a

certain time reveals more than the ordered details.